All-American Rebels

American Ways

General Editor: John David Smith, Charles H. Stone Distinguished Professor of American History, University of North Carolina at Charlotte

From the long arcs of America's history, to the short timeframes that convey larger stories, American Ways provides concise, accessible topical histories informed by the latest scholarship and written by scholars who are both leading experts in their fields and polished writers. Books in the series provide general readers and students with compelling introductions to America's social, cultural, political, and economic history, underscoring questions of class, gender, racial, and sectional diversity and inclusivity. The titles suggest the multiple ways that the past informs the present and shapes the future in often unforeseen ways.

Titles in the Series

All-American Rebels

The American Left from the Wobblies to Today

Robert C. Cottrell

ROWMAN & LITTLEFIELD
Lanham • Boulder • New York • London

Published by Rowman & Littlefield
An imprint of The Rowman & Littlefield Publishing Group, Inc.
4501 Forbes Boulevard, Suite 200, Lanham, Maryland 20706
www.rowman.com

6 Tinworth Street, London SE11 5AL, United Kingdom

British Library Cataloguing in Publication Information Available

Library of Congress Cataloging-in-Publication Data Available

ISBN 9781538112922 (cloth : alk. paper)
ISBN 9781538112939 (electronic)

∞ ™ The paper used in this publication meets the minimum requirements of American National Standard for Information Sciences Permanence of Paper for Printed Library Materials, ANSI/NISO Z39.48-1992.

To Sue and Jordan

Contents

Acknowledgments

As always, I want to express my gratitude to my wife Sue and my daughter Jordan.

I also want to thank the team at Rowman & Littlefield, especially Elaine McGarraugh, Jon Sisk, Dina Gulak, and Professor John David Smith, editor of The American Ways Series.

Introduction

The history of the modern American left is both storied and star-crossed. It includes genuinely luminous figures like Eugene V. Debs, Big Bill Haywood, Crystal Eastman, Inez Milholland, Randolph Bourne, John Reed, Roger Nash Baldwin, A. Philip Randolph, Dorothy Day, A. J. Muste, and I. F. "Izzy" Stone. Then there are Martin Luther King Jr., John Lewis, Bob Moses, Diane Nash, Sandra Cason Hayden, Cesar Chavez, Noam Chomsky, the Reverend William Barber II, and Alexandria Ocasio-Cortez, among others. The story of the American left involves the rise and fall of political movements that strove to empower the disfranchised as in the case of the anarchists, the socialists, and the Wobblies during the early portion of the twentieth century. It features the Communists and labor organizers who thrived before mid-century, and the antinuclear, civil rights, and New Left activists, as well as various countercultural participants, of the postwar period.

It also encompasses the wide array of movements that began to flourish during the 1960s, such as those agitating for the rights of women, gays, and Mother Earth in the 1970s and 1980s, through campaigns that highlighted local, national, and international issues, Latinos, Native Americans, Asian Americans, consumers, the elderly, the disabled, welfare recipients, and prisoners. Its distinct brand of radicalism covers the citizen activism that flourished in recent varieties of the American left including protests against globalization, violations of privacy, and assaults on human rights, whether pertaining to common citizens, LGBTQ representatives, people of color, women battling sexual abuse, children fighting for their very lives, and immigrants. Today, a revitalized American left is fighting back against an intemperate president easily given to belittling Muslims, Mexicans, a female presidential candidate, the handicapped, and left-of-center congresswomen, while consorting with white supremacists, neo-Nazis, and other anti-Semites. The battleground now includes the streets of America, sexual relationships, university campuses, the nation's public schools, social media, and the Internet.

Conveniently, from a historian's vantage point, the American left largely emerged at the start of the twentieth century, when anarchists, socialists, cultural radicals, and Wobblies—members of the Industrial Workers of the World (IWW)—thrived. They found particularly receptive audiences in Greenwich Village, which had long housed bohemians, other free spirits, and those who made up the Lyrical Left. However, American participation in World War I blunted, then debilitated the nation's first great left-wing movements, while providing seeds for others that endured for decades. The progressive administration of Woodrow Wilson targeted radical and antiwar groups and prominent figures, setting the stage for intolerant actions by federal operatives, state governments, municipalities, and vigilantes. And as the romanticism and innocence associated with the Lyrical Left dissipated, the repression and the example set by the Bolsheviks in post-czarist Russia convinced others of the need for radical, even revolutionary organizations in the United States. Both a communist and a non-communist left appeared, making up the Old Left that largely existed between 1919 and 1956.

During that nearly four-decade span of time, the Communist Party of the United States (CPUSA) dominated the American left, to the dismay of anti-communist radicals and liberals alike. American communism initially attracted independent thinkers like Reed and Max Eastman. But the party's subservience to Holy Mother Russia quickly became pronounced, resulting in otherwise inexplicable shifts in direction and leadership. The zenith of American communism occurred during the Great Depression and World War II, when Communist Party membership came close to matching that of both the Socialist Party of America (SPA) and the Industrial Workers of the World at their height. But the willingness to accept Soviet directives—including for some, instructions to engage in espionage—resulted in a discarding of the more successful Popular Front approach, involving accepting alliances with most, albeit not all, progressive forces. Sectarianism and dogmatism led many to leave the party, while the Cold War atmosphere prevailing after World War II proved catastrophic. By the mid-1950s, individuals associated with the Old Left but inclined to a critical perspective regarding the CPUSA began discussing the possibility of a revitalized American radicalism. The civil rights and antinuclear movements provided hope that both segregation and Cold War norms could be contested, as did the waning, though not the disappearance, of the postwar red scare. Radical pacifists helped to shape both campaigns, tendering the tactic of nonviolent direct action that Martin Luther King Jr. employed so deftly in the struggle to bring down Jim Crow barriers.

The longed for New Left began flourishing as a new decade opened, and eventually included youth-based organizations, Students for a Nonviolent Coordinating Committee (SNCC) and Students for a Democratic Society (SDS), envisioning a beloved community or participatory democracy, in which individuals would be actively engaged in social and political affairs on a continual basis. For a brief spell, the counterculture, with its heralding of sex, drugs, and rock 'n' roll, also seemed to promise radical, even revolutionary possibilities. A still more radical turn began occurring at the midpoint of the 1960s, as mounting frustration and despair intensified about the slow pace of change, political assassinations, and the Vietnam War, resulting in calls for black power, student syndicalism, resistance, and eventually, revolution. Groups like the Black Panthers, Weatherman, and the Vietnam Veterans Against the War (VVAW) appeared determined, however differently, to "bring the war home," while many hippies attempted to carve out alternative communities, both inside and beyond urban centers.

Both the radical fever and utopian hopes seemed to dissipate as U.S. withdrawal from Vietnam proceeded apace, but the decade of the 1960s ushered in a wide array of movements and dedicated individuals committed to carrying out "a long slow march through the institutions." Led at times by SNCC, SDS, and New Left veterans, activists by the last half of the 1960s participated in second-wave feminism, which contested male dominance, sexist stereotyping, and restricted opportunities for women. Battling persistent homophobia and discriminatory treatment, gay liberationists produced manifestoes, magazines, and newsletters, in addition to engaging in protests, including sip-ins patterned after labor and civil rights tactics and "zaps" or performance protests. Environmentalists insisted on the need for more holistic treatment of natural resources, spawning a mass movement that participated in Earth Day events. The Latino, Native American, and Asian American movements also flourished for a period during the late 1960s and the 1970s, and at various points afterward, striving for "brown power," "red power," and "yellow power," respectively.

As the women's, gay liberation, environmental, Latino, Native American, and Asian American movements burgeoned while the decade of the 1960s ended, all moved outside the confines of the New Left. But their inexorable departure from the Movement itself hardly meant the disappearance of the American left supposedly detected by many analysts, who clearly saw what they wanted to. Rather, the period ahead witnessed a proliferation of additional movements, some of them also coming out of the 1960s, and others appearing later. While not aligned in any formal manner, they demonstrated the strength of progressive, even radical ideas, but also a greater determination to avoid the internecine squabbles of American lefts that had come and gone. Together, they might be considered part of an Untethered Left that often proved highly influential, particularly at the local level. Citizen activism continued to flourish, including a consumer movement, as well as community-based organizations like the Association of Community Organizations for Reform Now (ACORN) and the Campaign for Economic Democracy (CED) that sought to curb the power of corporate interests. The elderly, the disabled, welfare recipients, and prisoners participated in movements of their own, to the amazement or chagrin of many. Remnants of the underground press and new progressive publications that flourished during the 1960s helped to spark interest in those movements and others. Alternative newspapers could be found in cities across America, many supporting grassroots drives or a "backyard revolution," as well as activism centering on national and international issues. At the end of the 1970s and the start of the following decade, antinuclear activists gained strength, amid a partial meltdown of a nuclear power plant in southeastern Pennsylvania and mounting concerns about the possibility of nuclear warfare.

President Ronald Reagan's massive increase in U.S. military spending and his support for rightwing governments and factions in Central America continued to trouble many and imperiled his presidency. His administration funneled assistance to anticommunist elements in El Salvador as a civil war raged there, and to the Contras, who sought to topple the radical Sandinista regime in Nicaragua. Identifying with the resistance movement, the Committee in Solidarity with the People of El Salvador (CISPES) opposed the Reagan administration's support for rightwing forces, including some associated with death squads, in El Salvador and other Central American states.

The aptly named Vietnam syndrome appeared to prevent the sending of large numbers of troops overseas, but that restraint disappeared during the presidencies of Reagan's successor, George Herbert Walker Bush, and the latter's son, George W. Bush. After ordering American soldiers into Panama to bring about the ouster of General Manuel Noriega, a former U.S. ally accused of drug trafficking, President Bush initiated Operation Desert Storm, to compel the removal of Iraqi troops from Kuwait. Massive protests took place around the world, in anticipation of an American-led attack against Iraq, which began in mid-January 1991. The same phenomenon occurred in late 2002 and early 2003, with more than ten million protestors urging a halt to the planned U.S. invasion of Iraq. While the early Gulf War ended quickly, preventing much in the way of a prolonged antiwar movement from emerging, the second conflict involving Iraq proved far more prolonged and soon went very badly. As war and sectarian strife tore apart Iraq and casualties soared, protests against the war surged too but the United States retained troops in both Iraq and Afghanistan as of 2020. Whether taking place in the United States or abroad, those protests were tied to a kind of Global Left, which had developed in response to intensifying inequities of power and wealth.

In addition to American troop deployments overseas, many of the other issues that sparked protest movements during the 1960s and 1970s continued to trouble activists. Racism, sexism, homophobia, environmental concerns, economic disparities, and issues confronting American consumers ensured that progressive, even radical ideas retained considerable resonance for many.

Women confronted sexist stereotypes and also efforts to prevent feminism from becoming more acceptable through ratification of the Equal Rights Amendment. Gays faced hysteria, particularly as they came out of the closet and when the HIV/AIDS epidemic began sweeping through American cities and even the heartland. As the federal government under Ronald Reagan initially failed to respond and never did so adequately, outraged gay activists responded with organizations like ACT UP (AIDS Coalition to Unleash Power) and Queer Nation. Environmentalists achieved noteworthy gains at times, through passage of long-overdue legislation and implementation of regulatory reforms. However, having adopted tactics like monkeywrenching involving deliberate sabotage, militant environmentalists through groups like Earth First! also experienced assaults on their character, sometimes their bodies, and generally the programs they espoused, as well as the environment itself.

Cultural issues proved divisive too, with charges of reverse discrimination leading to condemnations of affirmative action policies and federal court rulings that whittled away at their implementation. Members of the American left promoted progressive stances but were sometimes fragmented in their visions for the nation. They also hardly marched lock-step regarding their interpretations of constitutional protections, particularly those embedded in the First Amendment. Americans on the right and left viewed identity-rooted movements differently, with the latter generally more pleased about the possibility of cultural liberation. Education at all levels, both inside and outside classrooms, served as a battleground for debates swirling around "race, religion, gender, art, school curriculums, and history," indicates historian Seth Bartee. Although a public intellectual like Thomas Frank dismissed the culture wars, while acknowledging they shaped an increasingly charged political atmosphere, the controversy helped to pique grave concerns about many of the issues tied to progressive movements. It also sparked anger directed at supposed centers of left-of-center thinking, including the music industry, Hollywood, academia, portions of the mass media, and the American intelligentsia. A number of radical activists did indeed move into those realms, although hardly enough to monopolize any.

New popular movements continued to appear, like the Rainbow Coalition in Chicago that drew support from blacks, Latinos, less affluent poor whites, and the disabled to elect Harold Washington as mayor of Chicago in 1983. According to the journalist Ryan Grim, Washington's campaign favored "single-payer health care, gay rights . . . the Equal Rights Amendment, free community college, reparations for descendants of slaves, gender pay equity and an end to Reagan's drug war." The following year, Jesse Jackson, relying on the National Rainbow Coalition, undertook a spirited run for the Democratic Party presidential nomination. During the 1990s, an anti-globalization campaign appeared, leading to protests around the world, including massive demonstrations in Seattle as the century neared an end. Antiwar gatherings took place as the United States went to war in the Near East following the horrific attacks against New York City and Washington, D.C., on September 11, 2001. The later virtual collapse of the American economy eventually produced the Occupy Wall Street movement. The police killings of too many African Americans led to the #BlackLivesMatter crusade, while women responded to sexual abuse with the #MeToo movement. Even America's school children participated in a Never Again drive of their own, with a nationwide March for Our Lives effort and a readiness to challenge the political power of the National Rifle Association and the politicians who catered to it. Policies enacted by a xenophobic administration in Washington, D.C., led to outrage and massive protests concerning abusive treatment afforded immigrants, including children and their families. At the same time, democratic socialism acquired more adherents, as befitting Vermont Senator Bernie Sanders's spirited bids for the Democratic Party presidential nomination.

The greater acceptance of democratic socialism, however brief or extended it might prove to be, underscores the three core ideas coursing through this book, at least implicitly. The American left, with its outsider makeup, did not begin with Black Lives Matter, Me Too, or the Sanders's campaign, but rather has a long, memorable history. It succeeds best when it retains a democratic focus, and avoids association with authoritarian ideologies or practices. It resonates most clearly during the periods its proponents retain independent mindsets, even when those lean in the direction of internationalism.

Chapter 1

Socialists, Wobblies, and Village Rebels

The American left is largely a twentieth and early twenty-first century phenomenon. But its roots date back to colonial and revolutionary times, thanks to individuals ranging from Roger Williams and William Penn to Thomas Jefferson and Thomas Paine. Respectively, they propounded belief in religious freedom, freedom of conscience, egalitarianism, and the right, even the duty, to revolt against tyrannical authority. Democratic ideals took hold by the Jacksonian period, although what emerged was hardly a full-bodied democracy, given that few could participate in the political process other than adult white males. Antebellum reformers included communitarians, abolitionists, feminists, and labor activists, with some like Harriet Tubman, Elizabeth Cady Stanton, or Thomas Skidmore seeking wholesale transformation of American society.

Following the Civil War, the changes wrought by rapid modernization brought about labor and farmers' movements demanding a cooperative commonwealth. The short-lived Molly Maguires, Irish immigrants enamored with anarchism, appeared still more threatening to the powers that were. The United States experienced its "first nationwide strike," the Great Railroad Strike of 1877, amid the nationwide depression that started with the Panic of 1873. Reaching out to men and women, skilled and unskilled workers, whites and blacks, the Knights of Labor surged to a membership of 700,000 by 1886. But during a general strike called three days earlier on May 1 of that year, a bomb at Chicago's Haymarket Square that resulted in several deaths, including seven policemen, led to an association of the Knights with anarchism and violence.

Notwithstanding attempts to denigrate radicals altogether, the late nineteenth century witnessed the continued appearance of campaigns and movements that sought the radical restructuring of the social and economic system in the United States. Through their best-selling works—*Progress and Poverty, Looking Backward, 2000 – 1887*, and *Wealth Against Commonwealth*—Henry George, Edward Bellamy, and Henry Demarest Lloyd served as popularizers of vaguely socialist ideas. So did many ministers and laypersons involved with the social gospel movement, led by Washington Gladden, George Herron, Walter Rauschenbusch, and Harry F. Ward. Harking to the life and teachings of Jesus and insisting that those aspiring to the Kingdom of God had to engage in social betterment, Social Gospel advocates condemned laissez-faire capitalism. Some, like Herron, went so far as to condemn capitalism completely, warning that "a civilization based on self-interest, and securing itself through competition, has no power within itself to secure justice." The Social Gospel movement, which was called "social Christianity," dramatically impacted urban reform efforts, including those that occurred during the Progressive period. Various big city mayors, including Hazen Pingree in Detroit, and Samuel Milton "Golden Rule" Jones in Toledo, Ohio, drew from the movement as they attempted to grapple with problems resulting from rapid modernization.

More radical in his analysis of economic developments, Marxist theoretician and leader of the Socialist Labor Party (SLP) Daniel De Leon brooked little opposition as he led in a doctrinaire, sectarian way. He considered the United States an advanced capitalist nation, "ripe for the execution of Marxist revolutionary tactics." Few voters agreed and the SLP remained a minor political organization, never acquiring more than several thousand members. Little more successful was the Socialist Trade and Labor Alliance, a militant workers organization De Leon helped to spawn in opposition to the American Federation of Labor (AFL).

While De Leon's SLP remained a tiny sect, a series of radical movements briefly flourished during the 1890s, including when the severe depression that began in 1893 beset businesses, workers, and farmers across the United States. According to the historian Melvyn Dubofsky, miners in the nation's western sectors engaged in "armed war" against "capitalist adversaries." The miners' unions, including the Western Federation of Miners (WFM), bought and pilfered weapons and ammunition, conducted military-styled drilling, and anticipated clashes involving the "rifle, torch, and dynamite stick." Their opponents were equally determined and as ready to resort to violence, while also relying on Pinkerton detectives, *agents provocateurs*, even "private armies," which eventually helped to rout the WFM.

Another industrial federation, the American Railway Union (ARU), also appeared in 1893, intending to create "one, compact working force for legislative as well as industrial action," as one of its founders, Eugene V. Debs, indicated. The ARU optimistically promised to devote "itself to the great cause of industrial emancipation." A national boycott of Pullman cars resulted in federal injunctions against the union, which also confronted a large number of state and federal troops, and the jailing of Debs and other strike leaders.

During the spring of 1894, with the ARU routed and the WFM badly weakened, another display of widespread discontent with social and economic conditions developed through the carrying out of a protest march involving "Coxey's Army." A manufacturer from Massillon, Ohio, who joined the Populist Party, Jacob Coxey, determined to lead a group of jobless men to Washington, D.C., to demand a public works program. At its peak, Coxey's Army included 20,000 individuals from across the country, not the 100,000 he predicted, although even that smaller, yet still impressive number, rapidly dwindled, resulting in only 500 reaching, by May 1, the nation's capital. It was but one of a series of "industrial armies" that attempted to get to Washington, D.C., during that troubled period.

Frequently suffering through hard times of their own, farmers formed granges, Farmers Alliances, and, during the 1890s, the Populist Party. Initially, the granges were designed to lessen the social isolation many farm families experienced, but they soon pushed for legislative aid: Granger laws. Like the granges, the Alliances supported cooperative buying and marketing enterprises, while the Populist or People's Party began sending representatives to state assemblies and Congress. Its Omaha Platform in 1893 warned that the U.S. neared "moral, political, and material ruin," with "two great classes—tramps and millionaires"—appearing. Demanding a hefty increase in the money supply to assist debt-laden farmers, the Populists called for government ownership and operation of the railroads, telegraphs, and telephones. Fueled by fiery speakers like Mary Elizabeth Lease, who urged farmers to "raise less corn and more hell," and Tom Watson, the Populists performed well nationwide, but confronted strong, sometimes violent opposition, particularly from Southern Democrats, hardly disinclined to engage in fraud or to resort to racism to dilute the strength of the region's Populists. The Populists also made a politically disastrous decision to "fuse" with the Democratic Party, by backing William Jennings Bryan in his losing campaign for the presidency, in 1896, against William McKinley.

* * *

Prior to U.S. intervention in World War I, one of the three great American lefts of the twentieth century appeared, distinct from the radical movements of the late nineteenth century, and included democratic socialists, anarcho-syndicalists, and politically engaged bohemians. Their institutional founts were the Socialist Party; the IWW, representing radical laborers; and *The Masses* magazine, based appropriately enough, in Greenwich Village. The dominant players included many of American radicalism's greatest names:

Eugene V. Debs, Big Bill Haywood, Emma Goldman, Elizabeth Gurley Flynn, Crystal Eastman, Max Eastman, Inez Milholland, Randolph Bourne, and John Reed, among others. The ideological currents in vogue proved wide-ranging, moving from democratic socialism and anarcho-syndicalism to anarchism and feminism of a radical cast. The socialists, the Wobblies, and members of the Lyrical Left condemned capitalism, imperialism, racism, and patriarchy, while seeking expanded democracy politically and economically, along with cultural and sexual emancipation. Like their chronological forebears, these early twentieth century American radicals confronted hostility, legal assaults, and violence, blunting the possibility of a strong institutional left becoming entrenched in the United States. Nevertheless, the early twentieth century American left helped to sustain democracy, while insisting on its extension.

A native of Terre Haute, Indiana, who obtained a job as a locomotive fireman, served as a city clerk in his hometown, and became a member of the state legislature, Eugene V. Debs increasingly became attracted to radical ideas following his jailing during the Pullman Strike. Having identified with the Populist Party and fearing corporate dominance, Debs now warned that the extended "night of capitalism will be dark." At the same time, as his biographer Nick Salvatore reveals, Debs and many who followed him retained belief in republican ideals, individual worth, the dignity of citizenship, and "the redemptive power of the ballot." During a prison stint at Woodstock, Illinois, in the mid-1890s, Debs either did or did not experience a conversion to socialism. Following his jailing, Debs later declared, he was "a changed and charged man," who "became the advocate of revolt." Indeed, he recalled, accurately or not, being "baptized in Socialism in the roar of conflict." The violent confrontation, "the gleam of every bayonet and the flash of every rifle," Debs noted, concluded with the class struggle having been "revealed." However, near the end of his life, Debs insisted he considered himself a socialist before the strike. And yet shortly after the Pullman strike, Debs supported the possibility of a cooperative commonwealth but denied being a socialist, in testimony delivered to a federal commission. At the same time, Debs blasted a competitively-driven economic system, declaring, "Every man is entitled to all he produces with his brain and hands." The Social Gospel movement influenced Debs too, as he drew on George Herron's pronouncement that "the cross of Jesus" refuted "the competitive theory" purportedly derived from Cain.

Freed after six months of imprisonment, Debs spoke in the American vein to a crowd of more than 100,000 at a Chicago train station on November 22, 1895, affirming that "the spirit of '76 still survives." He referred to those in attendance as "lovers of liberty and as despisers of despotism." Delivering speeches around the country, and helping to pay off the debts incurred by the ARU, Debs continued to extol the virtues of the ballot box and conveyed support for Populism, while insisting on the need for "a fairer distribution of wealth." Following the defeat of William Jennings Bryan in the 1896 presidential election, Debs openly espoused a new path. "The issue is Socialism versus Capitalism. I am for Socialism because I am for humanity."

The former elected public official never discarded his faith in the electoral process. As Nick Salvatore reflects, Debs "was not born a Socialist, and he did not reject American values when he became one." He considered a commitment to the class struggle "the very fulfillment of the basic democratic promise of American life." Democratic to the very core, Debs stated, "I do not want you to follow me or anyone else. I would not lead you into the promised land if I could, because if I led you in, someone else would lead you out."

Favoring a socialist cooperative to enable laborers to acquire autonomy, Debs necessarily clashed with Daniel DeLeon of the Socialist Labor Party but also confronted Victor L. Berger, who helped, in 1897, to found the short-lived Socialist Democratic Party of America (SDPA). The SDPA was the latest attempt to establish a viable socialist organization in the United States, something that others had been striving for, including Morris Hillquit, a Latvian-born labor lawyer from New York City; editor Abraham Cahan of *The Jewish Daily Forward*, a Yiddish daily newspaper; and Julius Wayland, who published *Appeal to Reason*, a leftwing weekly. Berger, an immigrant born in Nieder-Rehbach, Austria-Hungary, who taught German in Milwaukee public schools and edited a pair of socialist newspapers, proved displeased with Debs's seeming failure to highlight class consciousness and his romantic insistence on viewing "'the people' as citizen-producers."

Nevertheless, it was the remarkably charismatic Debs who increasingly came to represent socialism for many American workers, farmers, and intellectuals. And it was Debs who declared at the same convention that ushered in the SDPA and terminated the American Railway Union, "The wage system . . . is the same in all ages, in all lands, and in all climes. Its victims work, propagate their species, bear all the burdens, and perish." The SDPA delivered its "Declaration of Principles" at the convention, insisting, in Debsian style, that "our despotic system of economics is the direct opposite of our democratic system of politics." The SDPA supported collective ownership of "all the means of production, transportation, and distribution, as well as a cooperative commonwealth to overcome "planless" capitalism, industrial conflagration, and social disarray.

That year, Debs undertook his first of a series of third-party campaigns for the American presidency. The party platform bemoaned the loss of autonomy accompanying the advent of corporate capitalism, which led to heightened economic insecurity, "poverty, misery, and degradation" for more and more Americans. As if following Karl Marx's admonition, the SDPA saw "two antagonistic classes" emerging: "the capitalist class and the propertyless class." At the same time, the previously potent middle class was vanishing. To this group of American socialists, political liberty was itself imperiled, becoming all but worthless without economic liberty too. As a minor party candidate, Debs managed to pull a mere 87,945 votes, only 0.63 percent of all the ones tabulated.

Populists and disaffected members of the SLP were among those who joined with SDPA members during the summer of 1901 at the "Unity Convention" that resulted in formation of the Socialist Party of America. A few weeks earlier, Debs had delivered a different kind of Fourth of July speech, asserting, "I am not of those who worship the flag. I have no respect for the stars and stripes, or for any other flag that symbolizes slavery." Now, with George Herron serving as convention chair, the delegates gathered in Indianapolis drew up a party platform, affirming belief in the tenets associated with International Socialism. They foresaw eventual collective ownership of the means of production and distribution, but exuded concern about ideological and cultural hegemony by "the capitalist class."

In early May 1904, the SPA's National Convention occurred in Chicago, naming Debs its presidential candidate and producing a platform articulating his expansive view of socialism. Also viewed by the historian Jack Ross as "very much the offspring of Populism," it deemed the SPA "the defender and preserver of the ideal of liberty and self-government." The platform supported "the eight-hour day, comprehensive social insurance, an income and inheritance tax, the abolition of child labor, women's suffrage, and the initiative, referendum, and recall," all favored by progressives. Debs's vote total in November mushroomed to over 400,000, as it would four years later.

* * *

Despite Debs's continued insistence that the SPA was "colorless," meaning colorblind, the American left at this point, and for some time afterward, continued to appear either oblivious to racial concerns or willing to harbor racism in its midst. Antagonists, playing the race card, had helped to divide the Populists and did the same in many labor unions. Leading early American socialists like Victor Berger and Jack London, who, due to his unmarried mother's illness, had been raised by a former slave, adhered to both social Darwinism and racial Darwinism, often labeled scientific racism.

Nevertheless, black luminaries like William Monroe Trotter and W. E. B. Du Bois contributed much to both American radicalism and public discourse. A recipient of two degrees from Harvard College in four years, Trotter founded *The Guardian* newspaper in 1901, designed to deliver "propaganda against discrimination." He soon allied with W. E. B. Du Bois, the first African American to receive a PhD from Harvard, who had written *The Souls of Black Folk* (1903), which declared "the problem of the Twentieth Century is the problem of the color line." "The Negro," Du Bois poignantly wrote, was afflicted with "double-consciousness. . . . One ever feels his two-ness—an American, a Negro . . . two thoughts, two unreconciled strivings; two warring ideals in one dark body, whose dogged strength alone keeps it from being torn asunder."

Trotter, who had helped to set up the National Negro Suffrage League, joined with Du Bois to found the Niagara Movement (1905), which brought together twenty-nine black leaders who, in a "Declaration of Principles," asserted, "We claim for ourselves every single right that belongs to a free-born American, political, civil and social." This contrasted with the approach of Booker T. Washington, who headed the Tuskegee Institute and urged his fellow African Americans to strive for economic gain, while seemingly accepting the social, political, and legal encumbrances that increasingly befell them in an age when the Supreme Court articulated the infamous separate but equal doctrine. The Niagara Movement insisted on attacking segregation and discriminatory practices involving unions, public facilities, and jurisprudence.

* * *

The same year that the Niagara Movement appeared, the Intercollegiate Socialist Society (ISS), building on earlier socialist clubs at the University of Wisconsin in Madison and the University of California at Berkeley, gathered in New York City for its initial session. The previous December, the writer Upton Sinclair, who was publishing a serialized version of *The Jungle*, his novel about the Chicago meatpacking industry, solicited signatures from socialist intellectuals supporting formation of such a group. Signatories included the radical attorney Clarence Darrow; Jack London, who had already published *The Call of the Wild, How I Became a Socialist*, and *The War of the Classes*; the millionaire socialist Graham Phelps Stokes; and William English Walling, another wealthy writer and founder of the National Women's Trade Union League. The social worker Florence Kelley and the radical feminist Charlotte Perkins Gilman, a proponent of both socialism and sexual emancipation, were founders, too, with Du Bois serving on the executive committee. The lawyer and social activist Crystal Eastman and the author Mary Beard were present at the opening assemblage, while Walter Lippmann, who attended Columbia University, was an early member. The ISS sought "to promote an intelligent interest in Socialism among college men and women."

The Intercollegiate Socialist Society proved influential on various college campuses, while the Christian Socialist Fellowship sought "to permeate churches, denominations, and other religious institutions with the social message of Jesus; to show that Socialism is the necessary economic expression

of the Christian life; to end the class struggle by establishing industrial democracy; and to hasten the reign of justice and brotherhood on the earth."

* * *

Before his next presidential campaign, Debs flirted with more radical possibilities. In contrast to other SPA leaders like Victor Berger and Morris
Hillquit, Debs viewed favorably the call in 1905 for a new "revolutionary
labor union." The founding convention for such an organization occurred in
Chicago in late June, resulting in the establishment of the Industrial Workers
of the World, whose members were known as the Wobblies and condemned
"the wages system." Debs saw the need for an industrial union associated
with "the class struggle," to assist "the political movement." He opposed the
"boring-from-within" tactic of existing labor unions supported by many others, including Berger. Speaking in South Chicago in late November, Debs
likened the IWW to the ARU, and extolled "class-conscious, revolutionary
workingmen . . . who" sought "the overthrow of the capitalist system, and the
emancipation of the working class from wage-slavery." He exclaimed, "We
have declared war upon the capitalist class, and upon the capitalist system. . . . We say: Arouse, you workingmen! . . . It is your duty to build up this
great revolutionary economic organization of your class, to seize and take
control of the tools with which you work, and make yourselves the masters
instead of being the slaves of industry."

Debs's direct association with the IWW proved short-lived but significant. Bill Haywood called the IWW's founding convention to order, proclaiming it "the Continental Congress of the working class." The gathering,
participated in by representatives from forty-three groups, was intended,
Haywood declared, to liberate workers from capitalism's "slave bondage."
The IWW aspired to place workers "in possession of the economic power,
the means of life, in control of the machinery of production and distribution,
without regard to capitalist masters." In contrast to the AFL and affiliated
organizations, the IWW welcomed black workers and foreign- and native-
born laborers. The group's manifesto pointed to increasingly fixed class divisions and ever sharper class antagonisms. His craftsmanship made "useless,"
the worker became a wage slave, suffering longer workdays and reduced
wages. While dividing workers, employers united "to crush," brutally, any
resistance, through injunctive relief and military might. The failure to unite
and display labor solidarity hurt Pennsylvanian textile workers, Chicago
butchers, Santa Fe machinists, and Colorado miners. Craft unions separated
workers, who required "a universal working class movement . . . one great
industrial union embracing all industries" rooted in the class struggle.
Among those affixing signatures to the IWW manifesto, which demanded

"an open union and a closed shop," were Debs, Haywood, Charles H. Moyer, William E. Trautmann, and Mother Jones.

The IWW soon became ensnared in an infamous murder trial that threatened to destroy the organization only months after its founding. On December 30, 1905, former Idaho governor Frank Steunenberg was fatally wounded in Caldwell, Idaho, by a bomb that exploded as he attempted to open the gate to his home. At one time viewed as pro-union, Steunenberg had enraged labor activists when, in the midst of bitter industrial conflict involving the WFM six years earlier, he declared martial law and requested federal troops. In justifying these actions, the governor stated, "We have taken the monster by the throat and we are going to choke the life out of it." Troopers rounded up more than 1,000 miners, placing them in detention centers where conditions were abominable. James McParland of the Pinkerton Detective Agency investigated Steunenberg's murder, quickly determining that key leaders in the WFM, Charles Moyer and Bill Haywood, along with another WFM member, George A. Pettibone, had plotted the assassination. Moyer was the WFM president, while Haywood served as secretary-treasurer. The charges against Moyer would be dropped, but before that happened Debs delivered a warning, headlined "Arouse, Ye Slaves." Recalling the Haymarket Square martyrs, Debs bristled, "If an attempt is made to repeat it, there will be a revolution and I will do all in my power to precipitate it. . . . If they attempt to murder Moyer, Haywood and Pettibone and their brothers, a million revolutionists will meet them with guns."

The trial, which attained national coverage, began in May 1907, with Clarence Darrow defending Haywood. In his lengthy closing statement, Darrow declared that Haywood had "risked his life" for the union cause, but warned, "Don't think for a moment that if you hang him you will crucify the labor movement of the world." Insisting he was not just representing Haywood, Darrow theatrically continued, "Gentlemen, it is not for him alone that I speak. I speak for the poor, for the weak, for the weary, for that long line of men who in darkness and despair have borne the labors of the human race." Newly elected to the U.S. Senate, prosecutor William Borah, who would become a renowned progressive legislator, saw anarchy unleashing "its first bloody triumph in Idaho." The jury rendered a "Not guilty" verdict, and Pettibone also won acquittal in a separate trial. Deeming the decision in the Haywood case "a gross miscarriage of justice," President Theodore Roosevelt suggested, "I suppose the jury was terrorized." Delighted by the verdict, the anarchist Emma Goldman and two colleagues telegrammed Roosevelt: "Undesirable citizens victorious. Rejoice." In an insightful, book-length analysis of the case, the journalist J. Anthony Lukas has determined that jury tampering occurred.

The IWW, having escaped a possible death blow, and the SPA each eventually attained a membership total of 100,000, the largest in the history

of the American left. Their philosophies and those of their leading representatives, Debs and Haywood, at times overlapped but also ultimately diverged.
As the historian Milton Cantor notes, American socialism drew from the
Bible, Jesus, Thomas Jefferson, and Thomas Paine, but appealed to both
farmers and workers. It included "social gospel Christians, utopians, Populists . . . anarchist-syndicalists, and . . . Marxist ideologues." The Socialist
Party at one point flourished in New York City and Milwaukee, and also in
the rural Southwest. The Wobblies subscribed to an eclectic mix of ideas and
theories, including both anarchism and syndicalism, while tending to those
near the bottom of the social strata, ill-affected by rapid modernization. Wobblies were white and black, native-stock Americans and immigrants, miners,
migratory laborers, dock workers, and textile workers. George Speed, an
organizer out West, conveyed the thinking behind the group's open admission policy: "One man is as good as another to me. I don't care whether he is
black, blue, green, or yellow, as long as he acts the man and acts true to his
economic interests as a worker."

Not democratic socialism, but anarcho-syndicalism was the ideology behind the IWW and Big Bill Haywood, who believed in One Big Union,
including white and black workers, and looked forward to a general strike
and industrial sabotage. While associated with "propaganda by the deed" and
bombastic rhetoric, IWW members nevertheless recognized that violence,
largely monopolized by governmental and corporate entities, was no path to
power. For their part, the Wobblies distrusted government operatives while
subscribing to "industrial unionism, labor solidarity, political nonpartisan-
ship, direct economic action and syndicalism," but "with a singularly
American patina," according to Melvyn Dubofsky. Romantically, Haywood
believed that in the future "there will be no such thing as the State or States."
Industrial unions would own and run their own industries, with the manageri-
al class selected by union members. The end result would be some version of
the cooperative commonwealth, industrial democracy, or "Industrial Communism."

By 1908, the IWW experienced the fate common to American leftwing
organizations: factional strife. One group, associated with Daniel DeLeon,
believed in the necessity of both political and economic activity to usher in
working-class dominance, while another faction, tied to Haywood and Vincent St. John, the IWW's general organizer, favored direct action. A miner
who became a WFM organizer, Frank H. Little denied that workers would
attain what they wanted through "sticking a piece of white paper into a
capitalist ballot box." The internecine battle occurred at the fourth IWW
convention, held in Chicago during late September, with removal from the
preamble of any reference to politics. DeLeon blasted the "new" version of
the IWW, dismissing its members as "bums, anarchists, and physical force
destroyers." Continuing to revile the IWW, DeLeon lambasted the "Overalls

Brigade," "Proletarian Rabble and Bummers," the "slum proletariat," the "bum brigade," and "hoboes" who formed its core. The WFM, the AFL, DeLeon's SLP, and the SPA also charged that "anarchists and bums" made up the IWW, and Debs, with little fanfare, walked away from the organization.

Some socialists, like Debs, did overcome the racism or disinterest that characterized too many of their compatriots. Several were involved with the new National Association for the Advancement of Colored People (NAACP), established in February 1909, only a few months following a terrible race riot in Springfield, Illinois, where Abraham Lincoln's tomb resided. Two reported assaults on white women by black men touched off lynchings, attacks on the homes of black families, and widespread property damage. Deeply distraught by recent events, white liberals and radicals, including Mary White Ovington, Oswald Garrison Villard, and William English Walling, issued a call for a gathering to explore racial issues. Sixty people, including seven African Americans led by W. E. B. Du Bois, Mary Church Terrell, and Ida B. Well-Barnett, signed the manifesto. The NACCP sought to safeguard constitutional rights, including those embedded in the 13th, 14th, and 15th Amendments, pertaining to slavery's abolition, equal protection of the law, and black suffrage. Prominent among the organization's early members were Jane Addams, Mary McLeod Bethune, Clarence Darrow, John Dewey, John Haynes Holmes, William Dean Howells, Florence Kelley, John Milholland, Henry Moskowitz, Charles Edward Russell, Lincoln Steffens, and Lillian Wald. Within a year, Du Bois began putting out *The Crisis* magazine, whose subtitle read "A Record of the Darker Races." The NAACP quickly became involved in different campaigns, including legal fights regarding the grandfather clause, intended to prevent anyone from voting whose grandfather had been unable to, legislative attempts to outlaw lynchings, and a direct action campaign concerning both William Trotter and *Birth of a Nation*, D. W. Griffith's epic but racist film.

Beginning in the fall of 1909, the IWW, with its more inclusive approach concerning race, became involved in a series of free speech fights, the first in Missoula, Montana, and another in Spokane, Washington. Fiery, nineteen-year-old Elizabeth Gurley Flynn, who joined the IWW while in high school and whose parents were working-class socialists, her organizer husband Jack Jones, and Wobbly agitator Frank Little participated in the free speech fight in Missoula. The IWW considered this its first free speech battle, and, one that, unlike so many others, proved successful. Arrest after arrest, including that of Flynn and Jones, charged with disturbing the peace, occurred, resulting in overloaded city jails. Flynn sent a message to the Wobbly office, located in Spokane, Washington, asking for "volunteers to go to jail." Wobbly supporters arrived from the Pacific Northwest, coming "on top of the trains and beneath the trains, and on the sides, in the box cars and every way that you didn't have to pay fare," Flynn recalled. Some went to a soapbox, and began reading from the U.S Constitution. Once behind bars, the Wobblies sang IWW songs and tossed out IWW slogans, receiving beatings in return. In another message, Flynn painted a gloomy picture of "the makeshift cell": "It's a filthy, dirty hole under the firehouse stable, where all the filthy excrement of the place pours down upon the prisoners." Matters were little better on the city streets, where the mayor demanded that the fire chief wield a water hose against protestors. As Wobblies continued pouring into Missoula, the city fathers backed down, dropping charges, releasing the prisoners, and allowing Wobbly speakers to have their say, provided they didn't impede traffic.

The battleground quickly shifted to Spokane, where the city council issued an ordinance prohibiting speaking on city streets, other than by those orating on behalf of the Salvation Army. *The Industrial Worker*, the Wobbly newspaper considered the voice of revolutionary industrial unionism, urged, "Big free speech fight in Spokane; come yourself if possible, and bring the boys with you!" On November 2, individual Wobblies followed one another in getting atop an overturned crate soapbox, and began talking. That day alone, police arrested over 100 Wobblies, often beating them in the process. Over the next several weeks, the number of arrests approached 600, while *The Industrial Worker* favored "passive resistance," opposing any attempt "to incite disorder or 'rioting.'" Among those placed in jail was Elizabeth Gurley Flynn. Soon called the Rebel Girl by IWW poet Joe Hill, Flynn offered an account in *The Industrial Worker* of the city jail's overcrowded and dangerous conditions. In March, the city council repealed the ordinance the Wobblies found so offensive. The historian Dale Raugust deems the Spokane action the "first significant free speech fight in the country."

From October 1910 to March 1911, the IWW waged another fight for free speech, one that featured Frank Little, in Fresno, California. The Wobbly chapter there was largely made up of migratory farm workers and casual laborers, and included Little's brother, W. F. By early October, the IWW National Office sent out a telegram declaring the fight in Fresno important, in the face of police "determined to crush organization." Another telegram, this one arriving from Fresno, promised, "Will fight to finish." Long attacked by the local press, the local Wobblies were driven out of their hall, forced to use a rented tent situated outside the city. As IWW members arrived in Fresno, having responded to solicitations from their union, the *Fresno Herald* suggested that "a whipping post and a cat-o-nine tails well seasoned by being soaked in salt water is none too harsh a treatment for peace-breakers." A succession of arrests began in the middle of the month, after Little spoke from a soapbox until "forcibly stopped" from doing so. However, the movement in Fresno initially failed to catch fire as had the Missoula and Spokane protests. Even the Wobblies' tirades while in jail seemingly only induced brutal treatment, including water hosing. But by late November, another campaign began, leading to scores of arrests. And on December 7, Little was acquitted after the court determined there existed "no law prohibiting speech without a permit in Fresno," writes the historian Matthew S. May.

Not all subsequent free speech fights proved as successful for the Wobblies, as evidenced by what transpired in San Diego in 1912. Downtown San Diego contained a section that served, in Melvyn Dubofsky's words, like "Hyde Park Speakers' Corner" in London. Radicals of various sorts, suffragists, religious believers, and non-believers waxed eloquently or not from E Street. Starting in late 1911, the San Diego city council shut down the speakers' area, leading to a clash with the California affiliate of the Free Speech League, founded nearly a decade earlier. The city's political leaders also employed vigilantes, who meted out considerable violence, and called on the Justice Department, which accused the Wobblies of engaging in "a criminally treasonous" conspiracy.

As free speech battles developed, the IWW also participated in a series of strikes across the nation, as it had since its inception. All the while, it acquired a romantic aura that appealed to any number of American writers, artists, and intellectuals, the group that would be called the Lyrical Left. The organization's association with poet-activists hardly hurt. Wobbly Ralph Chaplin penned "Solidarity Forever," its lyrics offered to the tune of "John Brown's Body" and "The Battle Hymn of the Republic." The anthem condemned "the greedy parasite," and celebrated workers who "plowed the prairies; built the cities. . . . Dug the mines and built the workshops, endless miles of railroad laid." The union, Chaplin insisted, "makes us strong." Another songwriter-activist, Joe Hill, crafted works like "The Preacher and the Slave," "The Tramp," and "The Rebel Girl," the latter an ode to Elizabeth Gurley Flynn. The first of those songs caustically referred to "long-haired preachers," "the Starvation Army," and "Holly Rollers and Jumpers," an obvious slap at the Salvation Army, its ministers, and fundamentalists, who made empty promises like "You'll get pie in the sky when you die." By contrast, workers worldwide needed to unite and demand freedom.

The IWW's "outlaw style," suggests the historian Michael Kazin, did not diminish its "heroic" campaign to assist the nation's most indigent workers. The Wobblies contested wage cuts in Goldfield, Nevada; bolstered sawmill workers, smeltermen, lumberjacks, and bakers out West; aided textile workers along the Eastern seaboard; helped out automobile and construction workers in the Midwest; and backed the racially integrated Brotherhood of Timber Workers in the American Southwest. The best remembered strike activities occurred in 1912 and 1913, taking place in Lawrence, Massachusetts; Paterson, New Jersey; and Wheatland, California. Called the "Bread and Roses" strike, the struggle in Lawrence, where the textile industry reigned, involved mostly immigrant laborers, particularly Italians, Lithuanians, and Poles, but also Armenians, Portuguese, and Russians. In response to a new state law capping the work week at fifty-four hours, employers sliced wages, and workers, on January 12, walked off the job. As they did so, a number engaged in acts of industrial sabotage. The following day, the IWW's Joseph Ettor appeared, urging workers to hold fast in demanding higher wages. At one point, all mills in the city shut down, with 25,000 workers on strike. Ettor, Elizabeth Gurley Flynn, and Bill Haywood provided guidance, emphasizing the need for solidarity. Women proved instrumental to the strike action, and also chose, in well-publicized fashion, to send their children out-of-town to be cared for as the labor clash continued. Despite the sending in of Pinkerton infiltrators, state militia, Marines, local police, and replacement laborers, reviled as "scabs," striking workers eventually prevailed in obtaining wage increases, overtime pay, and no retribution against strikers. They also overcame considerable violence, which included beatings of women and children, and the killing of a woman and a teenage boy.

* * *

The Lawrence strike occurred during a period when the American left appeared stronger than ever. In fact, American socialists, with their party membership having reached 118,000, never performed better nationwide than they did in 1912. That year's presidential election saw New Jersey Governor Woodrow Wilson, the Democratic candidate, prevail over the Republican incumbent, William Howard Taft, and former president Theodore Roosevelt, who was running on the Progressive or Bull Moose Party ticket. The fourth candidate in the race, Eugene Debs, attained a high point for the Socialist Party, taking 901,000 votes, nearly 6 percent of those cast. In several states— Arizona, California, Idaho, Montana, Nevada, Oklahoma, and Washington— Debs received over 10 percent of the votes.

Debs's presidential run was in line with electoral successes the Socialist Party had recently attained or would in 1912, which suggested that the organization might be on the path to becoming a significant factor in American politics. That year, 1,200 socialists were elected to municipal offices in over 300 cities, including a large number of mayoral posts. Socialism established seemingly firm roots in New York City and Berger's Milwaukee, where piecemeal or "sewer socialism" thrived, and also across parts of the American Southwest, where the ideology was linked to the familiar idea of the cooperative commonwealth. Nowhere was the SPA stronger than in Oklahoma, where socialists, for a number of years, became elected officials. Influenced by German-born editor Oscar Ameringer (soon expelled from the state branch) and Otto Branstetter, the Oklahoma party was a particularly potent force. Helping fuel the SPA's growth in the Southwest were regular encampments and a litany of charismatic speakers, including Ameringer, Debs, Kate Richards O'Hare, and Mother Jones.

By the spring of 1911, socialist momentum had appeared to be building, with socialists elected mayors in cities across the United States, ranging from Berkeley, California, and Eureka, Utah, to Rockaway, New Jersey, and Schenectady, New York. Victor Berger was sitting in Congress, the first socialist seated in the House of Representatives. Socialists held control of a growing number of labor unions, many affiliated, surprisingly or not, with the AFL. The next year's electoral results saw Berger defeated in his reelection bid, but party members continued to pile up offices nationwide, and Debs delivered an impressive showing in the presidential race. As James Weinstein, an astute chronicler of the American left, notes, socialists put out "more than 300 daily, weekly, and monthly publications," with *The Appeal to Reason* eventually attaining a weekly circulation of 761,000.

Socialists, in the all too typical manner of the American left, however, continued to display a propensity to fracture. Arguments over personalities, ideologies, and tactics beset the party and other left-of-center organizations. Egos and contrasting visions divided leaders like Debs, Berger, and Haywood. In his analysis of the American left, Milton Cantor discusses the separation between immediatists such as Berger, who believed in a gradual, reform-oriented path to socialism, and impossibilists like De Leon, who adhered to faith in the working class's international and revolutionary capabilities. Little caused greater sectarian divides than reliance on the ballot, radical unionism, and even rhetorical blandishments of a more militant cast. Some considered political action insufficient, and disputes continued regarding "boring from within" unions like the AFL or supporting dual unionism, which involved setting up new, radical confederations outside the purview of that seemingly conservative labor organization.

Even Haywood's attempt to meld socialism and industrial unionism proved unavailing, at least for very long. In 1912, he became a member of the SPA's National Executive Committee (NEC). But his open professions of belief in the need for sabotage to expel "the capitalistic class," and his seeming dismissal of "political Socialists," led to calls for his ouster from the NEC. In February 1913, his removal occurred, leading to Haywood's walking away from the party.

The general political atmosphere of the times drove many to willingly accept piecemeal reform, while others held out for wholesale social and economic transformation. For a time, socialism and even industrial unionism thrived as reform movements did likewise. From the close of the nineteenth century through World War I, progressivism dominated American political life, as attempts to ameliorate the worst aspects of industrial capitalism, to right many of the wrongs caused by rapid modernization, took hold. Ideologically, progressives ranged from just right of the ideological spectrum to a considerable distance on the left, skirting socialism's edges. Progressives were united in their disdain for socialist Darwinism and disbelief in laissez-faire capitalism. Rather, they subscribed to Reform Darwinism, reasoning that government, acting on behalf of the people, should steer the economy to ward off capitalism's greatest excesses, including monopolism; endemic corruption; and crass exploitation of land, resources, and human beings.

Progressivism developed in stages, beginning with urban reform under mayors like Detroit's Hazen Pingree, Toledo's Samuel "Golden Rule" Jones, Jersey City's Mark Fagan, and Cleveland's Tom Johnson. It moved to statehouses under governors Robert F. La Follette (Wisconsin), Hiram Johnson (California), Woodrow Wilson (New Jersey), and several others. Its pinnacle, for some, resided in the presidencies of Theodore Roosevelt and Wilson, as they laid a framework, however sketchily, incompletely, even unknowingly, for the American welfare state. Disproportionately, progressivism drew from the ranks of the well-educated middle class, and included social workers of the Jane Addams-Lillian Wald-Florence Kelly variety, legal realists like Oliver Wendell Holmes Jr. and Louis Brandeis, and new socialist scientists on the order of John Commons, Richard Ely, and Woodrow Wilson. Included too were environmentalists in both the John Muir and Gifford Pinchot camps, child-centric educators tied to John Dewey and his Laboratory School, the documentarian Lewis Hine, and muckraking journalists David Graham Phillips, Lincoln Steffens, and Ida Tarbell. The feminist drive, dominated by suffragists led by Harriet Stanton Blatch and Alice Paul, proved influential too. Champions of birth control, celebrated by Margaret Sanger and her *Birth Control Review*, made up another important contingent of early twentieth century American progressivism. On a less positive note, progressivism was also associated with more restrictive, even reactionary movements, including prohibition and nativism, the latter of which spurred anti-immigration drives.

For a period, progressives, the SPA, and the IWW coexisted, however uneasily. Progressivism, socialism, and anarchism, if not anarcho-syndicalism, appealed to many of the same constituencies. That tenuous relationship, if it can be called that, would not last, and the early twentieth century American left paid an enormous price as a consequence. But during the first decade and a half or so of the new century, American progressives and radicals would exist, if not side-by-side, then through an ever evolving dance that saw the former incorporate many ideas and portions of programs from the socialists, at least. All of this enabled individuals and sometimes groups to flirt with both progressivism and radicalism, to the obvious dismay of more conservative forces, including within the progressive movement.

* * *

Fascinated by both the socialists and the Wobblies, left-inclined intellectuals during the period before U.S. entrance into World War I were often drawn to militant postures, while very much influenced by romantic sensibilities. Drawing on Floyd Dell's encapsulation of 1912 as the "Lyrical Year," the historian John P. Diggins, in discussing the radical intellectuals of the pre-war era, lucidly writes about the Greenwich Village rooted Lyrical Left. Those intellectuals included Anglo-Saxon Protestants and Jews, middle-class and poorer sorts, the elite-educated and products of "tuition-free schooling," political radicals and apolitical types, Marxists and those influenced by the virtues extolled by Benjamin Franklin, writes Milton Cantor. Greenwich Village provided a nurturing backdrop, offering cheap rent and food, welcoming the avante-garde, and containing a raft of "bookshops, art studios, saloons, and salons."

No institutional fount carried more weight among the artists and radicals who congregated to the Village than *The Masses*, which had started as a socialist publication in 1911 but acquired a sharper edge when the strikingly handsome Max Eastman became editor at the end of the following year. Eastman quickly delivered a defining statement regarding the magazine's purpose:

> This magazine is owned and published cooperatively by its editors. It has no dividends to pay, and nobody is trying to make money out of it. A revolutionary and not a reform magazine: a magazine with a sense of humour and no respect for the respectable: frank, arrogant, impertinent, searching for true causes: a magazine directed against rigidity and dogma wherever it is found: printing what is too naked or true for a money-making press: a magazine whose final policy is to do as it pleases and conciliate nobody, not even its readers.

Its readers, *The Masses* also insisted, needed to "enjoy the revolution." Over the next five years, *The Masses* presented politically-charged artwork by such renowned artists as George Bellows, Stuart Davis, Robert Henri, Rockwell Kent, Robert Minor, Boardman Robinson, John Sloan, and Art Young. Writers for the publications included another Who's Who of the American left: Sherwood Anderson, Randolph Bourne, Louise Bryant, Dorothy Day, Floyd Dell, Mabel Dodge, Crystal Eastman, Arturo Giovannitti, Michael Gold, Helen Keller, John Reed, Carl Sandburg, Upton Sinclair, and Mary Heaton Vorse.

Young activists like lawyer-social work proponent Crystal Eastman, the suffragist-journalist Inez Milholland, the writer Randolph Bourne, and the journalist-political activist John Reed—all of whom contributed, in some manner, to *The Masses*—exemplified the Lyrical Left's dogged commitment to socialism, feminism, labor rights, internationalism, and, perhaps most of all, individualism. They displayed the kind of independence of mind that later versions of the American left were not identified with, fairly or not. Perhaps their early deaths—Eastman died at the age of forty-seven, while Milholland, Bourne, and Reed never reached their thirty-third birthdays— prevented the disillusionment with radical ideals others, including Crystal's brother Max, eventually experienced or the ideological stultification that beset various members of the early twentieth century American left and would afflict the Old Left and the New Left as well. On the other hand, Crystal Eastman, Milholland, Bourne, and Reed might have continued to personify the cultural sensibility that bound them together and distinguished them from other editions of the American left.

No matter the acclaim they acquired or the controversies that inevitably swirled about them, at times even among their allies, their independent cast of mind set Eastman, Milholland, Bourne, and Reed apart, even from certain of their generational and ideological cohorts. It certainly did so in relation to many later American radicals who seemingly worshipped at the altar of communism or national liberation fronts, leading them to pay homage toward Moscow, Beijing, Havana, Hanoi, or Managua. Discarding their independent cast of mind was something that Crystal Eastman, Inez Milholland, Randolph Bourne, and John Reed refused to do, like mentors on the order of Max Eastman, Emma Goldman, Debs, and Haywood. Like Max, his sister Crystal, Milholland, Bourne, and Reed reveled in the spirit of liberation that coursed through American radical circles during the twentieth century's first two decades. All four partook of—or wished to, in Bourne's case—the more open attitude about sexuality and intimate relations between men and women, celebrated by Goldman. Similar to Debs, they favored a brand of socialism that was open, inclusive, and democratic, although Reed ended up in the communist camp in the last two years of his life, and Haywood landed in Soviet Russia. Along with Haywood, they championed workers' rights, with particular concern for those viewed as members of the lumpenproletariat in Marxian terms, albeit in quasi-anarchist fashion.

Had their short lives been longer, Eastman, Milholland, Bourne, and Reed perhaps would have experienced the hard turn leftward or the disillusionment with radicalism that others of their generation, again like Max Eastman, underwent. On the other hand, they might have helped to leaven a sharp shift in either direction, while retaining their twin-fold commitment to personal liberation and community—interclass and transnational. The American Left could thereby possibly have avoided the tendency to genuflect to Holy Mother Russia or to divide into hardline pro-Soviet and anti-communist groupings. That in turn would have enabled radical voices to possess both continuity and integrity across the various generations of the twentieth century American left. Eastman, Milholland, Bourne, and Reed did cede legacies to later iterations of the left, including a profound belief in economic democracy, citizen engagement, the inherent dangers in war being waged by a democratic state, and the sensibility that the personal was indeed political. In the process, Crystal Eastman, Inez Milholland, Randolph Bourne, and John Reed left behind personal models for acting, living, and thinking differently, including as cultural and political radicals in early twentieth century America. Their very existence, friendships, alliances, and writings offered unique perspectives on socialism, anarchism, communism, feminism, and anti-imperialism. They presented telling analyses of labor and class, feminism and sexuality, personal liberation and cultural advances, education, war and imperialism, the state and militarism, civil liberties, and reform and revolution. Eastman, Milholland, Bourne, and Reed delivered much of substance, through their work and their very lives, in a too stunningly brief amount of time. It is fascinating to conjecture what more they might have accomplished and how that could have impacted the American left and American society as a whole.

Eastman, Milholland, Bourne, and Reed intersected with the era's dominant radical currents: socialism and industrial unionism. They also, at different points, expressed sympathy with anarchism of the sort associated with Emma Goldman, more than any other individual. But for a short time, Big Bill Haywood loomed largest in the hearts of Lyrical Leftists, celebrated in their foremost publications and feted at salons, particularly Greenwich Village's leading one, Mabel Dodge's at 23 Fifth Avenue. Haywood's celebrity followed his reengagement with the IWW after a number of years when he largely agitated on behalf of the Socialist Party as much as he did for industrial unionism. His participation in the Lawrence textile strike was succeeded by his involvement the next year in Paterson, where silk mill workers engaged in a work stoppage of their own. The strike in Paterson culminated in nearly 2,000 arrests, the shutting down of hundreds of mills and dye houses, and the appearance of radical figures. Fighting off increased workloads, laborers, led by the IWW's Haywood, Elizabeth Gurley Flynn, Patrick Quinlan, and Carlo Tresca, demanded better working conditions, including an eight-hour work day. Once again, women were key participants, understanding, as Haywood put it, that "the great feminist movement in the world" required economic freedom.

The labor left and the cultural left came together, as embodied by John Reed, a Harvard graduate who had been radicalized, thanks to mentoring by Lincoln Steffens, but also due to encountering what he did on the streets of New York City and in places like Paterson. "I couldn't help but observe the ugliness of poverty and all its train of evil, the cruel inequality between rich people who had too many motor-cars and poor people who didn't have enough to eat," Reed revealed. Writing in *The Masses*, Reed indicated, "There's war in Paterson. But it's a curious kind of war. All the violence is the work of one side—the Mill Owners." As Reed noted, "their servants" and "paid mercenaries," referring to the police and Pinkertons, "ride down law-abiding people on horseback" or "shoot and kill innocent people."

Acting on Haywood's suggestion, Reed and Mabel Dodge, who would soon live together, helped put on the Paterson Strike Pageant, attended in Madison Square Garden by 15,000 people. To Randolph Bourne, the pageant, with an IWW band performing "La Marseillaise" and "The Internationale" and Wobbly regalia aplenty, "stamped into one's mind the idea that a new social art was in the American world, something genuinely and excitingly new." But it operated at a loss, while the Paterson strike concluded unhappily, with many strikers replaced or forced to accept other jobs.

The outbreak of war in Europe in 1914 increasingly compelled American radicals like John Reed, Crystal Eastman, Randolph Bourne, and Inez Milholland to attend to events overseas. They, like so many on the American left, were terribly disappointed as socialists throughout Europe rallied around their respective national flags championing the war effort. Few reacted in the manner once predicted, that socialists worldwide would refuse to back martial conflicts, particularly those involving imperial powers, but would, instead, support only class warfare. As matters turned out, many American socialists and the SPA did operate like that, which proved enormously costly to the organization and American socialism in general.

Among those who remained true to the ideal of internationalism and condemned the war, including when their own country entered it, were several of the individuals associated with the SPA, the IWW, and *The Masses*. Twenty-seven-year-old Randolph Bourne was traveling abroad when the war broke out. The five-foot tall Bourne, a hunchback whose face had been disfigured during a difficult birth, was only able to initially enroll at Columbia University four years earlier owing to familial financial difficulties, but then he performed exceptionally well, while beginning to make his mark as a cogent chronicler of contemporary events. His writings included an analysis of labor relations in the United States, with a discussion of the McNamara case involving two brothers, members of the International Association of Bridge and Structural Iron Workers, charged with bombing the *Los Angeles Times* building in 1911, which led to twenty deaths, another bombing involving the Llewellyn Iron Works, and a trial featuring Clarence Darrow. As the trial began, James and John McNamara quickly confessed, shocking the courtroom and union supporters. Bourne's account appeared in *The Masses*, warning that "industrial war and the open conflict of a submerged and eternal class-hostility is no mere figure of speech." Having attained both his BA and MA from Columbia, Bourne received a fellowship to spend a full year in Europe. In August 1914, he returned to the United States, and continued writing for the *Dial* and *The Atlantic Monthly*, and also *The New Republic*, a fledgling progressive publication established by Herbert Croly, Walter Weyl, and Walter Lippmann. Bourne offered insightful articles, with an early focus on both American youth and education.

But by 1916, Bourne was also presenting articles like "Trans-National America," which appeared in the July 1916 issue of *The Atlantic*. In the face of growing nativism, Bourne wrote, "We are all foreign-born or the descendants of foreign-born, and if distinctions are to be made between us, they should rightly be on some ground than indigenousness." Bourne declared that "the new peoples," among them the New Immigrants from Southern and Eastern Europe so reviled by nativists, would "save us from our own stagnation." He decried "the weary old nationalism,—belligerent, exclusive, inbreeding, the poison of which we are witnessing now in Europe," charging it only made "patriotism a hollow sham." Countering pseudo-patriotism and "thinly disguised militarism" named "preparedness," Bourne warned, "the cosmopolitan ideal" and a unique transnationalism needed to appear. Concluding his essay, Bourne offered, "All our idealisms must be those of future social goals in which all can participate, the good life of personality lived in the environment of the Beloved Community." To bring about a transnational America, he indicated, was "work for a younger *intelligentsia* of America."

By the time World War I started in Europe, John Reed was possibly the most famous journalist in the United States. His reputation was bolstered by his coverage of social conditions in New York City, labor strife, and the Mexican Revolution. In late 1913 and early 1914, while serving as a correspondent for *Metropolitan Magazine*, he rode with Pancho Villa's rebel forces. Those accounts and *Insurgent Mexico*, his book about his Mexican experiences, might well have enabled the now twenty-six-year-old journalist to become the nation's highest paid reporter. He went on to investigate the Ludlow massacre involving the killing of over twenty people, including wives and children of members of the United Mine Workers of America, during a bitter labor struggle in Southeastern Colorado tied to a mine owned by John D. Rockefeller Jr.

The *Metropolitan* sent Reed overseas after hostilities began, but he delivered a scathing analysis in *The Masses*. "We, who are Socialists, must hope—we may even expect—that out of this horror of bloodshed and dire destruction will come far-reaching social changes—and a long step towards our goal of peace among men. But we must not be duped by this editorial buncombe about Liberalism going forth to Holy War against Tyranny. This is not our war." A subsequent trip to Europe by Reed resulted in another blistering indictment in *The Masses*, "The Worst Thing in Europe." He referred to "the super-Mexican horrors that civilized Europe is inflicting upon itself." In Paris's "quiet, dark, saddened streets," he repeatedly encountered "some miserable wreck of a human being, or a madman who lost his reason in the trenches, being led around by his wife. I could tell you of the big hospital in Berlin full of German soldiers who went crazy from merely hearing the cries of the thirty thousand Russians drowning in the swamps of East Prussia after the battle of Tannenburg." Reed saw numbed, horribly demoralized men in the trenches. He also came across "holes torn in bodies with jagged pieces of melanite shells, of sounds that make deaf, of gases that destroy eye-sight, of wounded men dying day by day and hour by hour within forty yards of twenty thousand human beings, who won't stop killing each other long enough to gather them up."

Every bit as troubled by the outbreak of war was twenty-seven-year-old Inez Milholland Boissevain, a graduate of Vassar College and New York University School of Law, who was a leading suffragist, civil rights proponent, and political activist. A labor attorney, Milholland joined the NAACP, the Socialist Party, and the Women's Trade Union League. She stood up for the disenfranchised, condemning prison conditions, child labor, and the exploitation of both women and men in the workplace. Called the "American Joan of Arc," "the most beautiful suffragette" acquired notoriety on appearing at the head of a suffrage parade of 8,000 women, during which she sat astride a white horse while attired in a flowing white cape, as they headed down Pennsylvania Avenue to the White House. Her banner read "Forward Out of Darkness, Leave Behind the Night, Forward Out of Error, Forward Into Light," a slogan later adopted by the National Woman's Party (NWP). While married to Eugen Jan Boissevain, a Dutch businessman, whom she met through Max Eastman, both believed in an open marriage in tune with the free love celebrated by the Lyrical Left.

The embodiment of the New Woman of the early twentieth century, Milholland warned against possible U.S. entrance into World War I and became a member of the Woman's Peace Party (WPP), established in early 1915 by a group of feminists, including Jane Addams. At their founding conference, held in Washington, D.C., attendees favored arms limitations, mediation of the conflict in Europe, and addressing the economic factors that led to war. Operating as a freelance reporter, Milholland sailed to Europe in May 1915, intending to deliver an account of the fighting in Italy. The soldiers, she charged in the *New York Tribune*, were "led to the slaughter like dumb sheep. For that slavish stupidity perhaps, they deserve to be massacred like dumb sheep." The Italian prime minister informed her that she was being expelled from the country because of her antiwar commentary. Milholland later became a member of the American Union against Militarism (AUAM), headed by Lillian Wald and Crystal Eastman. But unfortunately, while undertaking a speaking tour for the NWP, Milholland collapsed on October 22, 1916, and died the following month, a thirty-year-old martyr to the cause of women's rights and peace.

A few years older than Bourne, Reed, and Milholland, Crystal Eastman was another Vassar graduate, receiving an MA in sociology from Columbia, and obtaining a law degree at NYU. She participated in Paul Kellogg's famed Pittsburgh Survey, which examined workplace casualties, served as secretary of the New York State Commission on Employee's Liability and

Causes of Industrial Accidents, Unemployment and Lack of Farm Labor, and published *Work Accidents and the Law*. Eventually, she operated as an investigating attorney for President Wilson's Commission on Industrial Relations. Along with her brother Max, Crystal also became involved in the fight for women's suffrage. Following a failed marriage that led to her temporary domicile in Milwaukee, Eastman, said to be "the most beautiful white woman I ever saw" by the African American poet Claude McKay, returned to New York City to participate in the national suffrage movement. That led to her travels abroad and ties to the International Woman Suffrage Alliance, which exposed her to mass demonstrations and picketing.

The start of World War I deeply troubled Eastman, as it did so many associated with the Lyrical Left. Together with Jane Addams and Lillian Wald, in early 1915 she helped to found the Henry Street Peace Committee, which would later be renamed the American Union Against Militarism, to oppose U.S. involvement in World War I. That same year, she joined with Addams in establishing the WPP, intended to protect First Amendment rights during wartime. The WPP favored nationalization of the arms industry, arms reductions, and anti-militarism. The AUAM became the focal point of anti-preparedness and was considered by Idaho Senator William E. Borah the "brains" of the peace movement. Its members included Addams, Kelly, Wald, and their fellow social worker Paul U. Kellogg, along with Protestant ministers John Haynes Holmes, John Nevin Sayre, and Norman Thomas. The social connections of the AUAM leadership allowed for access to top government officers, including President Wilson, who expressed determination to avoid U.S. entrance into the war. The AUAM credited itself with helping to prevent war with Mexico, convincing Eastman that similar examples of "people's diplomacy" could stave off all wars.

* * *

The pre-World War I left possessed a vibrancy that wouldn't be replicated by American radicals for a generation or even longer. The Socialist Party, the Industrial Workers of the World, and the Lyrical Left boasted thriving institutions and charismatic individuals of the sort that were unique. Eugene V. Debs, Big Bill Haywood, Max Eastman, Crystal Eastman, Inez Milholland, Randolph Bourne, and John Reed were especially vibrant figures, and so too were the anarchist Emma Goldman and the radical litigator Clarence Darrow. What made all of these figures, and others too, particularly attractive at the time and even more so with the advantage of hindsight were their impassioned and independent natures. None displayed dogmatism and almost all avoided the crass sectarianism that so long afflicted the American left. However, the relative period of grace that existed for many American radicals before U.S. engagement in World War I ultimately proved short-lived and would never exactly be repeated. Although it was not known at the time, socialism, syndicalism, and anarchism had reached their peaks in the United States, and their proponents soon experienced embittered assaults of both a legal and extra-legal nature. All too typically, the left would also break into pieces, making it still more vulnerable and ensuring that its temporary surge would indeed prove short-lived.

Chapter 2

Repression and the Postwar American Left

The American left appeared fairly robust, even in the wake of a disappointing performance by the 1916 Socialist Party presidential candidate, Allan L. Benson. With Eugene Debs declining to undertake another run, the SPA had turned to the *Appeal to Reason* editorialist, who strongly warned against U.S. involvement in the Great War, most emphatically taking place on the European continent. The response of socialists to World War I had proven disappointing and not only overseas. American socialists bickered too, with many retaining the SPA's prewar antimilitarist stance, but others viewed German autocracy as an evil that had to be surmounted. That split would, naturally, only heighten once the U.S. issued a declaration of war, but differences were pronounced even earlier.

Although Crystal Eastman, Inez Milholland, Randolph Bourne, and John Reed condemned U.S. intervention, other leading left-wingers responded differently. Founding SPA member Algie Simons accused Victor Berger and the Milwaukee socialists of being German agents, while Social Gospel minister George Herron deemed Morris Hillquit a German "sympathizer." Hillquit's purported neutrality, Herron charged, was "a delusion. . . . There are no neutrals in this war." The schisms regarding World War I were still more complex, with Simons and John Spargo, an English immigrant, editor, and lecturer, favoring the Allies, particularly England and France, but opposing preparedness. Despite Simons's inflammatory accusation, Berger supported preparedness, as did the journalist Charles Edward Russell, an NAACP founder.

For a short while, the Socialist Party surmounted fratricidal difficulties, performing well during the 1914 campaign season, when it underscored its opposition to "this and all other wars." "Every Socialist ballot is a protest against war" was the party slogan that year. Despite or perhaps owing to such opposition, that period became "a high-water mark," Jack Ross states, with thirty-three socialists elected to state legislative bodies in fourteen states, topped by a half-dozen in Oklahoma, and "more than two dozen new mayors" voted into office across the United States. The attorney Meyer London, a Russian Jewish immigrant, who had headed a garment workers strike in New York City, became the second socialist elected to Congress.

Radicals, however, continued to be viewed unsympathetically by many of their fellow Americans, and even worse than that by some. That could result in harassment, ridicule, and, on occasion, tragedy, as in the case of the thirty-six-year-old Swedish immigrant, Joe Hill, the songwriter and IWW organizer, best recalled for "Casey Jones—A Union Scab" and "The Preacher and the Slave." A participant in West Coast free speech fights, Hill was convicted, notwithstanding a paucity of evidence, of the murder of a grocer and the grocer's son that occurred in January 1914 in the vicinity of Salt Lake City. The subsequent trial and appeals process led to Hill's execution by a firing squad on November 19, 1915, despite President Wilson's having favored clemency. In a note to Bill Haywood, Hill stated, "Goodbye Bill. I die like a true blue rebel. Don't waste any time in mourning. Organize."

The antipathy directed toward radicals heightened as World War I wound on, and U.S. intervention threatened. Writing in *Appeal to Reason* on September 11, 1915, Eugene Debs admitted he was "not opposed to all war" but instead to "ruling class war," and would prefer to be "shot for treason" rather than participate in such a conflict. Bluntly, he wrote, "*I have no country to fight for; my country is the earth; and I am a citizen of the world.*" Although he refused to fight "*for the oppressors of the working class and the robbers of the poor, the thieves and looters, the brigands and murderers,*" he would do so to liberate "their victims." No "capitalist soldier," he was "a proletarian revolutionist" belonging "to the irregular army of the people." Emphatically, Debs stated, "I am opposed to every war but one; I am for that war with heart and soul, and that is the world-wide war of the social revolution. In that war I am prepared to fight in any way the ruling class may make it necessary, even to the barricades." That was the stance, Debs declared, the Socialist Party should adopt concerning the war.

A bombing on July 22, 1916, took ten lives and wounded forty other individuals during a preparedness parade on San Francisco's Market Street. It undermined radicals out West. The prosecution of labor activists, Thomas J. Mooney, Warren K. Billings, and two others followed, which, notwithstanding disputed testimony supposedly linking Mooney and Billings to the bombing, resulted in their conviction. Mooney was sentenced to death, and Billings to life imprisonment. The case became a cause celebre for the American left, with Mooney's death sentence eventually commuted.

In 1916, an unchastened IWW forthrightly declared at its national convention, "We condemn all wars, and, for the prevention of such, we proclaim anti-militarist propaganda in time of peace, thus promoting Class Solidarity among the workers of the entire world, and, in time of war, the General Strike in all industries." The Wobblies also expressed continued belief in industrial unionism, and the struggle to eradicate "wage slavery" and usher in "Industrial Democracy." The Socialist Party platform that year similarly affirmed "steadfast adherence to the principles of international brotherhood, world peace and industrial democracy." The SPA pledged to oppose militarism and war, and to strive for both disarmament and "industrial freedom." The party blasted the preparedness campaign, while arguing that both the class struggle and capitalism were international in scope.

Both the IWW and the SPA foresaw brighter days ahead after the 1916 elections. The IWW membership would reach 100,000 the following year, but Wobbly leaders were uncertain how to respond should the United States enter the war. Wanting "One Big Union . . . to come out of the conflict stronger and . . . more industrial control than previously," Ben H. Williams asked why the IWW should "sacrifice working class interests" to conduct senseless antiwar protests. Admitting that the Wobblies would have to contest the conscription that would inevitably occur, leading to the threat of their organization "being completely destroyed," James M. Slovick exhorted the IWW to engage in "an anti-war general strike." While equivocating, the organization's publication *Solidarity* posed the following query: "Who will be to blame if the workers of America are betrayed and led into the bloodiest slaughter of history?"

For its part, the SPA readied for an Emergency Convention in St. Louis on April 7, intending to discuss the seemingly inexorable drive to war. In early February, the party had responded to President Wilson's breaking of diplomatic relations with Germany, in the wake of unrestricted submarine attacks. Condemning war as "murder," and calling it "the climax of utter lawlessness," the SPA fired off correspondence to the president and Congress demanding the United States "not be plunged into war for the benefit of plundering capitalists." Defections from the party's antiwar stance increased in number, while a series of socialists, including Upton Sinclair, Graham Phelps Stokes, and William English Walling, expressed a readiness "to support the government in any sacrifice it may require." They excoriated those in the party who thought otherwise: "To refuse to resist international crime is to be unworthy of the name of Socialist." Countering their argument, Morris Hillquit warned that "our pro-war American Socialists" were helping construct "a new system of militarism, where practically none has heretofore existed."

Acting at President Wilson's behest, Congress issued a declaration of war on April 6. The next day, the SPA began its convention, where the vast majority of delegates supported a manifesto that came to be known as the St. Louis Platform. Explaining the rationale behind that agenda, the party reaffirmed belief in "internationalism and work class solidarity the world over," along with unwavering opposition to U.S. involvement in the war. The SPA urged "workers of all countries to refuse support to their governments in their wars," which were stoked by "capitalism, imperialism, and militarism." The St. Louis Platform denied that the conflict involved protection of American rights or honor, was intended to defeat the militarist Central Powers, or was designed to further democracy overseas. Rather, the SPA charged, "We brand the declaration of war by our government as a crime against the people of the United States and against the nations of the world."

John Spargo offered a minority report accepted by a tiny percentage of the delegates, which insisted, "We are internationalists and anti-militarists." But in blaming Germany autocracy, imperialism, and militarism for the war, Spargo offered that because the United States was now a combatant, socialists must undergo necessary sacrifices "to enable our national and its allies to win the war as speedily as possible." The SPA's recent presidential candidate, Allan Benson, dismissed the "young hotheads" and "pro-Germans" at the convention, and worried that should "a single unfortunate death" occur, "the signers of the report would be put to death and the Socialist Party disgraced for a generation." A. M. Simons charged that the majority position was tendered "by a combination of nationalistic pro-Germans, violent syndicalists, and foreign-speaking organizations ignorant of American institutions. It is an insulting slap in the face to every Socialist." Job Harriman, twice a strong candidate to being elected mayor of Los Angeles, wondered if the SPA were committing suicide, warning that the St. Louis Platform would "support a charge of conspiracy to violate the federal statutes."

Eugene Debs countered the charge that the majority resolution was "treasonable," dismissing such an accusation as "base and cowardly. Let the cowardly press, and not our own comrades bring this charge." He recognized that such accusations might well be forthcoming, engendered "by the servile hirelings of Wall Street who can construe the law to fasten the charge of treason upon any undesirable citizen." Denying being "pro-German or pro-Ally," Debs declared, "We are Socialists, international Socialists. . . . The class war is our war and our only war." Both expulsions and resignations of "pro-war" members continued during the first several weeks of U.S. engagement in the conflagration.

As the SPA membership geared up to officially adopt the St. Louis Platform, the American nation underwent a shift indicating that little in the way of radical dissidence would be tolerated. Warrantless raids were carried out against SPA headquarters, anti-literature was seized, and individuals were placed behind bars because of "anti-war utterances." Antiwar rallies were broken up. Passports were denied to socialists to attend a Peace Conference in Stockholm.

Early opposition revolved around the military draft, with John Reed explaining on April 21, "Why I Am Against Conscription: An Open Letter to Members of Congress." Reed noted that he had spent eighteen months as a war correspondent in Europe, and worried about the drift to war before the fighting began. He warned that "the leisure class will command" a conscript army, compelling "boys of unformed minds" to engage in trench warfare, would take "the flower of our young men" given the large number of physically unfit applicants, and was simply "Un-American," violating liberty of conscience. Conscription, Reed feared, would enfeeble democracy and stimulate militarism in the United States. In *The Masses*, Reed charged, "War means an ugly mob—madness crucifying the truth-tellers, choking the artists, side-tracking reforms, revolutions, and the working of social forces." Anti-conscription rallies took place across the country, to the dismay of those who viewed such gatherings as unpatriotic or worse.

On May 18, Congress issued the Selective Service Act, mandating registration by all men from the ages of 21–30. The U.S. Army had remained small, amounting to about 121,000 men, with another 181,000 in the National Guard. Even a month-and-a-half following the declaration of war, a mere 73,000 individuals had volunteered to serve, leading the Wilson administration to opt for a military draft. Allowance for conscientious objection on religious grounds was provided, but the statute declared, "No person so exempted shall be exempted from service in any capacity that the President shall declare to be noncombatant." The IWW, for its part, equivocated on how to respond to conscription, although some, like Frank Little, insisted it had to be opposed. Nevertheless, almost all of the Wobblies who were required to had registered and few declined to serve.

Probably no individual was more determined to provide protection for conscientious objectors and other antiwar critics than Roger Nash Baldwin, a Boston patrician, Harvard graduate, and leading figure in the field of social work. Asked for a second time to head the American Union Against Militariam, Baldwin had chosen to do so in March, replacing the pregnant Crystal Eastman Fuller. The AUAM, tied to "pacifist and civil libertarian principles" under Baldwin's tutelage, attempted "to moderate the war hysteria." As an unintended consequence, the modern civil liberties movement began to develop, with the first systematic campaign to protect the personal freedoms associated with the Bill of Rights. Instrumental in that quest was the well-heeled makeup of many AUAM members, who were able, at least at first, to obtain entrée to top government officials, including Wilson himself.

Following passage of the Selective Service Act, Baldwin helped to convince the AUAM to establish "a bureau for advice and help to conscientious objectors throughout the United States." The board of the Civil Liberties

Bureau (later the National Civil Liberties Bureau) included John Lovejoy Elliott from the Ethical Culture Society; Thomas, representing the Fellowship of Reconciliation (FOR); and Oswald Garrison Villard, an NAACP founder soon to become editor-owner of *The Nation* magazine. An AUAM pamphlet termed liberty of conscience "essentially an Anglo-American tradition for which our ancestors fought and died, and for which thousands emigrated to America." The organization became particularly concerned on learning, the historian Charles Chatfield reports, that various conscientious objectors had suffered "beatings, bayonets, torture, and unreasonable confinement."

In late May, many leading radicals were involved in a conference held in New York City that led to formation of the People's Council of America for Democracy and Peace. The People's Council sought to bring about "an early, democratic and general peace" of the kind that "New Russia," which had emerged with the czar's abdication, favored: "no forcible annexations, no punitive indemnities, [and] free development of all nationalities." The group also opposed "war profiteering," supported repeal of conscription laws, and favored the strengthening of American democracy and liberty. Committee members included Baldwin, Eugene Debs, Crystal Eastman, Max Eastman, Morris Hillquit, John Haynes Holmes, Scott Nearing, and Norman Thomas. Over 100 local councils appeared across the country, bringing together labor, socialist, and single tax organizations, among others.

To prevent anti-conscription and other antiwar messages from receiving an airing, the Wilson administration and members of Congress began pushing for the most restrictive federal legislation involving First Amendment rights since passage of the Alien and Sedition Acts during the Federalist era. On June 15, 1917, Congress approved of the Espionage Act, which provided for prison sentences as lengthy as twenty years and fines as hefty as $10,000 for anyone successfully prosecuted under the measure. It all but criminalized the providing of information designed to curb the United States' waging of the war or to assist the nation's foes. It was viewed as an instrument to be wielded against anyone supporting draft resistance or military insubordination. The U.S. Post Office also obtained authorization to preclude "treasonous" material from circulating through the mail. The AUAM declared its readiness to support "maintenance in war time of the rights of free press, free speech, peaceable assembly, liberty of conscience, and freedom from unlawful search and seizure."

Vocal expressions of opposition to the war hardly subsided. Only weeks after passage of the Espionage Act, the People's Council coordinated a massive antiwar rally on Boston Commons, with over 30,000 individuals participating. A draft riot in Butte, Montana, where labor wars had long raged, broke out in early June. Draft resistance, Michael Kazin notes, proved "rampant in Harlem," due to rage fueled by Jim Crow practices and a disinclination to assist Belgium because of what "King Leopold and his gang had done to the Congolese."

But police, soldiers, and vigilantes frequently targeted war opponents, while the federal government began removing second-class mailing subsidies from radical publications, crippling many. States passed criminal syndicalism acts, restricting freedom of speech and assemblage. Socialist and IWW offices continued to be ransacked, and Wobblies in particular suffered physical abuse in various instances. In Bisbee, Arizona, the local sheriff and armed vigilantes rounded up nearly 1,200 men, many of them striking mining workers associated with the IWW, and loaded them into boxcars, then dumped the men in the New Mexican desert without food or water. In Butte, vigilantes snatched Frank Little, the famed "hobo agitator," who had railed away at "capitalists" following a terrible accident earlier in the summer that left 168 miners dead. His kidnappers castrated Little, stabbed him repeatedly, and hung him. Little's headstone would read "Slain by capitalist interests for organizing and inspiring his fellow men."

The rhetoric emanating from radicals generally tended to be stronger than their acts, with rare exceptions. One example to the contrary involved tenant farmers in Oklahoma who, in August 1917, participated in the Green Corn Rebellion. A state with a potent Socialist Party, Oklahoma recently had its own branch of the Working Class Union, an organization rooted in nearby Arkansas concerned about tough times for farmers and now displaying considerable anger regarding conscription. Hundreds of armed white, black, and Native American men planned to march to Washington, D.C., to force the war's end. Intending to survive by eating green and barbecued beef along their trek, the rebels, who charged "Rich mans war, Poor mans fight," torched bridges and sliced telegraph lines but their march was quickly halted, with three killed and hundreds arrested. The state Socialist Party paid the price, its vote plummeting. Starting in September, the Justice Department began grabbing Wobbly documents and writings, soon indicting 162 IWW figures, among them Elizabeth Gurley Flynn, Arturo Giovannitti, and Bill Haywood, under the Espionage Act. That was followed by an assault on the SPA national headquarters.

Notwithstanding the mounting repression, the SPA performed well in municipal elections that November, with Morris Hillquit obtaining 22 percent of the vote in the New York City mayoral race and seven socialists voted in as city aldermen. Ten socialists were elected to the New York state assembly. A number of socialists won mayoral elections across the country, and the vote total for socialist candidates jumped noticeably in several cities. However, in several instances, particularly in New York, efforts were initiated to prevent socialists from holding office. There was even an attempt to remove Robert La Follette from the U.S. Senate, owing to his opposition to the war and conscription.

* * *

Announcement of the second revolution in Russia during 1917 initially provided inspiration to many American radicals, while upsetting the Wilson administration. The Bolshevik takeover that brought Vladimir Lenin and Leon Trotsky to power induced a temporary rallying around the red flag of the revolution. "The world stands amazed, astounded, awe-inspired, in the presence of Russia's stupendous historic achievement," Eugene Debs would write the following spring. "The Russian Revolution is without precedent or parallel in history. Monumental in its glory, it stands alone. Behold its sublime majesty, catch its holy spirit and join in its thrilling inspiring appeal to the oppressed of every land to rise in their might, shake off their fetters and proclaim their freedom to the world!"

The SPA's continued electoral success, the IWW's refusal to go away quietly, and the glowing response by the American left to the Bolshevik triumph only resulted in intensified repression. Postmaster General Albert Burleson and his top assistant, W. H. Lamar, banned IWW and SPA publications from being sent by mail, banned various issues of *The Nation* and *The Masses*, and impounded an NCLB pamphlet. Eventually, Burleson explained, "There is a limit. And that limit is reached when it begins to say that this government got into the war wrong, that it is in it for the wrong purpose, and anything that will impugn the motives of the Government for going into war." Moreover, "they cannot say that this government is a tool of Wall Street or the munitions makers." Additionally, supposedly nothing encouraging military insubordination, disloyalty, or draft resistance was allowable.

The Justice Department carried out three mass trials of IWW leaders and prosecuted many of the leading figures on the American left, including Alexander Berkman, Emma Goldman, Eugene Debs, John Reed, and Max Eastman. The trial of Berkman and Goldman was one of the first, with the defendants prosecuted for having published a *No-Conscription Manifesto*, which denounced conscription, and for their general campaign condemning both American involvement in the war and the draft. The IWW conspiracy trials occurred in Chicago, Sacramento, and Wichita, Kansas. Prosecutors charged the Wobblies with conspiring to hinder the American war effort through sabotage and the destruction of property and by opposing the war and conscription. Contributors to *The Masses* such as Floyd Dell, Eastman, Reed, and Art Young, also were charged with conspiring to obstruct enlistment. The socialists Kate Richard O'Hare and Rose Pastor Stokes were prosecuted, the former because of an antiwar talk and the latter for sending a letter to the *Kansas City Star* asserting, "No government which is for the profiteers can also be for the people, and I am for the people while the government is for the profiteers." The government indicted a series of SPA leaders, including Debs and Victor Berger.

In keeping with the patriotic fervor that bordered on hysteria, virtually all of these defendants were convicted, many handed lengthy sentences; only *The Masses'* staff members avoided that fate. Several delivered memorable statements. Goldman purportedly likened Berkman and herself to "Jesus, Socrates, Galileo, Bruno, John Brown and scores of others" who had been viewed as criminals. During his testimony, Eastman, editor of *The Masses*, explained, "I was brought up with the utmost love for the character and the beauty of the teachings of Jesus of Nazareth, and I count Him much nearer in His faith and His influence to the message of the Socialists than to the message of any other political body of men." He compared socialists to the Founders, as they subscribed to "liberty and democracy exactly in the same way." Debs's statement at his sentencing hearing became the most celebrated, and began with his declaration, "Your Honor, years ago I recognized my kinship with all living beings, and I made up my mind that I was not one bit better than the meanest on earth. I said then, and I say now, that while there is a lower class, I am in it, and while there is a criminal element I am of it, and while there is a soul in prison, I am not free." Notwithstanding his eloquence, Debs was convicted. Only *The Masses'* defendants avoided incarceration, with two trials (the first, a mistrial) producing no guilty verdicts. But the publication perished, with Floyd Dell, Max Eastman, Merrill Rogers, and Art Young presenting a statement: "There is no room in the United States at this time for a free magazine," based on what "we are, a luxury like truth and beauty, a child of play and energetic idleness."

The persecution and prosecutions, coupled with vigilantism, broke the early twentieth century left, the one exemplified by the SPA, the IWW, and the Lyrical Left. Membership in the SPA and the IWW descended, precipitously, the SPA also weakened through internal struggles involving both U.S. participation in the war and the Bolshevik Revolution. The SPA soon divided, with a number of its more radical elements, including John Reed, breaking away to form one of two American communist parties.

* * *

Randolph Bourne weathered his own travails as the United States entered the war. *The New Republic*, which had long published Bourne's work, largely refused to do so any longer, having adopted a pro-war stance under co-founder Herbert Croly. *The Dial* also stripped away Bourne's editorial involvement. Consequently, he relied on a smaller outlet, *The Seven Arts*, to deliver some of the finest, most trenchant analyses of war, militarism, and repression ever offered by an American intellectual. Beginning in June 1917, Bourne scathingly examined "The War and the Intellectuals," which included a reflection in *The Seven Arts*, on his one-time mentor at Columbia, the philosopher John Dewey. That article bemoaned the easy turn of virtually all of the American intelligentsia toward a favorable reading of U.S. martial engagement. Many, in fact, appeared delighted with "a war made deliberately by the intellectuals!" Other warring states had required "predatory craft or popular hysteria or militarist madness," but American intellectuals believed they could bring about "the triumph of democracy and internationalize the world." He considered it ironic that the same individuals who were little concerned about capitalistic exploitation and racism in America were supposedly so troubled by the mistreatment of "oppressed nationalities and ravaged villages of Europe." In the process, repression intensified on the home front, fed by American intellectuals, who scolded pacifists and other war critics. Going further, they "excommunicated" dissenters, and made "irreconcilable radicals" out to be "the most despicable and impotent of men." To Bourne, his fellow intellectuals failed to remember "that the real enemy is War rather than imperial Germany."

Bourne, who had written so intelligently and movingly about American youth, worried that the war would engender bitterness among that group, eventually staining the generation. He feared "if the enterprise goes on endlessly, the work, so blithely undertaken for the defence (sic) of democracy, will have crushed out the only genuinely precious thing in a nation, the hope and ardent idealism of its youth." Continuing to express such concerns in "A War Diary," which appeared in the September 1917 issue of *The Seven Arts*, Bourne charged that "there was something incredibly mean and plebian about that abasement in which the war-partisans tried to throw us all," as they cultivated "the poison of war." He also warned, "The war—or American promise: one must choose. One cannot be interested in both," no matter what liberals suggested.

Even *The Seven Arts* soon succumbed to the war fever, shutting down in October 1917, but not before Bourne produced another masterwork, "Twilight of Idols," in which he took to task Dewey, even more fully. Dewey's philosophy of pragmatism, Bourne indicated, was "inspiring enough for a society at peace, prosperous and with a fund of progressive good-will. It is a philosophy of hope, of clear-sighted comprehension." It didn't succeed as well in an atmosphere in which war no longer appeared "gallant" and American democracy seemed increasingly imperiled by crusades to "stamp out the 'enemies within.'"

The influenza pandemic of 1918–1919 that took the lives of as many as fifty million people included Bourne as one of its victims. Succumbing at the age of thirty-two, Bourne left behind an impressive, impassioned legacy, including an unfinished work, "The State," which would be published posthumously. He raged, "War is the health of the State. It automatically sets in motion throughout society those irresistible forces for uniformity, for passionate cooperation with the Government in coercing into obedience the minority groups and individuals which lack the larger herd sense." War produced "herd feeling," as exemplified by the drive for "one hundred per cent Americanism, among one hundred per cent of the population." Critics turned into "outlaws" and minorities were oppressed, as "the herd becomes divided into the hunters and the hunted."

* * *

As Bourne feared, it proved difficult to shut off the spigot of repression once it was opened. Both progressive and regressive forces poured forth when the war ended. Pent-up desires and ambitions drove workers—white and black—farmers, and radicals, into a new frenzy of labor activism and the formation of new organizations. The AFL, headed by Samuel Gompers, had made its peace with the Wilson administration during the war, agreeing to no-strike pledges, while the IWW, led by the now imprisoned Bill Haywood, appeared shattered. Nevertheless, labor activism surged in the months following the Armistice in November 1918, with a general strike in Seattle, a walkout by 350,000 steelworkers in September 1919, and a strike by policemen in Boston. Farmers were at least equally disgruntled, as prices for their crops seldom matched costs. The Nonpartisan League, led by the socialist Arthur C. Townley, had appeared in North Dakota in 1915, and attained a membership of 200,000 within three years. It favored state ownership of farming instrumentalities ranging from flour mills to packing plants. Its founder was successfully prosecuted for anti-enlistment activity, and jailed for ninety days. Despite suffering from disaffection, repression, and the prosecution of several key figures, the SPA still had a substantial membership at war's end. The sectarian splits only deepened, however, as Bolshevik rule in Russia hardened and the Russian Civil War resulted.

From Seattle to Boston, politicians waved a red flag, charging that a conspiracy was afoot to destroy the social order. Seattle Mayor Ole Hanson declared that it was time for each individual in the city "to show his Americanism," and he fired off a telegram to the *New York Times* equating the general strike in his city to the Bolshevik Revolution. The *Times* indicated that Hanson proved "that Americanism, that respect for law, is not dead." Responding to the walkout by Boston policemen, Massachusetts Governor Calvin Coolidge ordered out the National Guard, and supported the police commissioner's decision to fire striking policemen. Coolidge stated, "There is no right to strike against the public safety by anybody, anywhere, anytime." The strike wave didn't entirely abate, with over four million workers, some 20 percent all told, participating in work stoppages over a seven-year period that had started in 1915. The Great Steel Strike of 1919 involved 365,000 workers, and another walkout involved 400,000 miners. But eventually the strikes subsided and union membership dropped 40 percent over the next decade, to three million, as company unions, blacklists, and repression abounded.

Too few organizations on the left paid attention to the needs of African Americans, including the 370,000 who served in the U.S. military during World War I, with about 40,000 experiencing combat. Black veterans were among those identified with the concept of the New Negro, proud and assertive, extolled by the socialist labor activist A. Philip Randolph and the economist Chandler Owen in their new publication, *The Messenger*. African American soldiers received no better treatment than their civilian counterparts, as attested by a series of race riots during the era, including while the country was at war. A four-day explosion occurred in St. Louis in early July, leaving as many as 125 African American residents dead. At the end of the month, the NAACP conducted a Silent Protest Parade in New York City, with 8,000 marching and signs reading, "Mr. President, why not make America safe for democracy." The following month saw another eruption, this time in Houston, Texas, involving black soldiers angered by mistreatment. Sixteen white residents and police officers, along with four black soldiers, were killed. Courts-martial rulings led to sixty-three life sentences and thirteen hangings.

But following the war, homecoming parades welcomed back black soldiers, with 250,000 gathering in New York City to see the famed 369th Infantry Regiment from New York, the Harlem Hellfighters. In the NAACP publication, the *Crisis* magazine, editor W. E. B. Du Bois discussed the black veterans, writing, "*We return. We return from fighting. We return fighting.* Make way for Democracy! We saved it in France, and by the Great Jehovah, we will save it in the United States of America, or know the reason why." The terrible riots that swept through American cities, particularly Washington, D.C., and Chicago, during the summer of 1919, enraged Du Bois, Randolph, and other black leaders. In both Washington, D.C. and Chicago, African Americans fought back, ensuring that victims were both white and black. It was as though whites and blacks were battling for breathing space, with housing and jobs difficult to acquire. Two years later, Tulsa, Oklahoma, was the scene of a mob assault on the Greenwood District, an affluent black community, which resulted in clashes between armed mobs, martial law, the holding of more than 6,000 people, the death of between 100–300 people, and immense property damage.

Riddled by sectarianism, the SPA, whose record regarding African American remained hardly ideal, tore itself apart over the war, the Russian Revolution, and ideology. Some left the party or were booted out owing to their pro-war stances, while others wrestled with how to respond to the materialization of what appeared to be the world's first socialist state. The earliest reaction by many leading American radicals to the Bolshevik triumph was one of elation. Writing from a prison cell, Eugene Debs proclaimed in February 1919, "From the crown of my head to the soles of my feet I am a Bolshevik, and proud of it." John Reed, able to write much of *Ten Days That Shook the World*, his account of the Bolshevik takeover, from personal observations, indicated, "Instead of being a destructive force, it seems to me that the Bolsheviki were the only party in Russia with a constructive program and the power to impose it on the country." Writing in *The Liberator*, which replaced *The Masses*, Reed relayed a message from Lenin and Trotsky "to the revolutionary proletariat of the world . . . Comrades! Greetings from the first proletariat republic of the world. We call you to arms for the international social revolution."

Returning to the United States, Reed helped to both split the SPA and father one of two communist parties, the Communist Labor Party; the other, the Communist Party of America, was dominated by foreign federations. That ensured a long-developing trend, the loss of members by the SPA, would worsen and do so dramatically. The SPA's high point of 118,000 members appeared as if a distant memory, with membership dipping below 35,000 in 1919 before plunging to 11,000 three years later. Internal divisions didn't help, while the prosecution of Debs, Berger, and other leaders and the labeling of radicals of any stripe as unpatriotic proved politically toxic for the early postwar left. Literal assaults on headquarters, individuals, and organizations by federal, state, municipal, and vigilante forces grievously damaged radical organizations, particularly the SPA and the IWW, but also lesser known anarchist groups, many tied to immigrant communities.

Those attacks took place in the wake of terrorist incidents and the fear of even more. On May 1 (May Day), 1919, riots occurred in Cleveland as socialists and trade union members conducted a parade to condemn the jailing of Debs and to back SPA mayoral candidate Charles Ruthenberg. A mob attacked the gathering, with violence breaking out, leading to two deaths, forty people injured, and over 100 arrests. That same day, bombs were slated for delivery to several well-known individuals, including Seattle Mayor Ole Hanson; Supreme Court Justice Oliver Wendell Holmes Jr.; the banker J. Pierpont Morgan; Attorney General A. Mitchell Palmer; the industrialist John D. Rockefeller; and Postmaster General Albert Burleson. By chance, a postal clerk uncovered the plot, although the wife of Georgia Senator Thomas W. Hardwick and their housekeeper were both injured when a package exploded at the Hardwick residence. Anarchists connected to Luigi Galleani, a proponent of propaganda of the deed, would be blamed for the May Day deliveries and for subsequent bombings that occurred in early June. The latter involved the sending of large bombs to officials in eight cities across the country. One bomber blew himself up at the home of Attorney General Palmer, which was located across the street from one occupied by Assistant

Secretary of the Navy Franklin Delano Roosevelt, his wife Eleanor, and their children.

That fall, following intensified labor strife, Palmer initiated a series of raids, leading to the arrest and eventual deportation of hundreds of immigrant radicals. Assisting the attorney general was a young Department of Justice attorney, J. Edgar Hoover, who became chief of the new General Intelligence Division, tasked with investigating how much of a threat radical organizations posed in the United States. Among those shipped aboard a boat called the Soviet Ark were Alexander Berkman and Emma Goldman, headed for the new Soviet state. On January 2 and 3, thousands of additional individuals were rounded up. Hoping to capture the Democratic Party presidential nomination, Palmer warned of a revolution that would be unleashed on May Day 1920, but his credibility was damaged when that failed to take place. A massive bombing did occur in the Manhattan Financial District on September 16, killing thirty-eight and wounding hundreds more. The case was never solved, although Galleani-related anarchists have been seen as likely culprits.

As radical movements weakened, the red scare dissipated, with release of various political prisoners, including Eugene Debs, by President Warren G. Harding, although neither radicalism nor repression entirely vanished over the course of the new decade. The story of Nicola Sacco and Bartolomeo Vanzetti, two Italian anarchist immigrants, demonstrated that. In 1921, notwithstanding a dearth of solid evidence, they were convicted of two felony murders that had taken place the previous year. The appeal process went on for the next half-dozen years, and the case served as a rallying point for radicals and intellectuals around the world. Nevertheless, the defendants were executed on August 23, 1927. Harvard law professor Felix Frankfurter was among those contending that justice was not being served, while the novelist John Dos Passos later delivered a loving eulogy, "We Stand Defeated," in his *U.S.A.* trilogy. Ben Shahn also produced *Bartolomeo Vanzetti and Nicola Sacco*, a moving piece of art.

* * *

Sixteen leading labor unions established the Conference for Progressive Political Action (CPPA), hoping to empower a farmer-labor political movement. At its founding conference in Chicago in February 1922, the CPPA warned of an "'invisible government' of plutocracy and privilege," "a campaign of ruthless imperialism in Haiti and San Domingo," and use of the military and police "to crush labor" as it fought to retain constitutionally guaranteed rights. The CPPA backed a presidential bid by Wisconsin Senator Robert M. La Follette, who, through the Progressive Party, supported public ownership of the railways and waterpower, labor's right to organize and bargain collectively, prohibition of child labor, and assistance to farmers' cooperatives. La Follette won his home state, and collected nearly five million votes, 16.6 percent of the total. But his death the following year largely terminated the Progressive Party.

The Palmer raids had spurred the establishment on January 20, 1920, of the American Civil Liberties Union (ACLU), whose executive director Roger Baldwin became intimately involved with the Sacco and Vanzetti case. The ACLU national committee contained stalwart progressive figures: Jane Addams, Crystal Eastman, Elizabeth Gurley Flynn, the AFL's William Z. Foster, Professor Felix Frankfurter, Scott Nearing, Norman Thomas, Oswald Garrison Villard, and Harry Ward. By the middle of the decade, top litigators for the ACLU included Albert DeSilver, Arthur Garfield Hays, and Walter Nelles, and also an array of attorneys associated with affiliates around the country. Under the board's tutelage and that of Baldwin, the ACLU soon demonstrated a readiness to defend First Amendment rights across the political spectrum, which eventually led to its involvement in a series of noteworthy cases including that of John T. Scopes, the Tennessee science teacher charged with violating a state statute precluding the teaching of evolution in public classrooms. Once again, Clarence Darrow appeared as an attorney of record for the defense, doing battle with none other than William Jennings Bryan, the old reformer who was also a diehard fundamentalist.

The ACLU, often spurred by Baldwin, joined in other seminal cases, particularly those pertaining to First Amendment rights, during the 1920s and early 1930s. Some of those helped to advance the doctrine of incorporation that Chief Justice John Marshall had long ago denied in *Barron v. Mayor & City of Baltimore* (1833). The doctrine declared that the Bill of Rights applied to state governments, and the U.S. Supreme Court, encouraged by ACLU attorneys like DeSilver, Hays, and Nelles, now began to proclaim "fundamental" various facets of the First Amendment. The *Gitlow* ruling (1925), with a CPUSA founder, Benjamin Gitlow, as the defendant, saw Chief Justice Edward T. Sanford declare, "We may and do assume that freedom of speech and of the press—which are protected by the First Amendment from abridgment by Congress—are among the fundamental personal rights and 'liberties' protected by the due process clause of the 14th Amendment from impairment by the states."

The ACLU, again under Baldwin's tutelage, participated in a series of other cases that held aloft the banner of the First Amendment, as the Wobblies had a generation earlier. In *Whitney v. California* (1927), Justice Louis D. Brandeis relied on the free speech standard first articulated by Justice Holmes in *Schenck v. United States* (1919): "The question . . . is whether the words used are used in such circumstances and are of such a nature as to create a clear and present danger that they will bring about the substantive evils that Congress has a right to prevent." *Stromberg v. California* (1931) protected symbolic speech. *Powell v. Alabama* (1932) and *Patterson v. Ala-*

bama (1935) both centered on the "Scottsboro Boys," nine African American youngsters falsely charged with having raped a pair of white women aboard a train close to Scottsboro, Alabama. The ACLU and the NAACP provided support, as did the communist-driven International Labor Defense.

Baldwin and other important figures in the early twentieth century American left became involved with another endeavor, the American Fund for Public Service or Garland Fund, which provided seed money for radical causes for nearly two decades. Incorporated in 1921, the fund was created by a young man, Charles Garland, determined to rid himself of a fortune and to help create a "new social order." Board members again spanned the left side of the nation's political spectrum, including Communist Labor Party co-founder Benjamin Gitlow; Freda Kirchwey, an editor with *The Nation*; Flynn; Nearing; Thomas; and Ward. "Garland's Million" provided funds to the American Birth Control League; the Federated Press, a syndicate for the radical press; the Vanguard Press, which initially published materials connected to labor and liberal groups; *The Messenger*; leftwing labor unions such as A. Philip Randolph's Brotherhood of Sleeping Car Porters; the International Ladies' Garment Workers' Union; and the League for Industrial Democracy. The Fund additionally delivered financial support for the NAACP; the National Urban League; communist enterprises ranging from the International Labor Defense to the *Daily Worker* and the *New Masses*; the labor school Commonwealth College; Brookwood Labor College; and the socialist Rand School. Despite the resources the board allocated, the Garland Fund grew throughout much of the 1920s, ironically perhaps, due to stock investments.

The economic downturn that beset the American nation, beginning with the stock market crash in late 1929, greatly reduced the resources the Garland Fund had at its disposal. That was hardly insignificant because, as the fund's historian, Gloria Garret Sampson, reflects, it distributed nearly $2 million to almost 100 "enterprises of pioneer character directly or indirectly related to building up the power of the unorganized working class."

* * *

The American left suffered additional blows and underwent substantial changes during the 1920s, with the deaths of John Reed (1920), Robert La Follette (1925), Eugene Debs (1926), Bill Haywood (1928), and Crystal Eastman (1928), among others. The losses of Reed and Eastman were particularly significant because of their fierce independence and youth in Reed's case, and relative youth in Eastman's. Robert La Follette and Eugene Debs were fabled characters, representing the best of the American progressive and socialist movements, respectively, and proved irreplaceable although Norman Thomas did become the leading exemplar of American socialism for decades to come. But La Follette was the greatest progressive legislator and a contender for the presidency, and Debs exemplified socialism in the United States at its finest with his insistence on democratic practices. Thomas, through his eloquence and carefully-mannered ways, reached out to a different and smaller constituency than Debs had, one that was more intellectual and affluent. Haywood was, of course, the Wobblies' Wobbly, but jumped bail as the Chicago conspiracy trial was going through the appeals process. He obtained refuge in Moscow, joining a trade union. Experiencing poor health, he died in the new Soviet Union, apparently having been an unhappy guest in the new communist state. His ashes were split, half placed near the Kremlin Wall close to Lenin's tomb and the burial site of John Reed, half shipped to Chicago to be interred next to a monument for the Haymarket anarchists.

With the SPA reduced to a shell of its former self and the IWW's membership similarly cascading in a downward spiral, the future of American radicalism at the beginning of the 1920s appeared to reside with the new communist parties and other recently established institutions like the ACLU and the Garland Fund. But the story of American communism was foreshadowed by the early turn of events that led to an ordered merger of the two parties, reflecting an immediate readiness to accept Russian mandates. Following the direction of the Communist International (Comintern), the Workers Party of America appeared in 1922; at decade's end, it would be renamed the Communist Party of the United States. Avoiding another trial in the United States, Reed had returned to Russia during the midst of its Civil War, to become involved in sectarian battles. Beset by typhus, the thirty-two-year-old Reed succumbed on October 19, 1920, and was afforded a state funeral, attended by Nickolai Bukharin and Alexandra Kollontai, before his burial at the Kremlin Wall. Disputes would arise as to whether Reed would have accepted directives from abroad or from anywhere else, given his fiercely independent nature. His good friend Max Eastman had also become enamored with the Russian Revolution but was displeased when Joseph Stalin prevailed in the succession struggle that followed the death in 1924 of Vladimir Lenin. Eastman, like Reed, was a strong-willed individual, beholden to no one, and not easily accepting of party commands. The obeisance displayed toward the Soviet Union hardly aided American communists, with the CPUSA's membership totaling, by decade's end, only a few thousand. Little helpful was the Comintern's insistence on removing talented individuals from the party like Max Schachtman, Jay Lovestone, and James Cannon. The first two were associated with the Left Opposition in the Soviet Union, identified with Trotsky, and Lovestone supported their ouster before he was also forced out by a Stalinist group tied to William Foster.

Max's sister Crystal was at least as determined, and her death from nephritis on July 8, 1928, at the age of forty-seven was equally unfortunate in many regards. Roger Baldwin recalled her as being "a natural leader: out-spoken (often tactless), determined, charming, beautiful, courageous." She helped to found the National Woman's Party, the American Union Against Militarism, the National Civil Liberties Bureau, and the ACLU. Along with Max, she established *The Liberator*, intended to replace *The Masses*, again confronting problems with the Postmaster General. A leading suffragist, she fought for voting rights in both the United States and England, where she lived with her husband for five years before his death, a year before she died. *The Nation*'s Freda Kirchwey sang her praises, while declaring that her absence would be felt worldwide, in the struggles for sexual equality, peace, social justice, and human liberty.

A more hopeful sign appeared in New York City in December 1928, with the establishment of the League for Independent Political Action (LIPA) by the economist Paul H. Douglas, the Protestant missionary Sherwood Eddy, and Norman Thomas. Believing in the necessity of a new "political alignment," the LIPA's national committee selected John Dewey as chair, and championed progressive taxation and "social insurance from the hazards of accident, ill health, unemployment, and old age." Refusing to support candidates from the major political parties, it backed instead the Minnesota Farm-Labor Party ticket in 1930, candidates like Thomas and the journalist Heywood Broun running with the blessing of the Socialist Party in New York state, and left-of-center figures elsewhere.

Also beginning in the late 1920s, A. J. Muste, a Congregational minister, pacifist, and founder of the Brookwood Labor College, set up the Conference for Progressive Labor Action (CPLA), outside the purview of both the AFL and the CPUSA. Favoring industrial unionism, the CPLA conducted strikes and engaged in worker insurgencies as in the case of the United Mineworkers. The CPLA organized in the American South, finding support among African Americans. As the Nonpartisan League faltered, the cooperative movement again gained support in agrarian communities, resulting in the formation of the National Council of Farmer Cooperatives in 1929.

* * *

Repression, sectarianism, and mortality tore apart the early American left of the twentieth century. Even before the war and intensifying both during and immediately after the period of U.S. engagement, vigilante forces and government operatives came down hard on the left's leading institutions: the Socialist Party, the Industrial Workers of the World, and *The Masses*, the embodiment of the Lyrical Left. Mortality also struck down too many young radicals, with Crystal Eastman, Inez Milholland, Randolph Bourne, and John Reed passing from the scene far too early. Max Eastman avoided such a fate, but the dissipating of pre-war cultural radicalism left him adrift, as he initially underwent a sharp turn in the direction of communism but found the pushing aside of Leon Trotsky disconcerting. The Stalinist preeminence in the world's lone socialist state upset Eastman, whose iconoclastic characteristics ensured that he wouldn't fit comfortably within any ideological camp for an extended period. The Old Left, though it lasted far longer in certain guises, lacked the brilliance of its Lyrical Left predecessors. The later New Left contained a number of remarkable individuals, but its finest moments proved as short-lived as those of the American cultural radicals who shone so radiantly during the century's first couple of decades. And it is questionable if the New Left could match the Lyrical Left for its collection of remarkable artists, writers, and activists who were seeking, in their own ways, to usher in a new world pertaining to race and gender relations, war and peace, and the American economic system.

The early interwar left is too little acknowledged but its impact was larger and more lasting than is generally appreciated. It too endured repression, including the red scare that helped to weaken the SPA, the IWW, and the Lyrical Left. New left-of-center groups appeared, including a pair of communist parties: the Workers Party, and finally, the CPUSA. Those communist variants, unfortunately, proved all too willing to demonstrate fealty to Russia or the new Soviet Union. Fellow traveling, involving non-member radicals supporting the CPUSA or joining in alliances with it, became a phenomenon that would recur more frequently beginning in the 1930s. On their boards of directors, both the Garland Fund and the ACLU contained fellow travelers, including Roger Nash Baldwin, who founded each, determined to assist radical organizations and individuals in the United States. But most remarkably, Baldwin helped to create the modern civil liberties movement, which involved providing protections for little-liked groups and actors on all sides of the political spectrum.

Chapter 3

Heyday of the Old Left

The lifespan of the Old Left was lengthy, covering nearly four decades between the end of World War I and the midpoint of the 1950s. Its greatest influence, however, was concentrated within a shorter period of time, from the height of the Great Depression in 1932 and 1933 to the onset of the red scare in the United States during the early Cold War. Sadly, tragically, and sometimes pathetically, among the dominant factors influencing and shaping the American Old Left were the Moscow-based communist empire, communism, and Joseph Stalin. That unholy trinity helped to misdirect and stain large portions of the American left for generations, while providing fuel for its antagonists, including those of a rabidly reactionary sort. It led to genuflecting eastward, and the repeated reshaping of what came to be the CPU-SA, with the discarding of longtime radicals, the readiness to turn on a dime at the Comintern's directives, and the linking up with brutal regimes and despots, including at one point, Nazi Germany and Adolf Hitler himself.

The brilliant English historian Eric Hobsbawn framed the communist worldview poetically, if far too romantically, in referring to the alterations communists underwent, including by supporting the Nazi-Soviet Nonaggression Pact (the Molotov-Ribbentrop Pact) during the summer of 1939.

> Communists, it was agreed, would never behave like international social democracy in 1914, abandoning its flag to follow the banners of nationalism, into mutual massacre. And, it must be said, they did not. There is something heroic about the British and French CPs in September 1939. Nationalism, political calculation, even common sense, pulled one way, yet they unhesitatingly chose to put the interests of the international movement first. As it happens, they were tragically and absurdly wrong. . . . It was not their fault that the International should have told them to do something else.

51

Historians generally indicate that the two largest issues facing the American Old Left, communists and non-communists alike, even before the advent of World War II, were the economic calamity that struck worldwide and the threat posed by rightwing aggressor states. This book contends that of equal importance was how the Old Left reacted to Stalinism and the Soviet Union's own role in international affairs.

The American left appeared at low ebb as the 1930s began, apparently lacking the vibrancy or hopefulness present a generation earlier when the SPA, the IWW, and the Lyrical Left thrived. U.S. entrance into the war, repression during the nineteen-month period of direct engagement followed by a postwar red scare, and sectarian divides, including those induced by the Bolshevik revolution and the revolutionary surges that followed in its wake, came close to decimating the American left. By 1930, the once vibrant SPA had a membership of less than 10,000. The IWW claimed only about 10,000 members, and the CPUSA had just over 7,000. The renowned figures of the pre-World War I era were almost all gone, or, as was the case with Max Eastman, no longer appeared at the forefront of American radicalism.

However, thanks to the advent of the Great Depression, the rise of fascism, and the seeming successes playing out in the USSR, radicalism in the United States and other Western states became revitalized. Marx's predictions about capitalism's inevitable demise appeared borne out by the economic calamities that befell too many countries during the early 1930s. Few countries were hit harder than the United States, where breadlines, soup kitchens, bank deposit disappearances, and foreclosures proved all too common. Malnutrition occurred, along with cases of starvation, albeit few in number, in what was still the world's richest nation. A million or more individuals rode the rails, not because they desired to undertake roles as tramps or hoboes, while shantytowns, ingloriously named Hoovervilles after the increasingly disliked President Herbert Hoover, turned up in city after city across the American landscape. By early 1933, the rock bottom of the Great Depression in the United States, 5,000 banks had shuttered, taking with them an untold number of savings accounts, thousands of homes and farms had been foreclosed on, 100,000 businesses had gone belly up, and unemployment soared to twenty-five percent, at a minimum. After initial tendencies on the part of many characteristically individualistic Americans, even those who were down and out, to blame themselves for their misfortunes, anger brewed and threatened to spill over in rural and urban sectors alike. During the first stages of the nation's worst depression, the major political parties, but particularly the governing Republican Party, seemingly had little to offer other than platitudes. Even the Hoover administration's willingness to discard laissez-faire economics in favor of federal assistance to large corporations appeared in keeping with trickle-down, social Darwinian mantras.

The resulting political and intellectual vacuum afforded an opportunity for those with contrasting ideas, even radical ones. The Democratic Party, under New York Governor Franklin Delano Roosevelt, delivered vague promises, including of "a new deal for the American people" were he elected president. The enormity of the Great Depression, the ineptitude of the Hoover administration's response to it, and the apparently brutal response to destitute veterans ensured a landslide victory for FDR, whose smiling, winning personality also proved far more pleasing than that of the sour and dour Hoover, who had repeatedly promised that prosperity was just around the corner. Particularly damaging for Hoover was the sending of federal troops to roust the Bonus Expeditionary Force or Bonus Army, which descended on Washington, D.C., in the manner of Coxey's band or how the Green Corn Rebellion activists once envisioned a states' long trek would end. Some 2,000–5,000 veterans, led by Walter W. Waters, sought fulfillment of an earlier congressional promise to pay World War I veterans a one-time bonus, but that wouldn't come due until 1945. Tanks and tear gas routed the veterans, with one killed and several wounded, as were a number of policemen.

This was the period when many American intellectuals, possibly more than during the high point of the Lyrical Left, gravitated to the left. That had not been the case during the 1920s, when many writers and artists appeared politically disengaged, possibly disillusioned along the lines of the Lost Generation of F. Scott Fitzgerald and Ernest Hemingway regarding both "the war to end all wars" and the political conservatism that supplanted progressivism as the nation's dominant ideological strand. The change in intellectual temperament induced a number of intellectuals, in 1932, to support not FDR but William Foster, the CPUSA presidential candidate.

A small number of writers and artists, foremost of them Joseph Freeman, Hugo Gellert, and Michael Gold, had joined the Communist Party during the 1920s. They contributed to publications like *The Liberator* and the *New Masses*, set up in May 1926 by Gold and Freeman. Within two years, the *New Masses* proclaimed itself a vehicle for proletarian literature. Some left-wing writers and artists joined the John Reed Clubs, established in 1929 and directed by the CPUSA. Many were impressed with the party's backing of labor militancy, as displayed amid bitter labor clashes in Gastonia, North Caroline, in 1929, and in Western Pennsylvania and Harlan, Kentucky, two years later. The party was also associated with heated demonstrations involving mass unemployment or hunger marches in New York, Detroit, St. Louis, Washington, D.C., and other cities from 1930 through the 1932 election. Party membership passed the 10,000 mark, while William Foster and union activist and party organizer James W. Ford were its national candidates. The League of Professional Groups for Foster and Ford issued an "Open Letter," declaring, "A vote for any party but the Communist Party is worse than a wasted vote. It is a vote for the class enemies of the workers." Signatories included Sherwood Anderson, Erskine Caldwell, Robert Cantwell, Malcolm Cowley, Countee Cullen, John Dos Passos, Theodore Dreiser, Waldo Frank, Granville Hicks, Sidney Hook, Langston Hughes, Matthew Josephson, Lincoln Steffens, Edmund Wilson, and Ella Winter.

Dos Passos, already renowned for the anti-militarist novel, *Three Soldiers,* the experimental *Manhattan Transfer,* and the first two volumes of his *USA* trilogy, likened the Socialist Party to "near beer." Nevertheless, that organization was also being revitalized, with Norman Thomas's presidential run in 1932 far exceeding Foster's. While the communist candidate amassed just under 103,000 votes, Thomas's total approached 885,000, the most by a socialist since Debs, despite being confined to a federal penitentiary, received nearly a million three elections earlier. A Committee of One Hundred Thousand backed Thomas and his running mate, James Hudson Maurer, a union activist and former Pennsylvania state legislator. It included Stuart Chase, Elmer Davis, John Dewey, Joseph Wood Krutch, and Reinhold Niebuhr. Three months before the election, *Time* magazine's cover featured the handsome, distinguished looking Thomas, who, along with Morris Hillquit, would be greeted cordially on March 14, 1933, by President Roosevelt at the White House. Thomas believed the program Roosevelt discussed with his visitors "far more nearly resembled the Socialist . . . than his own platform."

FDR continued to befuddle American radicals throughout his lengthy presidency. During its early stages, when Roosevelt acted decisively to shore up the national economy, harsh critics emerged from right to left. Groups like the American Liberty League, which drew on the du Pont fortune, but also included John J. Raskob, onetime Democratic Party chair and a business colleague of the du Pont brothers, and former Democratic Party presidential nominees John W. Davis and Alfred E. Smith, castigated the extension of federal power and restraints on corporations. A series of charismatic individuals, tied to movements of their own, also condemned Roosevelt and his attempt to usher in relief, recovery, and reform. They included Father Charles E. Coughlin, a Catholic priest stationed in Royal Oak, Michigan, a Detroit suburb, who acquired a national radio audience, which initially heard him praise the new president and New Deal attempts to pull the country out of the worst depths of the depression. Soon, however, Coughlin delivered blistering attacks on both FDR and his wife Eleanor, while adopting an anti-Semitic tenor and a message that increasingly bordered on fascism.

Louisiana Senator Huey Long, a radical populist, was engaged in his own Share Our Wealth program, which demanded that the federal government provide a sizable guaranteed annual income to every American family and limit individual incomes, legacies, and fortunes. A physician in Long Beach, California, Dr. Francis E. Townsend, put forth a plan to provide Americans sixty years of age and older with substantial monthly payments. Also out in the Golden State, Upton Sinclair ran for governor, calling on his End Poverty in California movement, which envisioned the state government running idle farms and factories collectively, striving for "production for use," rather than profit, and offering monthly pensions for the elderly. Minnesota's Floyd Olson, the state's first Farmer-Labor Party governor, supported progressive income taxation, a state program of unemployment insurance, and major public relief programs to stimulate the economy and put Minnesotans back to work. Denying he was a liberal, Olson proclaimed, "I am a radical." In nearby Wisconsin, La Follette progressivism still reigned, with brothers Robert M. La Follette Jr. and Philip La Follette occupying the seats in the Senate and the statehouse once filled by their father. Philip favored active government engagement in economic affairs, including the "little Wagner Act," which set up a state labor relations board to mediate labor disputes; a "little TVA," a public power agency; and bills to help farmers, homeowners, and cities from the ravages of the depression. The Commonwealth Federations appeared in Washington State and Oregon, holding office while adopting programs like those of Canadian social democrats. North Dakota's Nonpartisan League also became revitalized, winning a number of elections during the 1930s. Subscribing to tenets articulated through the Sermon on the Mount, Dorothy Day and Peter Maurin's Catholic Worker movement sought to bring about "a new society within the shell of the old, a society in which it will be easier to be good." Founded at the worst depths of the Great Depression in 1933, the movement exuded an anarchistic feel, celebrated volunteer poverty, and remained firmly committed to nonviolence. The interracial-socialist inclined Southern Tenant Farmers' Union (STFU), established by H. L. Mitchell in 1934, demanded relief from the Roosevelt administration for tenant farmers and sharecroppers. Within two years, the STFU included over 25,000 members across several southern states.

* * *

Roosevelt's New Deal borrowed liberally from both the progressive movement, through which the president began his political career, and more radical ideas, including socialism, at least to a degree. In the process, Roosevelt helped to save American capitalism by transforming it, laying the structural foundation for the welfare state. Radical nostrums and political actors on the order of Coughlin, Long, Townsend, Sinclair, Olson, and the La Follette brothers possessed considerable appeal to many Americans, as both CPUSA and the SPA experienced rebirths. According to Raymond Moley, one of the initial members of the president's "brain trust," FDR sought to ameliorate conditions for America's down-and-outers, while stabilizing the economic system. As analyzed by Roosevelt biographers, Arthur Schlesinger Jr., James McGregor Burns, and William Leuchtenburg, the New Deal underwent different phases. The first New Deal included an initial attempt to prevent the continued crashing of the economy, resulting in planning measures targeting the industrial and agrarian sectors, as well as one of the nation's most dilapidated areas, but also reform initiatives designed to stabilize the banking system and protect deposits, ward off foreclosures, avoid starvation, and put millions of forgotten men back to work. As the economy improved, criticism only mounted from the right and the left, leading to a second New Deal involving additional work relief, including that directed at artists, historians, writers, and actors; progressive income taxation; Social Security; and labor organizing. A third New Deal followed another economic downturn that came after Roosevelt attempted to stop priming the pump so vigorously; it featured housing programs, relief assistance, and additional deficit spending.

The American left, bluntly put, didn't know what to make of Franklin Roosevelt, with the CPUSA proving particularly distrustful. But then his early presidency followed the wrongheaded decision on the part of the Comintern to maintain its policy of deeming socialists "social fascists," as it had in Germany, thus ensuring a division of the left and Hitler's ascendancy to power. In both Spain and France, leftists began insisting on the need for collaboration between left-of-center elements to prevent takeover by right-wing movements. But in the United States, several radicals, including the young journalist Isadore Feinstein (soon to rename himself I. F. Stone), continued to parrot a communist line that the New Deal was fascist. Some, mostly communists, saw socialists in the same light. In February 1934, communists caused a riot at an SPA rally at Madison Square Garden held to honor Viennese socialist workers murdered by Austrian chancellor Engelbert Dollfuss's troops. An "Open Letter to the Communist Party" condemned the communist instigators. Responding to criticism that he had signed that note, John Dos Passos explained he believed "the growth of unintelligent fanaticism" could only result in separating "the conscious elements of the exploited classes into impotent brawling sects" and hinder movement toward "a sanely organized society."

The possibility of an alliance of left-wing forces was certainly not new, particularly gathering support among college students attracted to an antiwar movement. Disillusionment with what World War I had wrought lingered, as recent literary and film explorations demonstrated. Ernest Hemingway's *A Farewell to Arms* and Eric Maria Remarque's *All Quiet on the Western Front*, both issued in 1929, presented the unhappy ponderings of an American veteran and a German veteran, with both novels soon turned into Academy Award winning films. The Committee on Militarism in Education, originating through the pacifist Fellowship of Reconciliation, contested the establishment of Reserve Officers' Training Corps (ROTCs) in colleges and universities throughout the United States. American pacifists Kirby Page and Richard Gregg drew on Mohandas Gandhi's nonresistant campaign in British-ruled India. Starting in early 1934, the United States Senate conducted prolonged hearings through a committee headed by North Dakota's Gerald P. Nye but encouraged by the Women's International League for Peace and Freedom, into the purported influence of munitions makers and financial interests in compelling U.S. entrance into World War I. Also, in 1934, 25,000 students in New York City alone, headed by members of the Student League for Industrial Democracy (SLID), tied to the SPA, and the communist-laden National Student League (NSL), participated in the National Student Strike Against War. They also adopted the equivalent of the Oxford Pledge, which Oxford University undergraduates had taken the previous year, attesting to their refusal to "fight for King and country in any war." Antiwar protests occurred on a series of campuses, among them City College of New York, Columbia, Harvard, Vassar, and Johns Hopkins. By 1935, 175,000 students joined in another nationwide strike, which now received the backing of the communist-heavy American Youth Congress (AYC) and the Youth Section of the American League Against War and Fascism. Students from the NSL and SLID agreed to form the American Student Union (ASU), hoping to bring together "all progressive, anti-fascist students," according to the historian Robert Cohen. Within a year, half-a-million students were participating in strike activities.

In the early stages of the depression decade, SLID and NSL thus dabbled in "coalition politics" of the sort their adult mentors later favored. They joined forces in antiwar and antifascist campaigns, before the Comintern gave approval to the Popular Front, which was similar to the coalition of leftwing forces emerging in Spain and France. The Comintern finally announced a new policy in 1935, calling for all antifascist elements to unite, but communists continued to view Trotskyists, followers of the exiled Bolshevik leader, with total disdain. The CPUSA only shifted course from its "social fascist" line after being instructed to by the Comintern during mid-1935, following its Seventh World Congress.

In Spain, an alliance of left-of-center forces swept into office in early 1936, only to confront implacable hostility from rightwing groups, eventually led by Generalissimo Francisco Franco, committed to destroy the Republic. To Spain headed leftists and rightists from around the globe, while the Soviet Union, Nazi Germany, and fascist Italy provided assistance as the Spanish Civil War eventuated. Paul Robeson, the gifted African American theatrical and film star spoke in support of the Republic at Royal Albert Hall, located in South Kensington, London, affirming, "The artist must elect to fight for freedom or slavery. I have made my choice. The history of the capitalist era is characterized by the degradation of my people." Spain's liberation from "fascist reactionaries," Robeson said, was "the common cause of all advanced and progressive humanity." Some 2,800 Americans, virtually all men of the far left, including many communists, made up the Abraham Lincoln Brigade, which was part of the much larger International

Brigades determined to battle fascism. Among those fighting for the Republic were the English poet John Cornford, his countryman Eric Blair (whose writing pseudonym was George Orwell), and the French author and aviator Andre Malraux. Cornford died in combat, and Blair, shot through the throat, nearly did so but went on to write *Homage to Catalonia* (1938), which critically examined communist machinations during the Spanish Civil War. Another literary classic about the conflict was *For Whom the Bell Tolls* (1940), Ernest Hemingway's lyrical presentation of a college instructor who fought for the Loyalists. Hemingway went to Spain during the war, as did John Dos Passos, but their friendship dissolved as the latter's disillusionment with communists intensified following the arrest and murder of Jose Robles, a poet and radical activist, absurdly accused of being a fascist spy.

Back in the United States, the CPUSA took advantage of the Popular Front, participating in a series of groups and organizations that harvested support from sympathetic liberals and non-communist radicals. The party was heavily involved with both the League of American Writers (1935) and the American Artists' Congress (1936). Both strongly supported anti-fascism and the Spanish Republic, as indicated by a later pamphlet, *Writers Take Side* (1938), which recorded only three authors out of 418 backing Franco. The list of members was long and distinguished, including James Agee, Conrad Aiken, Nelson Algren, Sherwood Anderson, W. H. Auden, Michael Blankfort, Bertolt Brecht, Van Wycks Brooks, Heywood Broun, Alexander Calder, Malcolm Cowley, Stuart Davis, John Dos Passos, Aaron Douglas, Theodore Dresier, James T. Farrell, Robert Frost, Dashiell Hammett, Lillian Hellman, Ernest Hemingway, Granville Hicks, Langston Hughes, Rockwelll Kent, Archibald MacLeish, Thomas Mann, Meyer Schapiro, Ben Shahn, David Alfaro Siqueiros, John Steinbeck, Nathanael West, William Carlos Williams, and Art Young.

But communists and socialist organizers were at the forefront of a series of labor battles, including by industrial workers and the unemployed. One of the major contests involved longshoremen and maritime laborers, who, guided by Australian-born Harry Bridges, engaged in a four-day general strike of 150,000 workers throughout the Bay Area. Newspapers across California railed away at the strikers with the *Los Angeles Times* charging, "What is actually in progress there [in San Francisco] is an insurrection, a Communist-inspired and led revolt against organized government." Armed vigilantes tore into homes and offices of local radicals, while the police arrested 300 on one day alone.

Changed circumstances, including alteration of CP policy and adoption of the sit-down strike, resulted in the formation, by 1935, of the Congress of Industrial Labor Organizations (CIO). A. J. Muste's CPLA, renamed the Workers Party (WP), participated in a number of labor battles, especially in Toledo and Akron. Trotskyist influences in the WP loomed so large that

Muste soon disavowed any association with Marxism-Leninism, reaffirming the pacifism he had temporarily abandoned. Challenging the AFL's preeminent stance among American labor unions, the CIO employed militant tactics, including sit-down strikes where workers threatened to destroy plant equipment if police forces and vigilantes were brandished against them. The CIO's new unions achieved successes against previously recalcitrant employers like General Motors, Ford, and Chrysler.

The relation between the CPUSA and the SPA remained uneasy, at best. With a crowd of 20,000 gathered in Madison Square Garden in February 1935, CP leader Earl Browder urged a united front against fascism, while the SPA's Thomas praised what the Soviet Union had accomplished but asked, "Is Russia so weak that it cannot afford, eighteen years after the revolution, to grant civil liberties to its citizens?" No longer claiming that President Roosevelt was a "social fascist," Browder and his 1936 presidential platform warned instead about "extreme reaction" propelling the United States "toward fascism and a world war." Communism, Browder now claimed, was "Twentieth Century Americanism" in line with "the revolutionary Lincoln," and he referred to socialists as "comrades." "The immediate issue," the CPUSA exclaimed, was "democracy or fascism." The SPA, which refused any formal alliance with the CPUSA, was riddled by sectarianism of its own involving the Militants, tied to Thomas, and the Old Guard. Its youth wing, the Young People's Socialist League, would be fractured as well, as some supported a partnership involving the Young Communist League (YCL) within the antiwar camp. Others, who remained committed to anti-interventionism, formed the Youth Committee for the Oxford Pledge, later called the Youth Committee Against War (YCAW).

The change in perspective enabled the Popular Front to thrive for a time, as a brand of radical culture made an appearance in the United States. Writers like John Dos Passos, Clifford Odets, briefly a CP member, Marc Blitzstein of the CPUSA, John Steinbeck, and Richard Wright, the African American author who was then in the party, produced riveting works like *USA* (1930, 1932, 1936), *Waiting for Lefty* (1935), *In Dubious Battle* (1936), *The Cradle Will Rock* (1937), *The Grapes of Wrath* (1939), and *Native Son* (1940). Containing stream of consciousness writing and brief biographies, Dos Passos's *USA* analyzed American society during the first third of the twentieth century. His vignettes included a pantheon of American radicals or near radicals: Debs, Haywood, Bryan, Robert La Follette, Reed, Bourne, Thorstein Veblen, Hill, and Isadora Duncan. Odets's play, *Waiting for Lefty*, highlighted a recent taxi union strike, while Blitzstein's theatrical offering, *The Cradle Will Rock*, celebrated radical labor activity. Steinbeck's *In Dubious Battle* and *The Grapes of Wrath* focused on the toil and living conditions of the dispossessed, and radical protagonists, the first containing communists so committed to the cause that they were willing to die for it, the second about the displaced Joad family's trek westward to California. Wright's *N ative Son* explored Bigger Thomas, a twenty-year-old black man dwelling in Chicago's mean streets whose involvement with the CPUSA also proved ambivalent at best.

All but Dos Passos were associated, to some extent, with the Works Progress Administration (WPA), which was established in 1935, and contained innovative programs involving writers, historians, musicians, theatrical performers, and visual artists. Other radicals who became WPA veterans included the writers Nelson Algren, Jack Conroy, Malcolm Cowley, and Claude McKay; the dancer-anthropologist Katherine Dunham; theatrical figures John Houseman, Joseph Losey, Rose McClendon, Nicholas Ray, and Orson Welles; painters Stuart Davis, William Gropper, Philip Guston, Willem de Kooning, Jacob Lawrence, Jack Levine, Jackson Pollock, and Anton Refregier; composers Ruth Crawford, Hanns Eisler, Earl Robinson, and Charles Seeger; and photojournalists Walker Evans, Dorothea Lange, and Ben Shahn. Among the iconic works produced on the WPA payroll were Lange's *Migrant Mother* (1936), the photograph of the young but worn mother and her two children, capturing the human costs of the Great Depression, and Virgil Thompson's musical score for *The Plow That Broke the Plains*, Pare Lorentz's documentary of the Great Plains. Under the auspices of the WPA, folklorist John A. Lomax was involved with the Slave Narrative Collection. His son Alan conducted interviews with folksinger Woody Guthrie, who delivered a column, "Woody Sez," that appeared in both the *Daily Worker* and its West Coast edition, the *People's World*, for the American Folklife Center, which received backing from the WPA and other New Deal programs.

In spite of mounting criticisms from conservative voices, which eventually brought about a shutting down of WPA projects, radical writers, artists, musicians, and photojournalists continued to deliver stellar work, as did those outside the CPUSA but supportive, knowingly or not, of the Popular Front. Initially appearing in *Life* magazine (1937), Margaret Bourke-White's "World's Highest Standard of Living" displayed those words atop a large billboard containing the image of a comfortable white family and a white dog riding in a car and the words "There's no way like the American Way," in front of a long line of African Americans, clearly less affluent. Having written "Brother, Can You Spare a Dime?" early in the decade, song lyricist Yip Harburg produced "Over the Rainbow," for the cinematic version of *The Wizard of Oz*, adapted from the book of the same name by prairie radical L. Frank Baum just after the hard times of the 1890s. Moved by Lawrence Beitler's famed photograph of a lynching in Marion, Indiana, Abe Meeropol, a teaching veteran of a New York public high school and a social activist, wrote "Strange Fruit" (1937), whose haunting lyrics would be sung by the great Billie Holiday. Meeropol referred to Southern trees containing "a strange fruit," with blood aplenty and a "black body swinging." Ironically, he wrote of "the gallant South" and its pastoral makeup, but also "the bulging eyes," "the twisted mouth," "the sudden smell of burning flesh!" Crafted for the Federal Theatre Project by lyricist John La Touche and composer Earl Robinson, "Ballad for Americans" (1939) referred to Revolutionary War heroes, including the Jew Haym Solomon, Tom Paine, and Crispus Attucks, a man of African and Native American descent, as well as the Boston Massacre's first victim.

By 1940, Woody Guthrie had already delivered a vast panoply of socially-driven music, including "Vigilante Man," "Pretty Boy Floyd," "Tom Joad," and "Dust Bowl Blues," talking about vigilantes chasing down-and-outers, an outlaw folk-hero, *The Grapes of Wrath* protagonist, and hard times for America's heartland. Guthrie also penned "This Land Is Your Land," his beautiful rendering of the American landscape from coast to coast, with the refrain "This land was made for you and me." The black folk and blues great Josh White often appeared at the integrated and, hence, controversial Café Society, a Greenwich Village nightclub called the "wrong place for the right people," where Holiday first offered "Strange Fruit." As folksinger Cynthia Gooding indicated, "What Josh was doing was very dangerous. . . . At that time a black singer working to white audiences and singing songs about racial equality was doing a very dangerous thing. . . . He was about the only one doing it." White's recordings included *Chain Gang* (1940) and *Southern Exposure: An Album of Jim Crow Blues* (1941).

Even Hollywood, that purveyor of American fantasies, got caught up in the radical culture of the era, although hardly as redbaiters would later charge. Rather, Jeffersonian liberalism was brought into the twentieth century with a radical tinge and resonated in the work of a small number of the most creative forces in the film industry, particularly Frank Capra and John Ford. Capra dealt with the economic terrors wrought by the Great Depression in *American Madness* (1932) and *Meet John Doe* (1941), which also contained a warning against home-brewed fascism, but he offered social democratic or liberal solutions in *Mr. Deeds Goes to Town* (1936), *You Can't Take It with You* (1938), and *Mr. Smith Goes to Washington* (1939). His *Lost Horizon* (1937) displayed, then withdrew from the utopia of Shangri-La. Ford's 1940 cinematic treatment of *The Grapes of Wrath* had its protagonist Tom Joad assure his mother, "Then it don't matter. I'll be around in the dark—I'll be everywhere. Wherever you can look—wherever there's a fight, so hungry people can eat, I'll be there. Wherever there's a cop beatin' up a guy, I'll be there. I'll be in the way guys yell when they're mad. I'll be in the way kids laugh when they're hungry and they know supper's ready, and when the people are eatin' the stuff they raise and livin' in the houses they build—I'll be there, too." Also, King Vidor's *Our Daily Bread* (1934) heralded a collective farm, while *The Adventures of Robin Hood* (1938), directed by Michael Curtiz, presented the story of the fabled outlaw bandit who stole from the rich and passed that bounty on to the poor.

* * *

Several observers point to the signing of the Nazi-Soviet nonaggression pact in late August 1939 as ushering in the Popular Front's demise. For many, it did indeed serve as a breaking point or "Kronstadt" in the manner the journalist Louis Fischer discusses in *The God That Failed*, a collection of essays explaining why six writers, including Fischer and Richard Wright, abandoned the Communist Party. In 1921, Russian sailors, soldiers, and civilians in Kronstadt had revolted against Bolshevik tyranny but were brutally suppressed, alienating individuals like the anarchists Emma Goldman and Alexander Berkman. Some, including a number in communist parties worldwide, now experienced their own Kronstadts. Granville Hicks, literary editor of the *New Masses*, resigned from the CPUSA, most troubled by that organization's bending of the knee to the Soviet Union.

For many others, earlier developments had caused them to disavow allegiance to the Soviet Union or communism. The signs of seemingly inalterable tyranny by the Bolsheviks had been there all along for those inclined to acknowledge the terrible abuses, exploitation, and repression associated with Lenin, which worsened immeasurably under Joseph Stalin. The Polish-German revolutionary Rosa Luxemburg, the British socialist, philosopher, and mathematician Bertrand Russell, and the anarchist Goldman had all worried about Lenin's despotism. Before she was murdered by German counterrevolutionaries, Luxemburg warned, "Freedom only for the supporters of the government, only of the members of one party—however numerous they may be—is no freedom at all. Freedom is always and exclusively freedom for the one who thinks differently."

Supporters of Trotsky had long fallen off the train of the revolution, at least that which was tied to Stalinism. An anti-Stalinist left developed, although those associated with it seldom were treated by CP members as anything other than pariahs, even during the Popular Front period. Party members and many fellow travelers continued to vilify Trotsky and those connected to him. The purges inside the communist world, particularly in the Soviet Union, infuriated a small but growing number of radicals. That sense of outrage intensified with the Moscow Trials that followed the assassination, in late 1934, of Leningrad party chief Sergey Kirov. In an astonishing turn of events, many Old Bolsheviks, including Nikolai Bukharin, editor-in-chief of *Pravda*, the leading party newspaper in the Soviet Union, were accused of having conspired with Japanese militarists or, especially, German fascists to overthrow the communist state.

Such developments increased the ranks of anti-Stalinists, with noteworthy withdrawals from either backing the CPUSA wholeheartedly or joining in Popular Front alliances as the Moscow Trials appeared ever more ludicrous to some on the American left. Under Philip Rahv and William Phillips, *The Partisan Review*, initially tied to the John Reed Club of New York City, but always adverse to a "literary counterpart of mechanical materialism," shifted course by late 1937. Its pages were open to anti-Stalinists, including Trotsky himself, Dos Passos, and James T. Farrell, each increasingly viewed with disdain by CP members. Most of *The Partisan Review*'s latest contributors, like its editors, were part of the anti-Stalinist left, many were intellectuals, and many were educated at colleges and universities in New York City. The *Modern Quarterly*, founded by the non-affiliated radical V. F. Calverton, provided a welcoming station for anti-Stalinists.

The divides on the left were characterized by varying responses to the Dewey Commission, which the American Committee for the Defense of Leon Trotsky and his son Leon Sedov set up in March 1937. As the Marxist theoretician George Novack notes, "Trotsky was the only one among the accused Bolshevik leaders . . . beyond Stalin's grip." Chaired by John Dewey and held during April 1937 in Coyoacan, Mexico, where Trotsky resided in a ramshackle compound and where a Stalinist agent subsequently murdered him, the Commission held a series of sessions, exploring the life of its subject, his perspective regarding leading Moscow Trial defendants, Stalinist policy in Spain, the history of the Soviet state, and its foreign policy. Before the sessions began, Trotsky pledged, "If this commission decides that I am guilty in the slightest degree of the crimes which Stalin imputes to me, I pledge in advance to place myself voluntarily in the hands of the executioners of the GPU [Soviet secret police]."

CPUSA members and fellow travelers bashed the Dewey Commission, with Michael Gold insisting on the soundness of "Soviet justice," and Corliss Lamont charging that the Commission was designed to "whitewash Trotsky." As the Moscow Trials continued, 150 self-styled "American Progressives" essentially lauded them. Along with usual signatories, the names of George Seldes, Irwin Shaw, and Max Weber could be found. *The Nation* and *The New Republic*, two of the era's leading left-liberal publications, continued to dance around concerning the trial's authenticity. To its credit, *The Nation* did admit that the trials of the Old Bolsheviks were foreclosing "the dream of anti-Fascist unity."

More and more, well-known intellectuals condemned both the trials and Stalinism. As the historian Frank Warren relates, these included "liberals like John Haynes Holmes, Oswald Garrison Villard, and John Dewey," as well as "anti-Stalinist radicals . . . Max Eastman, Sidney Hook, and James T. Farrell." During the spring of 1939, following collapse of the Spanish Republic and the Nazi takeover of Czechoslovakia, *The Nation* presented a document by the Committee for Cultural Freedom, which insisted that the Popular Front be ended and criticized those who condemned Nazism but defended Stalinism.

Quickly responding, approximately 400 intellectuals who still subscribed to the Popular Front demanded its continuance and blasted "the fantastic falsehood that the USSR and the totalitarian states are basically alike." They lauded the "steadily expanding democracy in every sphere" within the Soviet Union, and termed dictatorship there temporary. Among those signing this unfortunate manifesto, issued on August 14, were longtime Popular Fronters Roger Baldwin, Ernest Hemingway, Granville Hicks, Matthew Josephson, Corliss Lamont, Max Lerner, and I. F. Stone.

Announcement of the Nazi-Soviet Pact only days later stunned and enraged many on the left, including those who had continued to believe that the Soviet Union had to be defended as it was the lone socialist national instrument and the preeminent anti-fascist vehicle. The socialism that was actually prevailing in Stalin's Soviet Union, however, was more in keeping with totalitarianism in general where a new ruling class prevailed, as Milovan Djilas would later bemoan. And its foreign policy, under Stalin, Maxim Litvinov, and Viacheslav Molotov, was characterized by self-serving, continually shifting positions pertaining to Japan and Western Europe. Consistently, however, Stalin had sought an accord, behind the scenes, with Adolf Hitler's Germany.

As the Popular Front collapsed, many who had steadfastly subscribed to it responded with venom. *The Nation*'s Louis Fischer termed the pact "totally indefensible." I. F. Stone, situated as that magazine's Washington editor, condemned members of the CPUSA, accusing them of jumping once more "at the pull of Stalin's string." Roger Baldwin reacted as if "a bombshell" had gone off. The pact, he recalled, "made you feel that suddenly the Communists were different people. They had abandoned us and got into bed with Hitler." The subsequent Soviet invasion of Finland only deepened the anger many felt, although those who stuck by the party justified it, as they did the pact and insisted that the war involved rival imperialisms, obviously not including the Soviet Union in such an analysis. The ACLU underwent its own shift, passing a resolution removing anyone in a leadership capacity who supported totalitarianism. This was directed at Elizabeth Gurley Flynn, who had long ago joined the Communist Party. The decision proved controversial, with many ACLU members and adherents accusing it of redbaiting.

Those who remained in the CPUSA, its membership having grown during the Popular Front period to 75,000–100,000, abruptly shifted course, discarding support for "anti-fascist collective security." They quickly adhered to the new or latest line emanating from Moscow, championing isolationism and American neutrality regarding the war in Europe. The CP's slogans now included "Keep America Out of War" and "The Yanks Are Not Coming," indicate party historians Irving Howe and Lewis Coser. The *Daily Worker* serialized *Johnny Got His Gun*, Dalton Trumbo's stunning fictionalized account of a young soldier coming to grips with having lost his limbs and face. Communists attempted to construct new fronts, which involved linkage with rightwing groups and individuals like Father Coughlin and famed aviator turned apologist for fascism, Charles A. Lindbergh.

In early September 1940, the American Peace Mobilization (APM) emerged, seemingly led by Paul Robeson, Dr. Francis Townshend, and New York Congressman Vito Marcantonio. The APM planks called for the United States remaining out of the war, fighting "militarism and regimentation," restoring the Bill of Rights, quashing war profiteering, and ensuring that all Americans had a decent standard of living. To those ends, the APM opposed conscription, which was just beginning in the United States. By the following spring, the APM conducted "round the clock" vigils in front of the White House, demonstrating the organization's opposition to the providing of aid to England, which was experiencing the German Luftwaffe's Blitz.

An organization like the American Student Union also readily accepted the new stance, alienating non-party members. Joseph P. Lash, a young man who had served as the ASU executive secretary, recalled "a terrible sense of betrayal" they experienced. Communists went after Lash, calling him a "warmonger" and reactionary. But appalled ASU members, who were not tied to the CPUSA, refused to accept the changed position, ensuring the organization's marked decline. Communists proceeded to effect greater control over the American Youth Congress, which President Roosevelt felt compelled to lambast as he favored U.S. aid to Finland. CP head Earl Browder now charged that the president "has studied well the Hitlerian arts and bids fair to outdo the record of his teacher."

Browder clearly had little liking for America's commander-in-chief, who was striving, notwithstanding a series of neutrality laws passed in the 1930s, to mobilize the United States for what FDR considered to be his country's near certain entry, at some point, into the war. Along with other CP leaders, Browder also faced an indictment charge for passport fraud. Upon his conviction, he received a four-year jail sentence and a $2,000 fine. The Justice Department prosecuted as well the Fur Workers Union and an officer of the National Maritime Union, both communist-driven.

Anti-communist but leftwing and concerned about the pacifism associated with the SPU, the Union for Democratic Action (UDA) appeared in May 1941. Founders included the actor Melvyn Douglas, James I. Loeb, and Reinhold Niebuhr, while A. Philip Randolph, the United Auto Workers' Walter P. Reuther, and Eleanor Roosevelt were among the honorary sponsors. The UDA refused to admit communists as members.

The budding red scare altered course following the German invasion of the Soviet Union, which began on July 22, 1941. The Soviet Union was, suddenly, back on the side of the angels, and calls for a new united front could be heard. The CPUSA insisted on the need to "defend the Soviet Union." *The Nation* and *The New Republic* returned to supporting an anti-fascist alliance, but then others did so as well, including *PM*, a left-of-center, adless newspaper published in New York City and featuring exposes by I. F. Stone and editorials by Max Lerner. Some supported aligning with the Soviet Union but remained suspicious about American comrades. Favoring assistance to the communist state, British Prime Minister Winston Churchill affirmed, "If Hitler invaded hell I would make at least a favourable reference to the devil in the House of Commons." The following month, Churchill and President Roosevelt, recently elected to an unprecedented third term, met in Newfoundland, where they produced the Atlantic Charter, a series of Wilsonian-styled war aims: disarmament, self-determination, less encumbered trade, and collective security.

The CPUSA cheered as the Department of Justice now trained prosecutorial energies against the Socialist Workers Party, with twenty-nine Trotskyists, including James P. Cannon, Farrell Dobbs, and Vincent Ray Dunne, tried for conspiracy. Fifteen of the defendants were members of Teamsters Local 544 in Minneapolis, a militant Trot-dominated branch. The charges involved a Civil War statute regarding seeking to overthrow the government through force and violence, and the recently passed Smith Act that criminalized advocacy of such a coup. Eighteen defendants were convicted and received prison sentences. Shortly after the trial, President Roosevelt agreed to release Earl Browder from jail. The CPUSA also vilified Norman Thomas, who declined to condemn U.S. participation in the war following the Japanese attack on Pearl Harbor, choosing instead to direct the SPA to support "civil liberties, democratic Socialism, and an anti-imperialist Peace." Thomas was condemned as a "Fifth Columnist and spearhead of fascism," supposedly striving to bore from within, thereby damaging the war effort.

* * *

After the United States became a combatant, Roosevelt steadily agreed, even more than before, with Churchill's determination to align with the Soviet Union against Germany and its Axis allies, Italy and Japan. Eventually, the United States, Great Britain, and the Soviet Union participated in the Grand Alliance, through which American industrial might, British will, and Soviet lives eventually defeated Nazi Germany, militarist Japan, and fascist Italy. The anti-fascist partnership was never an easy one, with considerable distrust sometimes hindering the union of capitalist, democratic America, parliamentary, imperialistic England, and communist Russia.

The Roosevelt administration waged World War II as a consciously antifascist fight, while both the president and Vice-President Henry A. Wallace delivered oratory promises that had to be to the liking of liberals and radicals. In his 1941 State of the Union address, FDR, obviously articulating war aims, extolled the "Four Freedoms," insisting on the need for freedom of speech, of worship, from want, and from fear. In a speech at the Commodore Hotel in New York City on May 8, 1942, Wallace predicted "the century of the common man." Declaring that a fight existed "between a slave world and a free world," Wallace denounced demagogues like "one Satan-inspired Fuhrer" as "the curse of the modern world." By contrast, the "long-drawn-out people's revolution" extending from the American Revolution to the Russian uprising in 1917 demonstrated "the people are on the march." During his 1944 State of the Union talk, Roosevelt spoke of the United States' participation "in the world's greatest war against human slavery" and "gangster rule." But he also referred to the need for "a second Bill of Rights" that would afford "security and prosperity . . . for all regardless of station, race, or creed." This economic platform would include the right to productive, adequately compensated employment, sufficient income allowing for "adequate food and clothing and recreation," adequate compensation for the farmer's produce, business operations unencumbered by unfair trade or monopolies, "a decent home" for a family, decent medical care, "a good education," and protection against the economic ravages "of old age, sickness, accident, and unemployment."

To the delight of many in the American left, wartime exigencies allowed for a rebooting of the Popular Front, although it lacked much of the romantic flair and displayed even greater absurdities than had the earlier edition. Stalin was portrayed as "Uncle Joe," even by many conservative media sources, and the Soviet Union was depicted favorably, often in rose-colored fashion. Hollywood made a small number of genuinely pro-Soviet films, far more so than during what has been called the "Red Decade" of the 1930s. Michael Curtiz's *Mission to Moscow* (1943), Louis Milestone's *The North Star* (1943), and Gregory Ratoff and Lazlo Benedek's *Song of Russia* (1944) lacked subtleties, offering Ptomekin-like villages, heroic Russian fighters, and glorified Moscow Trials. Conservative media magnate Henry Luce affectionately referred to Stalin as "Uncle Joe."

By contrast, anti-Stalinists remained distrustful, although few held out as many more had during World War I in refusing to support their country while it was at war. The attack on American soil ensured that a rallying round the flag phenomenon often displayed during exigent circumstances occurred, and FDR's continued popularity probably didn't hurt. Committed pacifists remained true to their principles and sometimes paid the price, as a consequence. Provisions for conscientious objection during World War II were more generous, with allowance for those acting on moral grounds, not simply due to religious principles. For those who didn't enter the military, alternative service was possible on the home front provided it involved "work of national importance." Of 34.5 million draft registrants, just over 72,000 were classified as conscientious objectors, 27,000 of whom failed the requisite physical exam. Another 25,000 performed noncombatant jobs, twice the number who engaged in alternative service involving Civilian Public Service (CPS) camps, which operated through the peace churches, while more than 6,000 resisters opted for jail.

CPS enrollees carried out useful functions on the home front during the war. Effectively receiving no pay and required to cover their own expenses, CPS participants volunteered to serve as "human guinea pigs" for vital medical experiments, worked in mental hospitals and schools, assisted agricultural and construction endeavors, and served as fire fighters for the U.S. Forest Service. The CPS smokejumpers, less than 300 of them, opted for an alternative to war or a nonviolent way to fight.

Most absolute resisters landed behind bars, refusing to have anything to do with the Selective Service System and the U.S. Armed Forces. Some who served time during World War II, like David Dellinger, Roy Finch, George Houser, James Peck, and Bayard Rustin, subscribed to radical pacifism, which they envisioned being employed to usher in sweeping social and economic transformations. Displeasure with prison rules, including those mandating racial segregation, resulted in hunger strikes and other forms of nonviolent resistance, the kind that would increasingly be used by various political and social groups in the United States during ensuing decades. Civil rights, antinuclear, antiwar, and New Left groups were among those that would resort to such tactics.

Dellinger, a Yale graduate and student at the Union Theological Seminary, was associated with the Harlem Commune that drew on Gandhi's inspiration in adopting nonviolent resistance to reconfigure "unjust social orders." As the historian James Tracy indicates, radical pacifists like Dellinger displayed determined opposition not simply to the war and military service but to conscription itself, quickly protesting congressional passage of the first peacetime draft in U.S. history. In prison, they honed techniques soon applied through organizations like the Fellowship of Reconciliation and the Congress of Racial Equality (CORE). The latter group, founded in 1942 by James L. Farmer Jr., Bernice Fisher, Houser, and Homer Jack, among others, emerged from conscientious objection and confinement in prison or CPS centers. Influential too was A. Philip Randolph, who threatened a mass march by 100,000 African Americans on Washington, D.C., before FDR, in June 1941, issued Executive Order 8802, establishing the Committee on Fair Employment Practices and banning racial discrimination in both the federal government and defense plants. CORE nevertheless turned to direct action protests, including sit-ins, to contest segregation beyond the American South.

Dwight Macdonald, through his journal *Politics*, initially appearing in February 1944, offered an anarcho-pacifistic slant, extolling conscientious objectors. A remarkable experiment in independent radical journalism, *Politics* began with reference to the apparent dissolution of the CPUSA (to be converted into the Communist Political Association), which Macdonald declared had "long . . . been a branch office of the parent firm in Moscow rather than an American political party." Later issues that year, which contained the work of radicals from Europe and the United States, condemned the American army's Jim Crow makeup, extolled conscientious objectors conducting prison revolts, underscored the French Underground's revolutionary demands, and refused to keep mum about Soviet despotism. Macdonald himself declared, "It is precisely because I have more faith in men's ability to create a decent human society that I am able to remain hopeful about socialist revolution without having to close my eyes to the realities of what has happened in Russia." Near war's end, he warned "that such atrocities as The Bomb and the Nazi death camps are *right now* brutalizing, warping, deadening the human beings who are expected to change the world for the better." He applauded "resistance" against "The Bomb."

The death on April 12, 1945, of Franklin D. Roosevelt, who had just begun a fourth presidential term, and growing concerns about postwar Soviet designs diminished the possibility of maintaining amicable relations between Grand Alliance partners. However ironically, so did conservative Prime Minister Winston Churchill's electoral defeat and his replacement by the Labour Party's Clement Attlee, Deputy Prime Minister under the great British wartime leader. Little helping matters was the sweep into Eastern Europe by the liberating Red Army, accompanied by Communist Party commissars, and its evident intent to remain in place. That army didn't just liberate, it also engaged in wholesale pillaging and mass rapes, especially in Germany. Attlee supported his party's sharp turn leftward regarding establishment of National Health Service and nationalization of various industries but was also both a democratic socialist and a stalwart anti-communist, whose Foreign Secretary, Ernest Bevin, a former trade union head, was even more antagonist toward the Soviets. Yet another anti-communist, the new American president, Harry S. Truman, was less likely than his predecessor, the jaunty patrician FDR, to believe he could readily deal with his Soviet counterpart.

* * *

The Old Left flourished throughout much of the Great Depression and World War II, while always remaining controversial. That was due, in part, to its association with both the CPUSA and the Soviet Union, seen by some as a socialist utopia deserving of adulation, the revolutionary motherland, or an anti-fascist bulwark. Others, including many fellow travelers, were well aware of failings, even massive repression, associated with the communist state but felt compelled to deny those existed and to defend the Soviet Union against any criticisms, including from other progressives, liberals, or radicals.

The periods of the Popular Front, during the last half of the 1930s and after Germany attacked the Soviet Union, allowed the Old Left to acquire something of a mass following, at least in certain circles. The coming together of left-of-center forces saw a thriving in the cultural realm, as writers, artists, actors, and others participated in the radical culture of the era. That enabled individuals like Ernest Hemingway, Paul Robeson, Dorothea Lange, and Woody Guthrie to attain or cement iconic stature, but not all, including those on the left, were welcomed. Anti-Stalinists were often reviled by their fellow leftists, and pacifists were sometimes heralded and sometimes denigrated. The uncritical nature displayed by too many comrades or those close to them hardly served the American left well then or later, dividing it, producing charges of hypocrisy or worse and helping to provide precedents for perverse treatment of radicals when ideological currents shifted course.

Chapter 4

American Radicalism
and the Early Cold War

Different facets of the American left proved hopeful, albeit for contrasting reasons, as World War II ended. Looking at its expanded wartime membership of 75,000 or so, the Soviet Union's favorable standing with the American public, and the active role communists played in the wartime Resistance against Nazi hegemony in Europe, the newly reconstituted CPUSA foresaw favorable times ahead. Anti-Stalinist radicals were undoubtedly less hopeful, fearful that the CPUSA's reignited influence in various labor unions and among reconstituted fellow travelers would continue, if not intensify, during the postwar period. The mood of radical pacifists was somewhere in between, as the horrors of the war, most starkly exemplified by the death camps, Hiroshima, and Nagasaki, had to be juxtaposed against the commitment displayed by a small but impassioned group of activists determined to make a larger mark on national and international events.

In fact, positive feelings regarding the Soviet Union would soon sharply descend, fueled by events both abroad and at home. Even before the war ended in Europe, the Communist Information Bureau (Cominform, 1943), which had replaced the Comintern, sent out signals indicating that another sharp shift in policy was impending. Written in Moscow but issued under the name of Jacques Duclos, a French communist politician, a letter in April 1945 urged communist parties to come to the aid of the Soviet Union by condemning imperialist regimes. Clearly signally an end to the World War II version of the Popular Front, Duclos attacked the accommodating position of Earl Browder, head of the Communist Political Association, which had brought about the CPUSA's shuttering. By the summer, Browder was out, replaced by Eugene Dennis, a man he had mentored. Having previously praised the new president, the party now called Harry Truman a "militant imperialist" and the *Daily Worker* insisted that "the center of the reactionary forces in the world today rests in the United States." As historian Thomas W. Devine relates, Popular Front groups in the United States adopted increasingly pro-Soviet positions.

This occurred as the communization or Stalinization of Eastern Europe proceeded apace, including eventually in Hungary and Czechoslovakia, where elections of various legitimacy were held for a time. Other points of contention involved the ending of Lend-Lease assistance from the United States; northern Iran, where Soviet troops had yet to withdraw despite earlier promises to do so; unrest in Turkey; and a civil war in Greece, in which communist forces appeared potent. Stalin seemed to throw down the gauntlet, declaring that communism and capitalism could not coexist. First, in an 8,000-word telegram from Moscow in February 1946 and then in an article in the prestigious journal *Foreign Affairs* (July 1947), U.S. diplomat George F. Kennan warned of the Soviet Union's aggressive nature and called for a policy of containment. In March 1946, with President Truman in attendance, Winston Churchill delivered a speech in Fulton, Missouri, bemoaning the fact that "from Stettin in the Baltic to Trieste in the Adriatic, an iron curtain has descended across the continent" of Europe. As conditions there remained grave, with devastating war-generated economic dislocations, and trepidation about a communist surge, the president issued the Truman Doctrine on March 12, 1947, pledging that the United States would "support free people who are resisting attempted subjugation by armed minorities or by outside pressures."

Truman's pronouncement followed some difficult times for his administration, whose popularity dissipated as pent-up frustrations spilled over from the war, amid concerns that the country could slide back into another depression, and as events overseas proved bleaker yet again. Adding to these worries were attacks from both sides of the ideological spectrum with Republicans condemning labor unrest, rising prices, and apparent communist advances. Growing fears about communism of both the external and internal variety helped propel Republicans to victory in the 1946 congressional races. Accused of being soft on communism, Truman responded by mandating federal employees take a loyalty oath to display "complete and unswerving loyalty" to the American nation. Loyalty boards emerged, which relied on the Attorney General's List of "totalitarian, fascist, communist, or subversive" organizations. Truman was reviled by the CPUSA and its allies, which considered his response to the Soviet Union provocative. But Truman's actions in no way satisfied Republicans, who urged passage of the Taft-Hartley Act, which weakened the Wagner Act by proscribing supposedly unfair labor practices. The measure became law, with Congress overriding Truman's veto.

By contrast, non-communist, non-fellow-traveling liberals increasingly were casting themselves apart from the Old Left, particularly anything associated with the CPUSA or the Popular Front. Shortly after the ill-fated 1946 congressional elections, a group of well-known liberals such as Eleanor Roosevelt established Americans for Democratic Action (ADA). Prominent members included John Kenneth Galbraith, Hubert Humphrey, Reinhold Niebuhr, Joseph Rauh, Ronald Reagan, and Arthur Schlesinger Jr. The anticommunist ADA was committed to progressive ideals and causes, including an expansion of the welfare state, termination of Jim Crow, and the safeguarding of civil liberties. In keeping with the ADA's orientation, Schlesinger soon referred to the need to sustain what he called "a vital center," but what he actually considered the non-communist left. He dismissed socialist attempts to collaborate with communists, and declared that "a united Left is an illusion" for "the question of freedom v. totalitarianism cannot be compromised." Schlesinger's "vital center" involved fervent belief in civil liberties, democracy, and constitutionalism.

What Truman and the Old Left were both contending with, but also exacerbated in various ways, was the budding red scare of the early Cold War period. Actions by portions of the Old Left, those who continued to revere or at least apologize for the Soviet Union's tyranny and its expansionist designs, often fed what amounted to hysteria. Both recent developments and some now decades-old hardly assisted those desirous of viewing international and domestic developments rationally. From the onset of the Bolshevik Revolution, fears regarding the communist experiment's contagious nature produced calls for investigations of supposedly un-American elements, moves to deport radical aliens, witch hunts, and repressive legislation. All of that had occurred during World War I and its immediate aftermath and recurred at different points thereafter, including following the most recent worldwide conflict.

State and federal investigations of radicals long predated the postwar red scare. The New York state legislature, in 1919, established the Joint Legislative Committee to Investigate Seditious Activities. That same year, the U.S. Senate's Overman Committee, chaired by North Carolina's Lee S. Overman, sought to track Bolshevism's influence in America. The Special Committee to Investigate Communist Activities in the United States, led by New York Congressman Hamilton Fish Jr., conducted hearings around the country during the early 1930s, with particular concerns conveyed about communist efforts to organize the unemployed. In 1938, Congress set up the House Committee on Un-American Activities, chaired by Texas' Martin Dies Jr., to examine purported disloyalty and subversion by individuals and groups with communist or fascist connections. Scurrilous accusations often resulted from congressional sessions, ranging from exaggerated charges by the Overman Committee that Jews abounded among the Bolsheviks to the Dies Committee's fixation on communism and besmirching of the Roosevelt administration. HUAC member J. Parnell Thomas of New Jersey contended that the Federal Theatre Project was "infested by radicals from top to bottom." "Practically every play presented under the auspices of the Project," he stated, "is sheer propaganda for Communism of the New Deal."

While such committees often carelessly, even recklessly carried out hearings or issued reports damning radicals and liberals alike, there existed genuine cause for concern about the activities of certain individuals associated with the CPUSA, the Comintern, or the Cominform. Much was little known at the time specific events took place, and some of this has only recently come to light. Almost immediately following the revolution that brought Lenin and Trotsky to power, worries emerged about pipelines, financial and otherwise, to individuals and groups outside Russia. In the case of the United States and its various communist parties, such threads long existed, many of them ideological, even romantic, in nature, resulting in support for regimes led by first Lenin and then Stalin hardly deserving of such backing. But there also developed more disturbing patterns, the first the propensity, already discussed, of accepting directives from communist overlords, and the still more troubling willingness of some to go farther in displaying loyalty to the cause of the revolution. That could lead to money trails or to a readiness to engage in espionage. All of this has resulted in a historiographical debate about whether the American Communist Party possessed any legitimacy, a question particularly posed during the postwar red scare but more recently too.

What has become increasingly clear is that stories of "Moscow Gold" have been borne out, from the earliest days of American communism onward. Harvey Klehr charges, in fact, "From its founding in 1919 . . . until the demise of the Soviet Union in 1991, the Communist Party of the United States of America was an instrument of Soviet foreign policy." With his fellow historian John Earl Haynes, Klehr has authenticated the trail of financial largesse emanating from communist Russia. Early couriers included John Reed, founding party member Louis Fraina, the industrialist Armand Hammer, and the poet Carl Sandburg. By the 1930s, the Soviets employed "business fronts" to funnel money to the CPUSA, while by the close of the following decade, that subsidy amounted to $1,000,000 annually.

Most troubling is the indisputable fact that American comrades, like the infamous Cambridge Five, engaged in espionage to funnel information, sometimes involving industrial, technological, scientific, and military matters, to the Soviet Union. In a lengthy review on Soviet espionage in the United States, investigative journalist Thomas Powers writes, "The plain fact is that the Russians were running a good many spies in the United States in the 1930s and 1940s, that they recruited them from the ranks of the left, that they ran them to steal secrets, and when they got caught at it they went to ground and waited for a better day." In a devastating analysis, Powers indicates that while "some of the left had no illusions . . . many . . . were slow and grudging in admitting first the truth and then the significance of any given spy case." There were those who sought to dismiss all of this "as a witch hunt" and refused to accept that this was only possible because the Soviets had hijacked "the social idealism of the 1930s." Furthermore, the defensiveness displayed by many liberals intensified "the suspicions of the right, making it easier to argue that progressive causes and treason somehow went hand in hand."

A fuller reading of the CPUSA became possible with the opening up of archives after the collapse of the Soviet Union, and particularly the revelations in 1995 of Venona, the National Security Agency's secret project involving the decoding of over 25,000 intercepted Soviet telegrams. That allowed for apparent revelations about Soviet espionage occurring during the Roosevelt administration, including involving former high level State Department official Alger Hiss, infiltration of the Manhattan Project leading to construction of the atomic bomb, and a wide range of government activities. As was the case with the Cambridge Five, Americans who agreed to spy for the Soviet Union apparently usually did so because of belief in communism, anti-fascism, or the wartime alliance.

Earlier warnings about spy rings existing in Washington, D.C., were little heeded before the Cold War era. The poet and party activist turned espionage agent Whittaker Chambers, fearful for his own life as the Moscow Trials took place, broke from the communist underground and became, according to writer-editor William F. Buckley, "the most important American defector from communism." In September 1939, Chambers spoke to Assistant Secretary of State Adolf Berle about eighteen individuals he claimed were spies or communist sympathizers, including Alger Hiss, his brother Donald, and Laurence Duggan, all working for the State Department, and Lauchlin Currie, a special presidential assistant. Berle relayed the information to FDR, who didn't take it seriously, but Berle later talked to the FBI about Chambers's accusations. Although Berle reached out to the FBI yet again, and the agency interviewed Chambers twice, it failed to act on the accusations. That didn't change until after the war, when the atmosphere was far more conducive to charges of espionage involving the Soviet Union.

That was due, of course, to the Cold War, which altered both international affairs and domestic politics. Both the National Association of Manufacturers and the U.S. Chamber of Commerce expended considerable resources warning about "the menace of socialism." The Chamber issued pamphlets intended to ignite alarm: *Communist Infiltration of the United States*, *Communists Within the Labor Movement*, and *Program for Community Anti-Communist Action*. It demanded that communist influence in a wide array of areas be examined, and called for a federal loyalty oath program. FBI director J. Edgar Hoover, in testimony before HUAC on March 26, 1947, insisted that the CPUSA desired to destroy American democracy and capitalism, seeking "a 'Soviet of the United States'" side-by-side with revolution worldwide. Condemning "the mad march of red fascism," Hoover reported that "the deceit, the trickery, and the lies of the American communists" were returning to haunt them. The CPUSA, he continued, was "a fifth column if there ever was one."

Later that year, HUAC conducted hearings regarding purported communist influence in Hollywood. The culminating event centered on a group of screenwriters and directors, who came to be known as the Hollywood Ten, and included prominent figures like Ring Lardner Jr., John Howard Lawson, and Dalton Trumbo. Denouncing the congressional sessions, the group exclaimed that constitutional rights were being abridged, including freedom of association. Responding to the query, "Are you now or have you ever been a member of the Communist Party?" Lardner said, "I could answer the question exactly the way you want, but if I did, I would hate myself in the morning." The committee issued contempt citations, and all ten witnesses received prison sentences. While at the Federal Correctional Institution, located in Danbury, Connecticut, Lardner ran into former HUAC chair J. Parnell Thomas, convicted of having received a financial kickback.

The HUAC hearings would be repeated over the next decade, as were responses by Hollywood moguls, who created blacklists precluding the hiring of anyone connected to the American Communist Party. HUAC branched out, exploring government agencies, educational institutions, and supposedly suspect individuals. The damage done to various lives, reputations, and careers was not marginal, and included how the "investigations" seemed to hold certain activities or even thoughts suspect, while narrowing the scope of public discourse.

That was not immediately apparent when HUAC's postwar hearings began, or even during the domestic red scare's initial stages. The fellow traveling Old Left remained confident, possessing as many luminaries as its anti-Stalinist counterparts, and soon coalescing around Henry Wallace's presidential bid. After being pushed aside from the vice-presidency, Wallace served as Secretary of Commerce before being compelled to resign following a speech he offered at Madison Square Garden criticizing the drift toward hostilities with the Soviet Union. Fueling his campaign was the organization, the Progressive Citizens of America (PCA), which possessed 25,000 members by mid-1947, making up chapters in nineteen states.

As Wallace barnstormed that year, 200,000 people showed up as he railed about the Cold War and insisted on better relations with the communist behemoth. After a warmup talk by Oscar-winning actress Katherine Hepburn, who assailed HUAC's Hollywood investigation, Wallace spoke to 30,0000 supporters at Los Angeles' Gilmore Stadium, warning, "Today an ugly fear is spread across America—the fear of communism. I say those who fear communism lack faith in democracy." He then harked back to earlier, troubled events, including the burning of an innocent woman charged with witchcraft, the lynching of African Americans, the harassing of labor leaders and socialists, the interning of "100,000 innocent women and men" due to their Japanese ancestry, and the murdering of "two humble and glorious immigrants—Sacco and Vanzetti."

He worried about others attempting "to fasten new shame on America," referring to HUAC's "bigots." In late 1947, Wallace conveyed a readiness to run for the presidency, which many American radicals believed had been unfairly denied him by political bosses who tossed him off the 1944 Democratic Party presidential ticket in favor of Truman. His supporters, Wallace indicated, could boldly assert they were "voting peace and security for ourselves and our children's children . . . for old-fashioned Americanism . . . for freedom of speech and freedom of assembly . . . to end racial discrimination . . . for lower prices . . . for free labor unions, for jobs, and for homes in which we can decently live."

Wallace ran under the banner of the Progressive Party, which contained a number of liberals, fellow travelers, and communists, including Aaron Copland, Jo Davidson, W. E. B. Du Bois, Edna Ferber, Dashiell Hammett, Helen Keller, Gene Kelly, Thomas Mann, Fredric March, Arthur Miller, Florida Senator Claude Pepper, Lee Pressman, Paul Robeson, Idaho Senator Glen H. Taylor, Carl Van Doren, and Thornton Wilder. The former Vice President displayed considerable courage in delivering blistering attacks on racial discrimination, as he did at the end of 1947 in Tulsa, Oklahoma. Wallace stated forthrightly, "Jim Crow in America has simply got to go." Or else America's professed support for democracy, freedom, and justice would "ring hollow throughout the world." On a number of occasions, Wallace spoke in the American South, appearing with the likes of Paul Robeson and radical folksinger Peter Seeger, confronting hostile, violent crowds. His running mate, Senator Glenn Taylor was arrested by Birmingham police commissioner Bull Connor, for attempting to head an integrated campaign rally. Taylor attacked HUAC as "a fortress for the defense of Jim Crow," and "the cancerous disease of race hate," while demanding that the right to vote be protected, poll taxes forbidden, and federal legislation outlawing lynching passed.

The New Party, as Wallace's organization was sometimes called, proved, in many regards, the Popular Front's last gasp. Its platform supported Jim Crow's demise, a women's rights amendment, welfare state expansion, federal support for education, progressive income taxation, and public ownership of utilities. It also demanded more amicable relations with the Soviet Union and recognition of its right to "a sphere of influence in Eastern Europe." The communist influence within the Progressive Party bothered many, but Wallace proved unwilling to disavow the CPUSA's support. Red-baiting of Wallace continued, and his campaign foundered, concluding with a fourth-place finish, behind even South Carolina Governor Strom Thurmond's running on an openly pro-segregationist States' Right Democratic or Dixiecraft ticket.

Wallace's inability to amass more than 2.4 percent of the ballots cast with not a single electoral vote demonstrated the American Old Left's weakness, but that would be borne out still more starkly as the domestic Cold War intensified. This occurred despite Truman's surprising triumph in the presidential race and his promise to bring about a Fair Deal for America, which would have resulted in a stronger welfare state, including expanded public housing, and national health insurance. Having already issued an executive order desegregating the U.S. Armed Forces, Truman also called for a permanent Fair Employment Practices Commission.

However, both the international and domestic versions of the Cold War had heightened considerably. Communists carried out a coup in Czechoslovakia, the Soviets began blockading West Berlin on June 24, 1948, and only days later declined to participate in the Marshall Plan, designed to revitalize and stabilize war-torn Europe but dismissed by the USSR as an imperialist plan to envelope Eastern Europe. In late July, FBI agents began arresting CPUSA leaders, including Eugene Dennis and William Foster, charging them under the Smith Act with having conspired to "advocate the overthrow and destruction of the Government of the United States by force and violence." HUAC hearings continued, with sensational charges leveled by Whittaker Chambers on August 3 regarding Alger Hiss's purported role as a communist agent. While Western Allies were able to end an airlift to Western Berlin in May 1949, when Stalin called off the blockade, stunning news emerged in August that the Soviet Union had completed a successful atomic bomb test. A riot broke out on August 27 when Paul Robeson attempted to deliver an open-air concert close to Peekskill, New York. The great singer was hung in effigy, a cross was set afire, and expletives filled the air: "dirty nigger-lovers," "dirty commies," "dirty kikes."

More troubles occurred when the event actually took place on September 4, with a car carrying Woody Guthrie and Pete Seeger attacked. Then, on October 1, the Chinese civil war ended, with Mao Zedong and his communist forces establishing the People's Republic of China. On October 14, a jury, following a ten-month trial held at Manhattan Foley Square Courthouse, rendered guilty verdicts for eleven American communist leaders, leading to sentences for all but one of five years and fines of $10,000. War hero Robert G. Thompson was handed a reduced, three-year sentence. The defense attorneys, cited for contempt, were also sentenced to prison. The next month, the CIO expelled the United Electrical Workers, its third largest union, and later kicked out another eleven left-dominated unions. On January 21, 1950, Hiss, enduring a second trial for perjury as the statute of limitations for purported espionage had expired, was convicted and received a pair of concurrent five-year sentences.

Less than three weeks later, the latest postwar red scare entered a new, more virulent phase when Wisconsin Senator Joseph McCarthy, speaking in Wheeling, West Virginia, claimed, "I have in my hand a list of 205 cases of individuals who appear to be either card-carrying members or certainly loyal to the Communist Party" working for the State Department. The phenomenon of McCarthyism often involved wild brandishing of accusations regarding supposed disloyalty that included high-ranking government officials and military leaders. Abetted by young assistants Roy Cohn and David Schine, McCarthy engaged in a rhetorical reign of terror, often facilitated by the FBI and encouraged by Republican leaders, who again saw a chance to sully the Democratic Party and besmirch the reputations of Franklin Roosevelt and Harry Truman. Concerns about a vast communist conspiracy were magnified by the outbreak of the Korean War, which followed an attack across the 38th parallel by communist North Korean forces. Republican senatorial candidates—Congressman Richard M. Nixon in California and Representative George Smathers in Florida—successfully used redbaiting techniques to defeat their foes, liberal Congresswoman Helen Gahagan Douglas, painted as "the pink lady," and Senator Claude Pepper, a Popular Fronter derided as "Red Pepper" by his fellow Democrat.

Congress, local "Red squads," and U.S. Supreme Court rulings provided political and judicial leverage for the domestic Cold War, at this stage. The McCarran Internal Security Act (1950) mandated registration with the Department of Justice by "communist-action" and "communist front" groups, delivery of membership lists, establishment of a Subversive Activities Control Board, deportation of immigrants suspected of subversion or promoting totalitarian ideas, and detention by the president of those considered likely to engage in espionage or sabotage, or to conspire with others to do so. The McCarran-Walter Immigration Act (1952) set up a political litmus test for immigrants, banning those the attorney general deemed subversive, and allowed for the deportation of individuals connected to communist or communist-front groups. Congress overrode Truman's veto of each piece of legislation. HUAC continued another round of hearings. In 1954, Congress passed the Communist Control Act, although it too failed to outlaw the CPUSA. Police departments in a number of American cities, including Chicago, Detroit, Los Angeles, and New York, had intelligence units designed "to drive the pinks out of the country." Like the FBI, they conducted undercover work as part of surveillance operations.

The U.S. Supreme Court, in *Dennis v. United States* (1951), sustained the convictions of CPUSA leaders, notwithstanding the lack of evidence indicating any intention to undertake specific violent acts. Two justices, Hugo L. Black and William O. Douglas, dissented, with Black acknowledging that few would presently express concerns about the treatment afforded the defendants. He continued, "There is hope, however, that, in calmer times, when present pressures, passions and fears subside, this or some later Court will restore the First Amendment liberties to the high preferred place where they belong to a free society."

* * *

The altered atmosphere, actual repression, and the inept or cynical moves by the CPUSA all but finished it as a significant force in American political life. It was increasingly clear, or at least it would be later, how much the party depended on being viewed as legitimate or even, at times, a partner many non-communists were willing to accept. Membership dropped to around 5,000 by the middle of the 1950s. By that point, it was clear that not all was well in the communist world. Stalin's death in early March 1953 caused consternation among many true believers, but also resulted in signs of considerable discontent. On June 16 of that year, workers in East Berlin began protesting pressure by the East German government to augment productivity, but also general repression and economic difficulties, including severe food shortages resulting from collectivization. Almost a million people eventually participated in the protests, with rioting occurring in numerous cities and towns across East Germany, where a supposed "workers' paradise" had been put in place.

Three years later, tensions in the Soviet bloc proved still more explosive. At the Soviet Communist Party's Twentieth Congress, First Secretary Nikita Khrushchev condemned the mass terror waged by Stalin against other party members, the weakening of the Red Army through purges, deportation of nationality groups, the split with Yugoslavia, and postwar purges, including a purported Doctor's Plot just prior to the dictator's death. Supposedly intended as a secret speech, it was transmitted at party meetings and by the CIA and furthered the "Khrushchev thaw" that saw censorship lightened, the release of thousands of political prisoners, and thousands of Stalin's victims rehabilitated. But it produced other results, including the sparking of greater unrest in Eastern Europe, particularly in Poland and Hungary, and tremendous disillusionment among communists and fellow travelers elsewhere. Demanding higher wages, reduced food prices, and a curbing of work quotas, 30,000 demonstrators in Poznan marched, with riots unfolding. Military units put down the uprising, resulting in almost sixty deaths, and the Polish Communist Party returned to power the recently politically rehabilitated Wladyslaw Gomulka.

The situation in Hungary proved graver still, with a revolution taking hold in October, with former premier Imre Nagy also handed back his old job. Many Hungarian rebels appeared to desire a melding of socialism and democracy, while Nagy declared his nation's neutrality and sought the assistance of the United Nations (UN). None was forthcoming, including from the United States, whose President Dwight D. Eisenhower and Secretary of State John Foster Dulles had spoken of liberating people from the yoke of communist tyranny. On November 4, 200,000 Soviet troops, along with 2,500 tanks, began rolling into Hungary, and fierce fighting occurred, leading to 2,500 Hungarian deaths and the fleeing of 200,000 from the country. While armed resistance and strikes continued for an extended period, so did mass arrests and repression. Tried in secret for treason, Nagy was hanged.

Khrushchev's revelations of Stalinist terrors and the quashing of the Hungarian revolution, coupled with heavy-handed treatment of its leaders, ensured the effective demise of the CPUSA. Reduced to a shell of its former self, the party was beset by the large number of informers and FBI agents in its midst. It also confronted, starting in August 1956, an FBI Counterintelligence Program (COINTELPRO), intended to "increase factionalism, cause disruption and win defections." That disarray was already all but complete, given recent events and continued adherence to Stalinism on the part of party leaders, at least until word of Khrushchev's speech.

The shattering of the CPUSA and the end of the Popular Front led some veterans of each to discuss the need for a new leftwing movement in the United States, as a similar development was occurring in France and England. A. J. Muste was involved in such endeavors, appealing to reach out to the noncommunist left in 1955. Early that year, he discussed establishing a new journal to encourage thinking about "the effort to constitute or reconstitute a non-totalitarian movement of the left." Such a publication, he believed, should attempt "to reach out and speak to a wide circle of students, labor people, Socialists, former Socialists and Communists, farmers, peace workers, pacifists, progressive church people."

Subsequently, Muste joined with Dave Dellinger and Bayard Rustin, all proponents of radical pacifism, to form *Liberation*, a journal first appearing in March 1956. In an opening editorial, they bemoaned "the decline of independent radicalism and the gradual falling into silence of prophetic and rebellious voices." They saw "the failure of a new radicalism to emerge" as indicating that the ideas propelling the Old Left required reexamination. "Old labels," particularly those associated with Marxism and liberalism, no longer seemed appropriate. What was called for was "a creative synthesis of the individual ethical insights of the great religious leaders and the collective social concern of the great revolutionists." Denying that revolution or construction "of a better society" required attaining power—control of the State—in order "to transform society and human beings as well," they extolled instead "decentralization . . . direct participation of all workers or citizens in determining the conditions of life and work, and . . . the use of technology for human ends." As James Tracy notes, *Liberation* early contained contributions from Paul Goodman, Michael Harrington, Martin Luther King Jr., Sidney Lens, and William Appleman Williams, among others.

Still striving to obtain support for a non-communist left, Muste initiated a number of sessions under the umbrella of the Fellowship of Reconciliation, which the historian Maurice Isserman terms "the first and most publicized attempt at regroupment" following the McCarthyite phase of the red scare. On May 27, 1956, Muste initiated a debate at Carnegie Hall involving hundreds of American radicals. Roger Baldwin, Eugene Dennis, W. E. B. Du Bois, and Norman Thomas spoke at the event. Muste also soon operated through the American Forum for Socialist Education, which envisioned a new partnership of non-communist leftists and their sectarian brethren. Irving Howe, Dave McReynolds, C. Wright Mills, Max Schachtman, and I. F. Stone were among those participating at Forum gatherings.

Stone, a key figure in the Old Left through his work on a number of left-of-center publications, including *The Nation*, *PM*, the *New York Star*, and the *New York Daily Compass*, had branched out in early 1953 to form his own newsletter, *I. F. Stone's Weekly*. Khrushchev's revelations had amounted to, in Stone's words, "Communism's self-exposure" and demonstrated that "backward" Russia was no fit role model. Returning from his first visit to the Soviet Union, Stone finally acknowledged, the Soviet Union *"is not a good society, and it is not led by honest men.* No society is good in which men fear to think—much less speak—freely." And Stone admitted that it was not Stalinism alone but Leninism that laid seeds for the terror. His disillusionment with the Soviet Union only deepened when Soviet tanks entered Budapest. He believed, as would many others, that an era was ending, where defense of the Russian Revolution, no matter its failings and horrors, was required of progressive individuals. Stone also considered at stake the good name of socialism, which had been sullied by communist rule.

Stone consequently considered it essential to regenerate the American left. His newsletter hosted a public gathering at the Unitarian Community Church in Manhattan on December 14, 1956, to examine Eastern European ferment. He invited independent left and socialist editors, including *Liberation*'s A. J. Muste, the *Militant*'s Daniel Roberts, the *American Socialist*'s Bert Cochran, and *Labor Action*'s Hal Draper, to participate in "an ideological free-for-all" involving a series of issues: How could freedom be safeguarded under socialism? What could Iron Curtain countries take from the American experience? How could basic political liberties be protected?

It was hardly surprising that Stone and Muste were among those most insistent on the need to recast American radicalism. Each had supported the Popular Front, and each possessed complicated relationships with the CPUSA and other radical organizations. Stone long operated as a fellow traveler, at times offering analyses that amounted to apologetics, and at times appearing to follow the Soviet line. But he had also delivered critical commentary about Stalinism and purges all along. A controversy has swirled about whether Stone served as a paid agent for the Comintern and Cominform, while somehow retaining the fierce independence that obliged him to question the vilification of Trotskyists. Muste actually adopted the Trotskyist stance for a period during the 1930s, before reestablishing his pacifism and a quasi-anarchist bent. Both clearly saw merit in bringing together radicals with divergent viewpoints. But their efforts proved largely unavailing. By contrast, for a time it seemed as though attempts to construct "a radical peace movement," which Muste was also a part of, made more sense.

* * *

While the CPUSA had been, however unfortunately, the centerpiece of the Popular Front, the weakening of the party during the early Cold War era afforded opportunities for other radical actors and they were not entirely absent. Of particular note, considering how events played out in the latter stages of the 1950s and then throughout the 1960s, pacifist, antinuclear, and independent radical strands existed even before the Old Left disintegrated. Radical pacifists who fought against the draft, segregation in the federal prisons where they were incarcerated, and stereotypes regarding their purported lack of manliness and patriotism, made up a small, but influential cohort as World War II came to an end. David Dellinger, A. J. Muste, and Dorothy Day established *Direct Action*, a publication that condemned the dropping of atomic bombs on the Japanese cities of Hiroshima and Nagasaki. The lone issue, appearing in October 1945, referred to *Direct Action* as "a magazine devoted to an American Revolution by non-violent methods." In his editorial, "Declaration of War," Dellinger insisted on the need for "*total war* against the infamous economic, political, and social system which is so dominant in this country" and had allowed for atrocities amounting to "the sudden murder of 300,000 Japanese." He condemned the draft and also "the economic conscription" resulting from capitalism. Demanding "war for total brotherhood," Dellinger said it had to be conducted non-violently. He foresaw "strikes, sabotage, and seizure of public property" presently controlled by private interests. He urged both civil disobedience and the "uncompromising . . . treating" of "everyone, including the worst of our opponents, with all the respect and decency" each individual merited.

As advertised in *Direct Action*, radical pacifists convened in Chicago in early 1946. There, Lewis Hill, a wealthy young follower of Gandhi and nonviolence, whose CPS experience had radicalized him, insisted, "The modern state is the first enemy" and had to be disobeyed. Foreseeing a "revolutionary government," Hill believed it must hold civil liberties most dear. Attendees established the Committee for Non-Violent Revolution (CNVR), whose members included Dave Dellinger, Ralph DiGia, George

Houser, Igal Roodenko, and Bayard Rustin. While its steering committee was based in New York City, CNVR was made up of local groups of radical pacifists. Its founding statement, the historian Lawrence S. Wittner indicates, blended socialism, pacifism, and anarchism. CNVR favored local control of industrialism, "complete social and economic equality," a measure of private enterprise, and cooperatives. The society it hoped to usher in would safeguard "freedom of speech, press, movement, assembly, organization, education, religion, radio, and cinema." CNVR members intended to refuse military service or to adhere to the draft and promised to "appeal to workers to leave war jobs and to soldiers to desert." Viewing itself as "the instrument of mass revolution," CNVR believed "killing, maiming, and violent coercion of people is counter revolutionary, whenever and by whomever it is done."

Over the next few years, CNVR conducted a series of pickets and demonstrations, mostly in New York City, including at the UN, issued fliers and position papers, and held another major gathering in August 1947, focusing on "Radicalism in the Next Five Years." The conference attacked Stalinists, while seeking to appeal to independent, non-communist radicals, and favored grassroots efforts, particularly in opposing the arms race. As the conference wound down, a statement was issued, asserting, "We must be nonviolent revolutionists . . . against the existing system," employing "strikes, sit-downs, and campaigns of civil disobedience without resort to any violence against any human being." However, as the historian Andrew E. Hunts notes, the group's charged rhetoric and anarchistic thrust turned off many potential supporters.

Nevertheless, the determination of radical pacifists to bear witness hardly abated. In February 1947, the Break With Conscription group, associated with the War Resisters League, held twenty protests involving 1,000 demonstrators around the country. Approximately 200 individuals who had destroyed their own draft cards mailed them to the White House. At the gathering in New York City, Dellinger, Muste, and Dwight Macdonald spoke, after introductions by Bayard Rustin. Macdonald declared, "Pacifism to me is primarily a way of actively struggling against injustice and inhumanity. . . . My kind of pacifism may be called 'non-violent resistance.'" A number of cells affiliated with the Congress of Racial Equality had emerged, while George Houser and Bayard Rustin held interracial workshops teaching that the organization had "one method—interracial, direct non-violent action."

On April 9, sixteen members of CORE, eight white, eight black, initiated the Journey of Reconciliation, involving bus rides across the Upper South. They departed from Washington, D.C., determined to contest Jim Crow ordinances mandating segregation in interstate travel. Among the participants were Houser, Homer Jack, James Peck, Rustin, and William Worthy. Arrests occurred in Durham, North Carolina, while in Chapel Hill, several men were pulled off of the bus and beaten before being arrested. An obviously perturbed Judge Henry Whitfield told some of the defendants, "It's about time you Jews from New York learned that you can't come down here bringing your niggers with you to upset the customs of the South. Just to teach you a lesson, I gave your black boys thirty days, and I give you ninety." Whitfield was referring to segregated chain gangs that the defendants now had to join.

Also in 1947, the *Bulletin of Atomic Scientists* initially presented its Doomsday Clock, intended to convey the threat presented by nuclear armaments. As the publication itself explained, the Clock offered hints of the apocalypse, as represented by midnight, and of nuclear war, signified by the countdown toward zero. Begun shortly after World War II, the *Bulletin*'s first editorial urged the American people to strive "unceasingly for . . . establishment of international control of atomic weapons, as a first step toward permanent peace." One of its progenitors, Albert Einstein, delivered an early solicitation for the publication, stating, "The unleashed power of the atom has changed everything save our modes of thinking, and thus we drift toward unparalleled catastrophe." The world's most famous scientist served as chair of the Emergency Committee of Atomic Scientists, which included Linus Pauling and Leo Szilard, and insisted, "A world authority and an eventual world state are not just *desirable* in the name of brotherhood, they are *necessary* for survival."

Later that year, pacifists held a series of retreats at Pendle Hill, a Quaker center in a Philadelphia suburb, discussing the need for more radical engagement, including both civil disobedience and the formation of "cells" involving "simplified living" and peace work. Cecil Hinshaw, Milton Mayer, and A. J. Muste produced a manifesto urging a conference "of those interested in a more revolutionary pacifist movement." In early April 1948, approximately 250 individuals gathered in Chicago at a "Conference on More Distinguished and Revolutionary Pacifism." They opted to form Peacemakers, intended to tie together radical pacifist cells. Emphasizing the Gandhian approach more fully than had CNVR, Peacemakers championed employment of nonviolent approaches to conflicts, unilateral disarmament, full democracy politically and economically, and the individual's "inner transformation." The group lauded war-resistance and non-registrants. Regarding conscription, the organization expressed support for young men "to refuse to register or render any service under this iniquitous law," and for all others to support such "non-violent non-cooperation." One approach involved tax refusal, while another entailed residing in cooperative communities such as Macedonia, located in Georgia's Blue Ridge foothills. All but singularly, the Peacemakers expressed strong opposition to President Truman's call for Universal Military Training.

Radical pacifists also welcomed new radio stations established by the Pacifica Foundation, the first set up at KPFA-FM in Berkeley. A Quaker, poet, and CO during World War II, Lewis Hill had created the Foundation to prevent pacifism's marginalization. Relying extensively on the idea of listener-sponsored broadcasting, Hill and a band of pacifists, who thought "dialogue could save the world," wanted a forum for independent journalism, free speech, artistic expression, poetry, and creative thought. Hill drew on the University of California at Berkeley, bohemian North Beach in San Francisco, and the general Bay Area, which had held work camps for conscientious objectors. Hill's friend Roy Finch, another war resister imprisoned during the war, thought "this was the way we imagined pacifism. . . . We did not think of it as non-resistance; we thought of it as direct action of a non-violent character."

However, the heightening of the Cold War resulted in a thinning of radical pacifism's ranks. Nevertheless, both the Truman administration's decision to purse a hydrogen bomb and the advent of the Korean War resulted in small pacifist protests. And in 1951, David Dellinger, Ralph DeGia, Art Emery, and Bill Sutherland engaged in the Baden Action, which involved bicycling from Paris to Moscow, without passports and while expressing opposition to the Cold War. They got as far as Soviet-controlled Baden, Austria, receiving a certain amount of attention, but were forced to turn back.

* * *

Particularly later in the decade, pacifists appeared at the cutting edge of radical movements in the United States, influencing both civil rights and anti-nuclear efforts. Radical pacifists were drawn to the civil rights struggle, which increasingly had involved a campaign to challenge segregation's legal edifice. Black progressives of all types, including radicals like W. E. B. Du Bois, A. Philip Randolph, and Paul Robeson, welcomed the series of judicial decisions that weakened Jim Crow, at least constitutionally. From the mid-1930s, Charles Hamilton Houston and Thurgood Marshall had headed the NAACP's Legal Defense and Education Fund's drive to curb segregation, including in the spheres of graduate and professional education, voting rights, and fair housing. Eventually, Marshall and a team of NAACP attorneys turned to public education, where discriminatory practices and sparse funding for black schools ensured that even the *Plessy* (1896) separate but equal standard was never met. On May 17, 1954, Chief Justice Earl Warren of the U.S. Supreme Court overturned that precedent, issuing a unanimous ruling in the case of *Brown v. Board of Education*. Relying on the kind of sociological jurisprudence earlier associated with Justices Holmes and Brandeis, Warren declared the *Plessy* doctrine unconstitutional as educational segregation stimulated "a sense of inferiority" in black children. The following spring, Warren presented the implementation order, directing that desegregation proceed "with all deliberate speed."

Segregationists responded angrily, but that resistance, coupled with continued terror visited upon African Americans, alongside hopes engendered by the Warren Court, helped to sustain an already emerging civil rights movement. During the war, A. Philip Randolph not only threatened a March on Washington, but he established the National Council for a Permanent Fair Employment Practices Commission (1943) and the Committee against Jim Crow Military Services and Training (1945), which would be renamed the League for Nonviolent Civil Disobedience against Military Service. In 1947, W. E. B. Du Bois delivered "An Appeal to the World," in speaking to the UN about "the denial of human rights" to African Americans, warning that "a great nation, which today ought to be in the forefront of the march toward peace and democracy, finds itself continuously making common cause with race hate." Unfortunately, Du Bois's concerns were too often borne out, as exemplified by the killing of the forty-six-year-old Harry T. Moore, a teacher and Florida's NAACP Secretary, and Harriette, his forty-nine-year-old wife, when a bomb left by the KKK on Christmas Day 1951 exploded beneath their home. The murders were the first of the era that can be considered linked to the politics of assassination, which would afflict the American landscape for the next several decades, as it had earlier. Black resistance continued too, with an eight-day long bus boycott led by the Reverend T. J. Jemison conducted in Baton Rouge, Louisiana, in June 1953. As Christian Melton indicates, religious leaders increasingly now took the lead during civil rights protests.

White recalcitrance remained both debilitating and, all too frequently, deadly. Violence sometimes erupted, but it was also often organized and involved police officers. On May 7, 1955, three shotgun blasts tore into fifty-one-year-old George W. Lee, an African American Baptist minister and NAACP field worker from Belzoni, Mississippi, who had been warned to stop attempting to register blacks to vote. Sixty-three-year-old Lamar Smith, a black farmer and World War II veteran, was also killed, shot on August 13, 1955, near the courthouse in Brookhaven, Mississippi. Fifteen days later, a fourteen-year-old African American boy from Chicago visiting family members in Money, Mississippi, was tortured and murdered by two white men, angered by his supposed flirting with one of their wives. The black press relayed the horrifying image of Emmett Till's battered, unrecognizable face. In supposedly more reasonable fashion, the South also witnessed the appearance of White Citizens' Councils, viewed by some as an uptown version of the Klan. The Councils relied on economic pressure and social intimidation, but attempted to suppress the black vote and was not disinclined to spew out venomous language conducive to a violent climate. The KKK again resurfaced. Congress itself got involved, when 101 members, including a pair of Republicans, signed the Declaration of Constitutional Principles (1956) con-

demning racial integration, while attempting to delegitimize recent Supreme
Court rulings, particularly *Brown*.

During this same period, radical pacifists and other veterans of movements past and present joined in the crusade to make over the American
South, and the nation. In December 1955 and continuing for the next year,
African Americans in Montgomery, Alabama, participated in a lengthy bus
boycott following the arrest of forty-two-year-old Rosa Parks, a well-re-
spected African American woman who was secretary of the local NAACP
chapter. The arrest came after her refusal to relinquish her seat, in accordance
with a municipal Jim Crow ordinance, to a white passenger. What followed
was the beginning of a mass movement, one that propelled a twenty-six-year-
old Baptist preacher and the tactics of nonviolent resistance into the public
limelight. Dr. Martin Luther King Jr., son of one of the South's leading black
ministers, consciously steered protestors in a Gandhian direction, something
that was hardly ordained or foreseeable. Providing assistance to the Montgomery Improvement Association (MIA), which directed the boycott of city
buses, were radical pacifists William Stuart Nelson, Bayard Rustin, and
Glenn Smiley. Dean of Howard University, Dr. Nelson became something of
a mentor to King on "the Gandhian principles of nonviolent noncoopera-
tion." A white minister from Texas, Smiley reasoned, "If [King] can really be
won to a faith in non-violence there is no end to what he can do. Soon he will
be able to direct the movement by the sheer force of being the symbol of
resistance." King later acknowledged, "As the days unfolded I became more
and more convinced of the power of nonviolence, as well as the instrument of
love."

The MIA undertaking was arduous, with setbacks along the way before a
favorable Supreme Court ruling induced city leaders to agree to desegregate
buses. Prior to that occurrence, mass arrests took place, with Dr. King among
those jailed. His home was also among those bombed, resulting in angry,
armed blacks arriving to provide protection. Notwithstanding King's allegiance to nonviolence, the belief in armed resistance held by many African
Americans in the South, including various leaders of civil rights struggles,
continued. Nevertheless, public perception of the nonviolent nature of both
the bus boycott campaign and King proved instrumental in amassing support
for the movement. And King's allegiance to nonviolence was genuine, as
indicated by his founding, alongside other black ministers and activists, of
the Southern Leadership Conference (later renamed Southern Christian
Leadership Conference, SCLC) and involvement with the Prayer Pilgrimage
for Freedom held in Washington, D.C., in early 1957 at the Lincoln Memorial. Designed to coordinate local Southern affiliates, SCLC exalted King's
emphasis regarding nonviolent mass action. Having failed to convince the
Eisenhower administration to tackle the issue of noncompliance with the
Brown decision, SCLC participated in the Prayer Pilgrimage organized by

Bayard Rustin and A. Philip Randolph. On May 17, approximately 30,000 individuals congregated at the site of the Lincoln Memorial to take in a procession of songs and speeches, including praise for *Brown* and King's "Give Us the Ballot" offering. To the chagrin of various African American luminaries, James Hicks of the *New York Amsterdam News* had just written, "Date with Destiny in DC—Rev. King" and now affirmed, "King Emerges as Top Negro Leader."

While King's and his most intimate followers' dedication to non-violence could hardly be questioned, not all African Americans were in agreement with the young Baptist minister, including some close to him and others well outside his inner sanctum. International events were influential, including the anticolonial movements spurred by World War II and its aftermath. The rapidity with which decolonization occurred in Africa heartened many African Americans, including both W. E. B. Du Bois and Paul Robeson. The Afro-Asian Conference in Bandung in 1955 produced condemnations of racism and imperialism, and calls for a third bloc of nation-states not beholden to either the Soviet Union or the United States.

At home, the Nation of Islam (NOI), the Black Nationalist group led by Elijah Muhammad, acquired greater popularity by the latter stages of the 1950s, with Harlem serving, in historian Peniel E. Joseph's words, as "the movement's nerve center." Another terrific orator, the young Black Muslim minister, Malcolm X, began to acquire his own following and reputation. Not all were pleased, as was apparent when Malcolm twice intervened as mob violence beckoned following the beating in Harlem of NOI member Johnson X. After Malcolm simply waved his hand, leading to a dispersal of an angry crowd, one police officer remarked, "This is too much power for one man to have."

News of the *Brown* decision had thrilled Robert F. Williams, a World War II veteran and former Marine, who, writing in *Liberation* in 1959, indicated that he finally felt he "was a part of America and . . . belonged." However, he quickly became disillusioned by what he considered "open defiance to law and order" across the South. Nevertheless, he headed a chapter of the NAACP in Monroe, North Carolina, but soon recognized that the KKK was thriving in the area. Indeed, its members "became so brazen that mile-long motorcades started invading the Negro community," accompanied by police vehicles. As Klansmen shot at or attempted to run over blacks, Williams helped to form an armed guard, even returning fire at one point. The "great miscarriage of justice" sickened Williams, who declared, "Negroes must be willing to defend themselves, their women, their children and their homes." He also warned that "the turn-the-other-cheekism" of Martin Luther King Jr. offered "no match or repellent for a sadist."

As American Studies' scholar T. V. Reed smartly offers, "dozens of civil rights movements" appeared in the American South and elsewhere, sustained

Chapter 4

by "hundreds of grassroots organizers," with many "unsung" community activists engaging in "life-threatening" efforts. The movement as a whole, Reed notes, was "a fundamentally radical, grassroots, decentralized, mass-based, often women-led" campaign by African Americans determined to compel "a deeply racist society to grant them freedom, dignity, and economic justice."

* * *

While King, Malcolm X, and Williams offered different paths for responding to racial injustice and discrimination, radical pacifists continued to provide counsel to the young black preacher. Like King, they also maintained fervent opposition to war, while increasingly focusing on the threat of nuclear annihilation. The detonation of hydrogen bombs by both the United States and the Soviet Union provided a spur for antinuclear activism, as occurred following a test in the Pacific that contaminated a Japanese fishing boat. Bertrand Russell joined with Albert Einstein, Frederic Joliot-Curie, Linus Pauling, and other top scientists in issuing a manifesto on July 9, 1955. Warning of "the tragic situation which confronts humanity," the scientists spoke "as human beings, members of the species Man, whose continued existence is in doubt." They insisted on the need "to learn to think in a new way," to ask what could be done to prevent a nuclear calamity, with the new bomb "2,500 times as powerful as that which destroyed Hiroshima." On April 23, 1957, Dr. Albert Schweitzer, with the backing of the Nobel Peace Prize Committee, broadcast "A Declaration of Conscience" from Oslo, Norway, discussing how radioactive fallout from hydrogen bomb tests entered the food chain, particularly endangering small children. Urging public opposition to such testing, Schweitzer declared, "The end of further experiments with atom bombs would be like the sunrays of hope which suffering humanity is longing for."

  That spring, two new antinuclear groups appeared in the United States: the Non-Violent Action Against Nuclear Weapons (later renamed the Committee for Non-Violent Action, CNVA), and the National Committee for a SANE Nuclear Policy (SANE). A Quaker pacifist, Lawrence Scott, joined with Bayard Rustin and A. J. Muste, among others, to form what came to be known as CNVA, favoring radical nonviolent action to protest nuclear testing. Rustin and Muste, along with *Saturday Review of Literature* editor, Norman Cousins, and Clarence Pickett of the American Friends Service Committee (AFSC), were also involved in establishing the more mainstream SANE, which strove for an international test ban. Early prominent SANE supporters included Eleanor Roosevelt, A. Philip Randolph, and Walter Reuther.

On November 15, 1957, SANE ran a full-page advertisement in the *New York Times*, "We are Facing a Danger Unlike Any Danger That Has Ever Existed." Asserting that "the sovereignty of the human community" was paramount, the ad proclaimed, "In that community, man has natural rights. He has the right to live and to grow, to breathe unpoised air, to work on uncontaminated soil. He has the right to his sacred nature." By the following summer, 130 SANE chapters existed, with a membership of 25,000, which included that of Martin Luther King Jr. CNVA, for its part, had acquired a different kind of notoriety, firing off a petition to President Eisenhower condemning nuclear testing and carrying out nonviolent protests. The most striking involved *The Golden Rule*, a boat skippered by Albert Bigelow, a graduate of Harvard and the Massachusetts Institute of Technology and a naval war commander turned pacifist, who had been "absolutely awestruck" on hearing of the atomic bomb attack on Hiroshima. "Intuitively it was then that I realized for the first time that morally war is impossible." Seeking to sail with a small crew, labeled "Thoreauesque" by a Boston newspaper, to the South Pacific to prevent a nuclear test, Bigelow and his crew were arrested in Hawaii on May 1, 1958. Additional protests took place at U.S. missile and nuclear test sites, including in Cheyenne, Wyoming, and Omaha, Nebraska, where militant activists attempted to halt the building of ICBM sites. Brad Lyttle, seventy-four-year-old A. J. Muste, and Marj Swann were among those arrested because of the Omaha Action during the summer of 1959.

* * *

The latest postwar red scare, joined with self-inflicted disasters, ensured the effective evisceration of the American Old Left. While the period immediately following the end of the war proved hopeful for progressives, that quickly changed as the Cold War, both internationally and domestically, took place. The repression and the ever-escalating distancing of former allies helped to break the CPUSA, which was scarcely an innocent agent in its own demise. Yet even in the new red scare's darkest moments, including during McCarthyism's heyday, American radicals were not altogether absent. Radical pacifists, honing tactics learned or cultivated during wartime prison stays, employed direct action tactics later associated with the Movement of the latter part of the 1950s, the 1960s, and beyond. Both civil rights and antinuclear activists used those tactics, often in the face of furious, sometime ferocious opposition.

Chapter 5

Revolt of the Young (and Others)

Throughout the 1960s and for some time thereafter, young people joined radical political movements or formed ones of their own, as a third wave of twentieth-century activism took hold, during which the hoped for New Left rose and fell. That surge began at the onset of the decade and never abated altogether, while reaching different peaks at various points. Many considered themselves to be participating in the Movement, an amorphous, ever shifting array of left-of-center activists involved with one or more campaigns concerning civil rights, nuclear arms, the Vietnam War, and an array of other issues.

The first glimmerings of the New Left materialized earlier, but not through the gatherings A. J. Muste and I. F. Stone sponsored. At a number of colleges and universities around the country, left-liberal groups began appearing by 1960, including TASC (Towards an Active Student Community) and SLATE at the University of California at Berkeley, ACTION at Columbia, PLATFORM at the University of California at Los Angeles, POLIT at the University of Chicago, TOCSIN and the Student Peace Union at Harvard-Radcliffe, and VOICE at the University of Michigan. Then there were DECLARE at the University of California at Riverside, FOCUS at Reed, the Political Action Club at Swarthmore, the Progressive Student League at Oberlin, SCOPE at the University of Illinois and San Francisco State, TASC and SPUR at San Jose State, and THINK at the University of Oklahoma.

In keeping with the prominence it would come to hold in Movement circles, UC Berkeley first displayed signs that something was stirring among a new generation of college students, in contrast to the one that appeared quiescent during and shortly after the McCarthyite phase of the red scare. Now, student activism began to reemerge, however selectively. Concerned about racially and religiously discriminatory practices on campus, a small band of students established TASC in early 1957. That group and then SLATE also condemned South African apartheid, HUAC, loyalty oaths, compulsory ROTC, and restrictions on free speech at UC Berkeley. Later in the year, TASC put up a "slate" of candidates for student government. An eighteen-year-old freshman, Frederick Moore, explained the rationale for a two-day hunger strike he waged in 1959 against mandatory ROTC: "I refuse to take ROTC. . . . I am a conscientious objector."

In Madison, *Studies on the Left* was first published in 1959, with mentorship from the revisionist historian William Appleman Williams. Lloyd Gardner, Saul Landau, and Martin Sklar, along with fellow graduate students at the University of Wisconsin, served on the editorial board. *New University Thought* soon appeared at the University of Chicago, and like *Studies on the Left*, would be influenced by radical social critic Paul Goodman.

* * *

African American young people were on the march, both figuratively and literally, as when they, with assistance from U.S. Army troops, helped to integrate Central High School in Little Rock, Arkansas, or participated in the nation's capital in Youth Marches for Integrated Schools. A number of sit-ins preceded the acclaimed one that occurred in Greensboro, North Carolina, on February 1, 1960, and seemingly ushered in a surge of student activism. The sociologist Aldon Morris refutes the notion that Greensboro was the first sit-in, as others had taken place "in at least fifteen cities between 1957 and February 1960," including Durham, North Carolina (1957); Wichita, Kansas (1958); and Oklahoma City (1958).

Meanwhile, James Lawson, who had assisted with the Montgomery bus boycott, and was attending the Vanderbilt Divinity School, while serving in a CORE leadership capacity and guiding SCLC nonviolence training sessions, sought to turn Nashville into "a laboratory for demonstrating nonviolence" and to spawn "many Montgomerys." Recruits receiving an introduction to Southern history and the tenets of nonviolence included Fish University's Diane Nash and Marion Barry, in addition to divinity students James "Jim" Bevel, Bernard Lafayette, John Lewis, and C. T. Vivian. Lawson hoped to help cultivate what he—and Dr. King—referred to as "the beloved community," which the Nashville group came to appreciate as "the Christian concept of the kingdom of God on earth." By November 28, 1959, they initiated a preliminary sit-in at Harvey's Department Store in Nashville, soon followed by another a week later at Cain-Sloan's. SCLC's Nashville branch anticipated that the fight to desegregate the city's downtown sector could take a decade or even longer.

But four young students from North Carolina Agricultural and Technical College—Ezell Blair Jr., Franklin McCain, Joseph McNeil, and David Richmond—sped up such expectations when they sat down at a Woolworth's luncheon counter in downtown Greensboro and awaited service. Familiar with Gandhian tactics and the 1947 Journey of Reconciliation, the Greensboro Four triggered a procession of sit-ins in almost sixty cities, including Nashville, across thirteen states over the next three months. Additionally, as the historian Sascha Cohen records, the sit-in campaign prompted "wade-ins at pools and beaches, kneel-ins at churches, read-ins at libraries, and walk-ins at theaters and amusement parks." More than 70,000 black and white demonstrators participated by the end of the year, often enduring ridicule, expletives, and, on occasion, violence. Over 3,000 individuals suffered arrest. But the sit-ins accomplished a great deal, according to Aldon Morris, who indicates that they "pumped new life into the civil rights movement." In fact, they drew "many people, often entire communities, directly into the movement," while "making civil rights a towering issue throughout the nation."

The Nashville student movement included the remarkable array of activists Reverend Lawson trained. Explaining the refusal of eighty-one students to avoid jail, Nash declared, "We feel that if we pay these fines we would be contributing to, and supporting, the injustice and immoral practices that have been performed in the arrest and conviction of the defendants." In Martin Luther King Jr.'s hometown, students—among them Julian Bond and Lonnie King—formed the Atlanta University Center, which issued "An Appeal for Human Rights," condemning racism and discrimination. Warning "today's youth will not sit by submissively, while being denied all the rights, privileges, and joys of life," they promised to employ "every legal and nonviolent means at our disposal to secure full citizenship rights as members of this great Democracy of ours."

As the sit-in movement continued, SCLC director Ella Baker encouraged participants to establish their own, student-based organization, one not dominated by Dr. King. More than 200 individuals accepted her invitation to meet in mid-April at Shaw University in Raleigh, North Carolina. The gathering resulted in the creation of the Student Nonviolent Coordinating Committee, whose first chair would be Fish University's Marion Barry. The conference also produced a Statement of Purpose drafted by Lawson: "We affirm the philosophical or religious ideal of nonviolence as the foundation of our purpose, the presupposition of our faith, and the manner of our action. Nonviolence as it grows from Judaic-Christian traditions seeks a social order of justice permeated by love." In the spirit of the "beloved community," delegates delivered a new version of a gospel song, "We Shall Overcome," which Pete Seeger had refashioned. In an enthralling moment, they sang, "Oh, deep in my heart, I do believe/We shall overcome someday." They also saw their fellow activists as "a band of brothers and sisters, a circle of trust," according to SNCC cofounder Charles "Chuck" McDew.

Shortly following the founding of SNCC, another organization comprised of activist youth was established at an institution of higher learning, the University of Michigan in Ann Arbor. The Student League for Industrial Democracy had fallen on hard times, reduced to tiny chapters at Columbia, Yale, and Michigan. In January 1960, SLID leaders, without approval from its parent organization, the social democratic League for Industrial Democracy, changed its name to Students for a Democratic Society. Plans were in place to hold a conference in Ann Arbor titled "Human Rights in the North," with the sit-in movement providing a model. Importantly, a SLID leader at Michigan, Al Haber, believed "the citizen must take the initiative . . . provide the energy required for the social action program to effect permanent improvement." Following the lead of early twentieth century progressives, Haber considered the university "a laboratory where students test ideas and techniques which are later used in all areas of society."

Haber and another SDS delegate, Tom Hayden, a graduate student at Michigan and editor of the school newspaper, were fully cognizant of other signs that a student movement was possible or actually emerging. In mid-May, protestors gathered at San Francisco City Hall to protest a HUAC hearing. Following the sit-in movement's lead, students sang "We Shall Not Be Moved." On "Black Friday," May 13, police fire-hosed and clubbed several protestors, hauling off to jail sixty-four, including thirty-one UC Berkeley students. The press referred to a "Communist-led riot," and FBI director J. Edgar Hoover denounced the demonstrators as "Communist dupes." A protest committee called for HUAC's abolition, something that would have been virtually imaginable just a short while earlier.

In mid-June 1960, twenty-nine delegates, representing nine universities, gathered for SDS's initial national convention, at the Barbizon-Plaza Hotel in mid-Manhattan. Eleven of those delegates came from the University of Michigan, while approximately fifty other guests were present, including James Farmer, Dwight Macdonald, Norman Thomas, and the journalist Murray Kempton. The opening session, which went on for two days, featured "Student Radicalism: From the Close of World War I through the McCarthy Period." Discussion ranged widely, regarding the differences between liberal and radical activity and the possibility of student protests of civil defense drills. In his closing address, Macdonald emphasized "The Relevance of Anarchy."

Heartened by newly founded SNCC and SDS, forty-four-year-old C. Wright Mills delivered his latest manifesto, "Letter to the New Left," in the September-October issue of a fledging publication, *New Left Review*, published in London. The controversial radical sociologist, author of *The Power Elite*, emphasized that contemporary young radicals were little associated with "a Fanatical and Apocalyptic Vision . . . An Infallible and Monolithic Lever of Change . . . Dogmatic Ideology," or comparable "bogeymen" feared by "deadenders." He considered the socialists' longstanding belief in the working class as the instrument of historical agency "a legacy from Victorian Marxism . . . now quite unrealistic." Mills pointed to the fact that he viewed intellectuals as "a possible, immediate, radical agency of change." Bluntly, he asked, "Who is it that is getting fed up? Who is it that is getting disgusted with what Marx called 'all the old crap?' Who is it that is thinking and acting in radical ways?" Mills indicated that "all over the world," including in the Soviet bloc and the nations seeking a Third Way, young intellectuals were leading the charge.

By the spring of 1961, the civil rights movement moved beyond sit-ins to undertake Freedom Rides in the Deep South. Recalling the Journey of Reconciliation, CORE director James Farmer conceived of Freedom Rides being conducted throughout the heart of Old Dixie. He anticipated problems arising that would force the Kennedy administration to act. SNCC's Diane Nash, for her part, strongly believed "that the future of the movement was going to be cut short if the Freedom Rides . . . [were] stopped as a result of violence."

Civil rights activists experienced arrests and beatings at the hands of angry mobs. SNCC's John Lewis was among those suffering such indignities. A twenty-one-year-old seminary student, Lewis attempted to enter a waiting room with an attached sign emblazoned "White," at the Greyhound bus terminal in Rock Hill, South Carolina. At least two young white men told Lewis, "Other side, nigger," directing him to a door that held a different kind of sign, "Colored." Before Lewis could react, he was attacked. "A fist smashed the right side of my head. Then another hit me square in the face. As I fell to the floor I could feel feet kicking me hard in the sides. I could taste blood in my mouth." Other incidents included the firebombing of a Greyhound bus that carried freedom riders and beatings by Klansmen. Such acts compelled Attorney General Robert F. Kennedy to send John Seigenthaler to meet with Alabama Governor John Malcolm Patterson to prevent further violence, but Kennedy's administrative assistant was himself knocked unconscious by a pipe-wielding thug. Eventually, President John F. Kennedy threatened to order federal troops to Alabama until Patterson called out the Alabama National Guard to disperse a rampaging mob. King declared that the existing crisis in Alabama demanded "a full scale nonviolent assault on the system of segregation."

That same year, another young black activist—a graduate of both Hamilton College and Harvard and a teacher at the elite preparatory Horace Mann School in the Bronx—traveled to Mississippi to initiate SNCC's voting rights project there. Significantly, as Tom Hayden later revealed, Bob Moses "listened. When people asked him what to do, he asked them what they thought. At mass meetings, he usually sat in the back. In group discussions, he mostly spoke last. He slept on floors, wore sharecroppers' overalls, shared the risks, took the blows, went to jail, dug in deeply." Harlem-born Moses sought to make a difference in a state where nearly 70 percent of African Americans resided outside urban centers and many toiled as sharecroppers, tenant farmers, or farm laborers. As Moses noted, too many were "just rock bottom poor." And they were powerless. While over 40 percent of the residents of the state were black, few were registered to vote, with many counties containing black majorities having no African Americans registered. Moses initiated his work in McComb, located in Pike County, referred to as "Klan nation."

Resistance to the voting rights drive proved fierce and unrelenting. Arrests, beatings, and the murder of a fifteen-year-old high school student soon occurred, while in nearby Amite County, an ally of Moses, Herbert Lee, was also killed. The hulking E. H. Hurst, a member of the Mississippi House of Representatives, shot the 5'4", fifty-two-year-old father of nine. Klan members engaged in night riding, part of ongoing efforts to quell voter registration.

The black community held weapons of its own. As Moses came to appreciate, "Self-defense is so deeply ingrained in rural southern America that we as a small group can't affect it." Moses still insisted that SNCC staff members not carry guns, but local blacks remained determined to protect the young activists. And one black farmer, Hartman Turnbow, warned Martin Luther King Jr., "This nonviolent stuff is no good. It'll getcha killed."

SNCC activists continued to serve as role models for their counterparts in the other leading New Left organizations of the early 1960s, SDS. In late December 1961, SDS members gathered in Ann Arbor determined to draft "a political manifesto of the left." In preparation, SDS Field Secretary Tom Hayden read widely, including works by C. Wright Mills, Harold Taylor, Albert Camus, Erich Fromm, Michael Harrington, Norman O. Brown, and William Appleman Williams, as well as *Studies on the Left* and the *New Left Review*. Hayden proclaimed Mills "the first to see what was happening."

With input from several other SDS members, gathered in Port Huron, Michigan, for the group's national convention in June 1962, Hayden helped to complete *The Port Huron Statement*, comprised of nearly 26,000 words, and articulating SDS's vision of American society. The document propounded the need for personal engagement in social, economic, and political affairs, under the rubric of participatory democracy. That visionary ideal— like SNCC's beloved community—provided the initial ideological framework for the early American New Left, and exemplified SDS's determination to speak truth to power.

The Port Huron Statement opened elegantly with the simple observation, "We are people of this generation, bred in at least modest comfort, housed now in universities, looking uncomfortably to the world we inherit." Among its most remarkable statements was the declaration "We regard men as infinitely precious and possessed of unfulfilled capacities for reason, freedom, and love." The university provided the institutional foundation, but a need also existed to connect with "the less exotic but more lasting struggles for justice."

SDS soon printed 20,000 copies of *The Port Huron Statement*, which became an ideological framework for many New Leftists. As Rebecca E. Klatch notes, *The Port Huron Statement* "became the most widely read pamphlet of the 1960s generation." Barbara Jacobs considered it radical in its refusal to accept Old Left panaceas. Its progenitors seemed determined to "live . . . lives differently than [their] parents." As Jacobs put it, "We were going to use our lives as experiments."

* * *

Civil rights activists engaged in sit-ins, freedom rides, voting rights drives, and public demonstrations, often at great risk to themselves, as they strove to create the beloved community and shatter Jim Crow barriers. Combining the efforts of SNCC, CORE, and the NAACP, the Council of Federated Organizations (COFO) conducted civil rights activities in Mississippi, with Bob Moses serving as program director.

Martin Luther King Jr. had carried out his own operations in the Deep South, not always successfully, before targeting Birmingham in early 1963. As one of SCLC's leaders, Andrew Young, recalled, Birmingham "was probably the most violent city in America, and every family had an arsenal." Many in the Movement referred to "Bombingham," due to the number of bombs that beset affluent black homes. The Executive Director of SCLC, Wyatt T. Walker, devised Project "C," standing for confrontation, designed to attack segregation in that city and throughout the South. The plan sought to compel the Kennedy administration to act more forcefully and to engender support for major civil rights legislation; King declared, "The key to everything is federal commitment." The Reverend Fred Shuttlesworth urged that civil rights activists take to the streets nonviolently, although a number of blacks carried weapons as demonstrations took place. SCLC organizers gathered trash bins loaded with "knives, razors, and other weapons."

On April 12, Dr. King was arrested and placed in solitary confinement, soon drafting his "Letter from a Birmingham Jail," which was not initially released to the public. Defending the employment of nonviolent direct action to contest unjust laws, King went on to admonish his fellow religious leaders for failing to act. He praised black protestors "for their sublime courage, their willingness to suffer and their amazing discipline in the midst of the most inhuman provocation." They were the South's "real heroes," as would be eventually acknowledged, he predicted.

In seemingly sharp contrast between the forces of darkness and light, King; James Bevel, SCLC's Director of Direct Action and Nonviolent Education; Andrew Young; and other activists directed a Children's Crusade that soon confronted pugnacious Bull Connor, the city's Commissioner of Public Safety. Stark images of children, pummeled by police clubs, dogs, and high-pressure fire hoses, appeared in newspapers around the world. Those very images, President Kennedy admitted, made him "sick" and enabled him to understand why African Americans in Birmingham were fed up with the counsel of patience. Well-known activists arrived to lend support to the cause, including Ella Baker, James Forman, Dick Gregory, and David Dellinger, while folksingers Joan Baez and Guy Carawan also came to Birmingham. Thousands were jailed, as King, who had been released on bail, praised demonstrators for "making . . . and . . . experiencing history." An agreement on May 10 resulted in release of jailed demonstrators and a promise to desegregate a number of public facilities in Birmingham and to hire more black workers.

But violence continued, sometimes resulting in counter-violence. Immediately following the Birmingham agreement, a series of bombings occurred, which in turn led to the first of the era's mass racial eruptions. In early June, futile attempts by the Cambridge Nonviolent Action Committee to desegregate Maryland's Eastern shore devolved into armed conflicts between African Americans and whites. The torching of white-owned businesses followed. On June 12, in the midst of the Cambridge disturbances, Mississippi NAACP field secretary, Medgar Evers, was murdered while heading onto his driveway, holding sweatshirts emblazoned with "Jim Crow Must Go." Evers's slaying was but the first of a series of killings of well-known public figures during a decade when the politics of assassination would, unfortunately, be among its most noteworthy occurrences.

That summer witnessed the zenith of the nonviolent phase of the civil rights movement. As he had a generation earlier, A. Philip Randolph, assisted by Bayard Rustin, demanded a march on Washington to highlight the need for a major jobs program and civil rights legislation. Concerns expressed by the Kennedy administration resulted in SNCC leader John Lewis's speech being tempered, including removal of a question pondering, "Which side is the federal government on?" Also deleted was Lewis's fiery exhortation for civil rights activists to "march through the South, through the heart of Dixie, the way Sherman did," through "scorched earth" actions, thereby burning "Jim Crow to the ground—nonviolently." And yet Lewis exclaimed before the large crowd, "We are involved in serious social revolution."

More than 200,000 individuals showed up on August 28, 1963, for the March on Washington, as it came to be known. While banners called for jobs and freedom, the march became most celebrated for Martin Luther King Jr.'s seemingly extemporized but not unpracticed "I Have a Dream" oration. King contemplated a day when the American nation would adhere to its egalitarian creed, freedom and justice would prevail, and his four small children would "not be judged by the color of their skin but by the content of their character." He hoped for the day when "all of God's children" would unite and—drawing from an old African American spiritual—sing, "Free at last! Free at last! Thank God Almighty, we are free at last!"

The joy, even elation spawned by the March crumbled against the brutal reality of Birmingham, Alabama, once again. There, on the morning of September 15, a bomb tore apart the 16th Street Baptist Church, which boasted a largely black congregation. One eleven-year-old girl and three fourteen-year-olds were discovered underneath the basement rubble. Many other congregants were injured, some seriously. In response, SNCC activist Diane Nash, like John Lewis, envisioned creating "a nonviolent army" to sweep across Alabama, while demanding mass enfranchisement of African Americans.

During the period ahead, Malcolm X belittled the notion that revolution could be achieved without bloodshed. He questioned how employment of nonviolence could be justified in Mississippi and Alabama as churches were blown apart and "your little girls" murdered. He denied the possibility of "a turn-the-other-cheek revolution," and refuted the idea that desegregating luncheon counters, theaters, parks, and public toilets made for a revolution. According to Malcolm, revolution was "bloody . . . hostile," uncompromising, and destructive. As he saw it, "a revolutionary is a black nationalist." Thus, "if you love revolution, you love black nationalism."

In the nation's most segregated and most violent state, COFO maintained its campaign to bring about a peaceful revolution. Led by Bob Moses and Allard K. Lowenstein, ex-president of the National Student Association, who taught at North Carolina State University, COFO held a "Freedom Vote" involving mock elections for top state offices to refute the declaration by Mississippi Senators James Eastland and John C. Stennis that blacks were "not ready for the vote." The 1963 Freedom Vote received more than 80,000 votes at churches, beauty parlors, and other black-run establishments cast for Aaron Henry, the COFO president who also headed the state chapter of the NAACP, and Ed King, a white minister who worked at Tougaloo College.

The Freedom Vote drive led directly to the decision to carry out Mississippi Freedom Summer the next year. Also launched by Moses and Lowenstein, Freedom Summer involved 1,000–1,500 volunteers, including many white students from elite colleges and universities beyond the South, and resulted in nearly forty black churches and more than thirty black homes and businesses bombed or burned, countless numbers of blacks fired from their jobs, the arrest of more than 1,000 participants, emotional toll, eighty or more people assaulted by the police or white mobs, and no fewer than six murders. Among those killed were 24-year-old Mickey Schwerner, 20-year-old Andrew Goodman, and 21-year-old James Chaney, bearing out earlier fears and warnings that such violence would be forthcoming amid Freedom

Summer. As Moses and Lowenstein had predicted, the murder of the young white men brought considerable attention. It also resulted in a concerted effort by the FBI, following orders from Attorney General Robert Kennedy and President Lyndon B. Johnson, to initiate an investigation into their disappearance.

Despite the killings and relentless pressure, Freedom Summer continued, with many volunteers displaying dogged commitment. Moreover, as John Lewis recalled, "There was an all-pervading sense that one was involved in a movement larger than oneself, almost like a Holy Crusade, an idea whose time had come." Participants experienced, as sociologist Doug McAdam has recorded, a "freedom high." They assisted with three projects: voter registration, community centers, and Freedom Schools. Freedom Summer particularly revolved around voter registration, in a state where a mere 6.7 percent of age-eligible blacks in Mississippi were registered to vote. That fact, and the virtual exclusion of blacks from the state Democratic Party, had led SNCC to create the Mississippi Freedom Democratic Party (MFDP) during the spring.

SNCC and the MFDP also challenged the seating of Mississippi Democratic Party regulars at the national convention held in Atlantic City that summer. That experience proved disillusioning as the Johnson-controlled conclave only granted two at-large seats to MFDP representatives. Even delivery of riveting testimony by forty-six-year-old Fannie Lou Hamer about her arrest and the terrible beating she suffered at the behest of racist police failed to convince the Credentials Committee to back the MFDP. As klieg lights induced sweat to fall down her face, she warned, "If the Freedom Party is not seated now, I question America."

The refusal to seat MFDP representatives proved shattering for many, dispelling already evaporating illusions regarding liberals' readiness to support civil rights activists. That turn of events, coupled with growing anger about the violence inflicted on movement participants and Southern blacks in general, contributed to an already germinating development: further radicalization of many who had agreed to white involvement in the struggle and accepted nonviolence, at least tactically. Examining Freedom Summer volunteers later, psychiatrist Robert Coles encountered "battle fatigue . . . exhaustion, weariness, despair, frustration and rage." SNCC's Joyce Ladner offered, "For many people, Atlantic City was the end of innocence."

Both Freedom Summer and the growing radicalization of key civil rights activists soon impacted the white student left. Mario Savio and other MFS veterans proved instrumental in likening conditions in the American South and at an elite academic institution like UC Berkeley, which he attended. During the fall of 1964, Savio became involved with the Free Speech Movement (FSM) at UC Berkeley, which emerged as a change in university policy troubled a small but growing number of activist students and others in the Bay Area. Campus political groups had long engaged in recruitment and advocacy, such as relating to civil rights, near the campus entrance at Bancroft Avenue. When an administrator announced new restrictions on the use of university property, "including the 26-foot strip of brick walkway at the campus entrance on Bancroft Way and Telegraph Avenue," protest was ignited.

The resulting Free Speech Movement threatened to transform American higher education, with challenges to *in loco parentis*—the university's operating in a quasi-parental role—and limitations concerning political engagement. The charismatic Savio garnered attention, as when he delivered fiery oratory harking back to Thoreau and San Francisco Renaissance poet Kenneth Rexroth. Speaking before 800 demonstrators engaged in a campus sit-in, Savio declared, "There is a time when the operation of the machine becomes so odious, makes you so sick at heart, that you can't take part; you can't even passively take part, and you've got to put your bodies upon the gears and upon the wheels, upon the levers, upon all the apparatus, and you've got to make it stop. And you've got to indicate to the people who run it, to the people who own it, that unless you're free, the machine will be prevented from working at all!" Over the span of several months, clashes occurred between students and administrators, with more than 600 police arresting demonstrators engaged in a sit-in, and an eventual campus-wide strike.

* * *

Events in Mississippi, Atlantic City, and Berkeley proved disheartening to many young activists. A series of ensuing developments, both at home and abroad, only exacerbated mounting disillusionment regarding the American political order, including that seemingly associated with liberal policies. On the one hand, the Johnson administration, expanding on proposals made by the martyred John F. Kennedy, ushered in a dramatic expansion of the welfare state while calling for both a War on Poverty and the Great Society. Along with an array of progressive programs involving heath care, education, the environment, immigration, and consumer protection, LBJ worked for eradication of *de facto* segregation, through the 1964 Civil Rights Act and the 1965 Voting Rights Act, both monumental pieces of legislation. Nevertheless, rising expectations led to more urban explosions, including in Harlem and Watts, a largely African American neighborhood in South Los Angeles.

Additionally, President Johnson's decision to Americanize and intensify the war in Vietnam proved disastrous. As the United States conducted a systematic air campaign against North Vietnam, the building of air bases required American land troops, adding to the total number of U.S. forces that eventually soared past half-a-million. During the first three years of expanded operations, a disproportionate number of the infantrymen were black, brown, or working-class, further enraging many African Americans and Latinos. The determination of the U.S. military commander, General William Westmoreland, to conduct the war with an emphasis on attrition, body counts, search-and-destroy missions, chemical agents like Agent Orange, and numerous bombing runs over both North and South Vietnam, ensured that opposition would surge both in America and overseas. The prolonged nature of the conflict, which for a time seemed to demand ever-increasing numbers of call-ups and led to greater and greater casualties, hardly went over well with the American public, which was able to partake of the nation's first televised war. The exploding costs of the conflict also led to both a credibility gap for the Johnson administration, sometimes reluctant to deliver straightforward accounts, and a diverting of funds from domestic programs.

All of this ensured that opposition to the war would be lengthy, embittered, and portions of which, at least, increasingly radicalized. That proved particularly true among many already inclined to critical perspectives, whether in the civil rights, the New Left, the student movement, or the soon-to-be potent antiwar campaign. Civil rights activists Bob Parris, Julian Bond, and Stokely Carmichael were among the strongest opponents of American engagement in Vietnam. They questioned the federal government's willingness to expend countless resources on a counterrevolutionary campaign in a distant Southeast land, while the American people appeared leery of conducting a genuine antipoverty program at home. They wondered about the readiness to participate in costly struggles—both financially, and in terms of lives expended—in distant locales, and the disinclination to devote similar energy to eradicate *de facto* segregation and usher in LBJ's Great Society. They were appalled that young African American men could be conscripted to fight non-whites in a foreign land, but were not afforded the opportunity to join in a genuine struggle against racial injustice and exploitation in the rural South and urban centers around their own country. Militant civil rights figures began to champion conscientious objectors and general opposition to the war. Some identified more with foreign revolutionaries than with American soldiers attempting to quell Third World liberation movements.

Although similarly ill-disposed to the war in Vietnam, Martin Luther King Jr. during both 1965 and 1966 offered few thoughts about it in public. Initially, he concentrated on a voting rights campaign in Selma, Alabama, where the county population included 58 percent blacks, but only 2 percent of whom were registered voters. Sheriff James G. Clark led a mounted posse containing 200 volunteers, and that posse relied on bullwhips and cattle prods to corral demonstrators. During a clash on Sunday, February 18, an Alabama state trooper shot a local civil rights activist, twenty-six-year-old Jimmie Lee Jackson. The unarmed Jackson died eight days later. During a eulogy, Dr. King declared, "Jimmie Jackson wanted to be free. . . . We must be concerned not merely about who murdered him but about the system, the way of life, the philosophy which produced the murderer." Thousands turned out on March 7 as SNCC's John Lewis led a protest march bound for the state capital in Montgomery. When demonstrators refused to turn around on a bridge situated outside Selma, Clark's posse and Alabama state police sent by Governor George Wallace attacked them. "Bloody Sunday" resulted in forty injuries. Two days later, a white Unitarian minister, thirty-eight-year-old James Reeb, suffered a fatal blow to his skull delivered by a screaming mob that denounced him and two companions as "nigger-lovers." Another march, led by King, occurred without incident after the civil rights leader turned it around at the bridge. On March 25, the Klan killed thirty-nine-year-old Viola Liuzzo, an activist from Detroit who became the only white woman murdered during the civil rights movement. President Johnson responded by pushing for a voting rights bill, and moved King and John Lewis, among others, as he promised in a televised address, "We shall overcome."

Yet even before King carried his campaign beyond the South to undertake the Chicago Freedom Movement, opposition to his insistence on nonviolence and both his and SNCC's belief in the beloved community grew among black activists. Malcolm X saw no American dream but rather "an American nightmare." His call for what came to be known as black power increasingly appealed to many young African Americans. Then, on February 21, 1965, while readying for a speech in the Washington Heights neighborhood of Manhattan, thirty-nine-year-old Malcolm X was murdered by members of the Nation of Islam, whose leader Elijah Muhammad had increasingly become embittered about his former top assistant.

* * *

As black power proponents wrestled with nonviolent advocates, both groups were increasingly appalled by U.S. operations overseas, with a particular focus on the seemingly ever-expanding Vietnam War. In that regard, they shared much in common with white activists, many of whom began directing their energies to that conflict. Starting with the University of Michigan, a number of college and university campuses held teach-ins to examine the war. SDS, which had devoted considerable energy to community organizing, through its Economic Research and Action Program, soon put together the then largest antiwar rally in American history, held in Washington, D.C., on April 17, 1965. Responding to the dramatic escalation of U.S. operations in Vietnam, 25,000 congregated, spurred by peace groups like "Committee for Nonviolent Action, SANE, Student Peace Union, War Resisters League, Women Strike for Peace, Women's International League for Peace and Freedom," youth-based leftwing organizations such as "the DuBois Clubs, M2M, the Young People's Socialist League, and Youth Against War and Fascism," the Maoist Progressive Labor Movement, and SDS.

SDS president Paul Potter, a University of Michigan graduate student, delivered what was arguably the most stirring address, "The Incredible War," which contested the Johnson administration's rationale for the conflict. The war, Potter began, had produced "the razor, the terrifying sharp cutting edge that" had dissipated final illusions suggesting U.S. foreign policy was shaped by concerns about democracy and morality. Dismissing "the saccharine, self-righteous moralism" American policymakers exhibited, Potter all but denounced that policy as indecent. Additionally, he agreed with Senator Wayne Morse's assessment that his own country might "well be the greatest threat to peace in the world today." He pointed to napalm, gas, despoiled crops, and torture indiscriminately meted out to women and children, to both neutrals and guerrillas. Potter spoke of peasants being removed from their villages and housed "in concentration camps," euphemistically termed "sunrise villages." He referred to the rending of local ways and traditions, as well as the trampling upon that which afforded "dignity and purpose to life."

Indicating how radicalizing the war proved to be for many, Staughton Lynd, a pacifist and the rally's chairperson, who was teaching at Yale and editing *Liberation* magazine, discussed a march by various demonstrators toward the Capitol to present a petition to Congress urging an immediate end to the war. Then, somewhat remarkably, Lynd suggested, "Perhaps next time we should keep going."

The Vietnam War spurred the growth of the largest, most sustained antiwar movement in American history. During the next several years, the antiwar movement remained a vital force in American life, often seemingly experiencing growth and a change in tactics that paralleled escalation of the Vietnam conflict. Respectful and nonviolent rallies and protests continued to appear, but so did calls for and employment of more militant tactics. The vast majority of those who showed up for demonstrations, large or small, adhered to admonitions by monitors at rallies to remain peaceful. As frustration over the war grew, so did acceptance of nonviolent approaches, including civil disobedience. The media proved drawn to such antics, a fact recognized by various activists. Agent provocateurs sometimes urged greater militancy, as did a small, but at times growing number of dedicated opponents of the war and U.S. policies, both foreign and domestic.

The Johnson administration and its successor never really learned how to contend with war critics, vacillating between uneasy acceptance of the right of American citizens to protest even while their soldiers were fighting overseas and a sensibility that unpatriotic or even foreign elements were directing the antiwar movement. Ultimately, that resulted in use of intelligence agencies, which included reinvigorating the FBI's COINTELPRO, and initiating the first of the conspiracy trials undertaken against movement forces.

To the White House's dismay, the antiwar movement experienced several surges throughout the remainder of Johnson's presidency. In late May 1965, the largest teach-in, Vietnam Day, organized by Jerry Rubin, occurred at the University of California at Berkeley, with between 10,000 and 30,000 in attendance. Also in May, Mary Clarke and Lorraine Gordon of Women Strike for Peace (WSP) traveled to Hanoi, the first Americans to do so voluntarily during the war. WSP sponsored an advertisement in the *New York Times* displaying a young man, attired in cap and gown, along with the heading, "He graduates in June of '65. Will he die in Vietnam in June of '66?" On July 29, the very day President Johnson indicated monthly draft calls would more than double, approximately 400 marchers, sporting black armbands, headed for the military induction center located at 39 Whitehall Street near the bottom of Manhattan. Arriving there, a handful of young men burned their draft cards. In his opening statement to a mass gathering in Birmingham, Alabama, on August 12, Martin Luther King Jr. asserted, "Few events in my lifetime have stirred my conscience and pained my heart as much as the present conflict which is raging in Vietnam." On the West Coast, SDSers and Vietnam Day Committee (VDC) members sought to prevent soldiers from being shipped out from Oakland, as trains carrying them passed through Berkeley.

The VDC, led by Rubin and Stephen Smale, planned the International Days of Protest, scheduled for the fall. Activists resorted to increasingly confrontational tactics and mass civil disobedience to support their antiwar stance. The VDC, Rubin later reflected, "taught us to believe in the Apocalyptic Action. History could be changed in a day. An hour. A second. By the right action at the right time. Our tactics was exaggeration. Everything was 'the biggest,' 'the most massive.' Our goal was to create crises which would grab everybody's attention and force people to change their lives overnight."

The International Days of Protest in mid-October included protests in scores of cities around the world, with some 300 demonstrators showing up at the Whitehall induction center in New York City. They watched as a twenty-two-year-old Catholic pacifist, David Miller, burned his draft card, deliberately violating the new federal law prohibiting such an act. More than 20,000, including A. J. Muste, joined in the Fifth Avenue Peace Committee march in mid-Manhattan, encountering brickbats, eggs, paint, and violence, along the way. During the following month, President Johnson became the target of a telling chant, "Hey, hey, LBJ, how many kids did you kill today?"

On November 2, thirty-one-year-old Norman Morrison, a Quaker and the father of three young children, read that a French priest had exclaimed on discovering Vietnamese parishioners had been bombed, "I have seen my faithful burned up in napalm." Morrison positioned himself near Secretary of Defense Robert McNamara's Pentagon office. Having left a note for his wife, "Know that I love thee but must act for the children of the priest's village," Morrison engaged in an act of self-immolation. A week later, twenty-one-year-old Roger LaPorte, a member of the Catholic Worker movement, set

himself afire in the Hammarskjold Plaza near the UN. Before he died, La-
Porte explained, "I'm a Catholic Worker. I'm against war, all wars. I did this
as a religious action."

The murder on January 3, 1966, of twenty-one-year-old civil rights activist Sammy Younge Jr., who had served on the aircraft carrier, the *USS
Independence*, which helped to carry out a naval blockade during the Cuban
missile crisis, enraged civil rights proponents. Within three days, SNCC, now
headed by Carmichael, issued a "Statement on Vietnam." SNCC considered
civil rights work a genuine alternative to conscription and called for "all
Americans to seek this alternative, knowing full well that it may cost them
their lives—as painfully as in Vietnam."

After Julian Bond, overwhelmingly elected to the George House of Representatives, expressed approval for SNCC's antiwar pronouncement, the
Georgia legislative body voted 184–12 in early January to deny him a seat.
Bond's support for the anti-draft campaign was called "totally and completely repugnant to and inconsistent with the mandatory oath presented by the"
state constitution. Bond initiated legal action in a federal district court.

Lending credence to growing charges regarding atrocities committed by
American soldiers in Southeast Asia was an article appearing in the February
issue of *Ramparts* magazine, authored by Donald Duncan, a former Green
Beret Master Sergeant with eighteen months of combat duty in Vietnam.
Increasingly linked to the New Left, the San Francisco-based publication had
recently unveiled ties between Michigan State University and Saigon. "The
Whole Thing Was a Lie!" discussed use of torture techniques against captured Vietcong, depiction of Vietnamese as "'slopes' and 'gooks,'" and
American support for a repressive South Vietnamese regime. *Ramparts*
caused another sensation with its expose of the CIA's secret funding of
educational organizations, including the National Student Association, which
had received financial assistance since the early fifties.

That late winter and early spring, heavyweight boxing champion Muhammad Ali, who had become a lightning rod on proclaiming himself a Black
Muslim, became more controversial still after stating, "Man, I ain't got no
quarrel with them Vietcong." He also filed for conscientious objector status,
leading to his being denounced as a "cowardly, turncoat black rat" and a
"black bastard."

Antiwar opposition continued to surge throughout 1966. Thousands, including A. J. Muste and folksinger-activist Joan Baez, refused to pay the
portion of their income taxes directed toward military purposes. "Read-ins"
were conducted by the American Writers and Artists Against the War in
Vietnam. SANE convinced many to support antiwar congressional candidates. To call attention to the employment in the Vietnam War of napalm,
produced by Dow, housewives out West attempted to halt shipments of the

controversial chemical. They initiated a boycott of Saran Wrap, the Dow kitchen product.

In late June, the case of the Fort Hood Three drew national attention. Three young soldiers—one black; another, the son of Lithuanian and Italian parents; the third, Puerto Rican—issued a statement on June 30, condemning the Vietnam War as "immoral, illegal, and unjust." James Johnson, Dennis Mora, and David Samas had undertaken legal action to preclude Secretary of Defense McNamara and Secretary of the Army Stanley R. Resor from shipping them off to Vietnam. Purporting to stand for "a cross section of the Army and of America," the Fort Hood Three declared, "We will not be a part of this unjust, immoral, and illegal war. We want no part of a war of extermination. We oppose the criminal waste of American lives and resources. We refuse to go to Vietnam!!!!!!!"

The SDS National Convention, held in Clear Lake, Iowa, during the late summer of 1966, conveyed support for the Fort Hood Three and demonstrated prairie power's surging influence. The latter involved members from the American heartland, who came attired in "blue workshirts, denim jackets, and boots," and appeared "more aligned to the frontier, more violent, more individualistic, more bare-knuckled and callus-handed, than that of the early SDSers," in the words of Kirkpatrick Sale. SDS' new vice-president, Carl Davidson, from a working-class family in Pennsylvania, who attended graduate school at the University of Nebraska, presented a position paper, "Towards a Student Syndicalist Movement, or, University Reform Revisited," demonstrating that the New Left organization was in flux, while tapping into ideas linked to both SDS founders and anarcho-syndicalists like the Wobblies. He considered the fight against *in loco parentis* and the antiwar movement intertwined and feared "assembly lines in the universities" were producing "a new kind of scab." Like Carl Oglesby, just completing his term as SDS president, Davidson blamed corporate liberalism for having sired a "dehumanized and oppressive system."

Protest against the war reached the hallowed grounds of Harvard University in early November, where protestors confronted Secretary of Defense McNamara, an MBA recipient and former assistant professor there. As he attempted to leave campus in a university police vehicle, several hundred demonstrators, including Robert Scheer, an editor at *Ramparts* and recent congressional candidate, compelled it to halt.

In late November 1966, the just formed Spring Mobilization Committee to End the War in Vietnam, meeting in Cleveland, agreed to hold massive rallies in New York City and San Francisco the following April. Chairing the new organization was A. J. Muste, while David Dellinger, Sidney Peck, *Ramparts* founder Edward Keating, and Cornell University's Robert Greenblatt served as vice-chairs. SANE national co-chair Benjamin Spock, notwithstanding concerns within his organization regarding the Spring Mobe's non-exclusionary policy, showed up in Cleveland, lending a degree of legitimacy to the undertaking. But the eighty-one year-old Muste was the star of the proceeding, standing, in Peck's words, as "the father" of the peace movement. Within a month, a complementary group appeared, the Student Mobilization Committee to End the War in Vietnam.

Also emerging were small We Won't Go groups, antidraft unions on college campus or in major urban centers. A We Won't Go conference was held in Chicago on December 4, with speakers on the order of early SDS member Richard Flacks, a sociology professor at the University of Chicago, the Central Committee for Conscientious Objectors' Arlo Tatum, longtime draft resister David Mitchell, SCLC's James Bevel, and Yale University history professor Staughton Lynd.

The *New York Times* edition of December 29, 1966, referred to a twenty-nine-year-old dermatologist from Brooklyn, Captain Howard B. Levy, who had been charged with fomenting "disloyalty and disaffection among the troops," subjecting him to possible court-martial proceedings that could result in a lengthy prison sentence. He was accused of having publicly declared, "The United States is wrong in being involved in the Vietnam War. I would refuse to go to Vietnam if ordered to do so." He stated, "Special Forces personnel are liars and thieves and killers of peasants and murderers of women and children."

SDS, at its National Council meeting in Berkeley at the end of the year, backed a strong antiwar program, while damning both conscription and the "immoral, illegal, and genocidal war." Decrying all conscription as "coercive and anti-democratic," SDS supported the setting up of "unions of draft resisters." This indicated, as National Secretary Greg Calvert put it, that the organization had shifted "from protest to resistance." While exploring the draft for SDS' Radical Education Project, Peter Henig uncovered a Selective Service memorandum from Director Lewis Hersey discussing "the threat of loss of deferment" compelling young men to apply skills "in an essential activity in the national interest." Soon referred to as the "channeling memo," it became infamous for the expressed determination to engage in coercive social engineering. The New Left organization responded by embossing buttons with the words, "NOT WITH MY LIFE YOU DON'T."

As the fighting in Vietnam became even deadlier, opposition to the war at home and abroad again quickened. The antiwar movement suffered an enormous loss in early February when A. J. Muste, once called by the theologian Reinhold Niebuhr "a perfect innocent" and long referred to as "the American Gandhi," died. Muste had recently engaged in a two-hour talk with North Vietnamese President Ho Chi Minh in Hanoi.

While Muste was in some ways irreplaceable, the antiwar movement scarcely slackened. MIT linguist Noam Chomsky provided intellectual ammunition for the antiwar movement, while presenting a devastating critique of many of his fellow intellectuals in a seminal essay appearing on February 23 in *The New York Review of Books*. "The Responsibility of Intellectuals" insisted they possessed an obligation "to speak the truth and to expose lies." Chomsky particularly emphasized what he considered duplicitous statements by Arthur Schlesinger Jr., Walt Rostow, Henry Kissinger, and McGeorge Bundy. The intellectual possessed the responsibility, Chomsky wrote, "to insist on the truth," and "to see events in their historical perspective."

Significantly, Martin Luther King Jr. began expressing more overt opposition to the war in Vietnam. On February 25, while addressing a crowd of 1,500 at a conference dealing with the conflict, sponsored by The Nation Institute and held in Beverly Hills, Dr. King spoke of "The Casualties of the War in Vietnam." He discussed general awareness regarding "nightmarish" physical casualties: trampled and burned Asian rice fields, anguished mothers holding crying babies amid torched bamboo huts, blood soaked battlefields and valleys, countless "broken bodies," physically and psychically wrecked young veterans, and saddest of all, "mutilated and incinerated children," victims of napalm and bombs. King exclaimed, "A war in which children are incinerated, in which American soldiers die in mounting numbers is a war that mutilates the conscience." With the United States failing to tackle "the triple evils of racism, extreme materialism and militarism," King reasoned, "We must demonstrate, teach and preach, until the very foundations of our nation are shaken."

Beginning a speech on April 4 to an overflow crowd at Riverside Church, located in Morningside Heights, skirting New York City's Upper West Side, Reverend King indicated that his conscience compelled him to do so. His address was sponsored by Clergy and Laymen Concerned about Vietnam (CALCAV), an organization that declared, "A time comes when silence is betrayal." He had spoken in Northern ghettoes with "desperate, rejected and angry young men," whom he attempted to convince "that Molotov cocktails and rifles would not solve their problems." They had asked, "What about Vietnam?" King determined, "I knew that I could never again raise my voice against the violence of the oppressed in the ghettos without having first spoken clearly to the greatest purveyor of violence in the world today—my own government."

On April 15, 1967, King participated in the Spring Mobilization to End the War in Vietnam, which civil rights activist James Bevel helped to lead. Prominent figures on the American left served as sponsors, including Harry Belafonte, Father Daniel Berrigan, Dorothy Day, James Farmer, John Lewis, Staughton Lynd, Carl Oglesby, Norman Mailer, Linus Pauling, and Fred Shuttlesworth. Of note too was participation by hundreds of World War II and Korean War veterans, as well as by members of Veterans for Peace in America, who wielded signs demanding negotiations with the National Liberation Front (NLF) and displayed support for American soldiers in insisting they immediately be brought home. Some 400,000 people marched along with Dr. King, Benjamin Spock, and Rabbi Abraham Heschel in New York City, while 100,000 assembled in San Francisco. Chants of "Hell, no, we won't go" and "Hey, Hey, LBJ, how many kids did you kill today?" rang out from the marchers in Manhattan.

Another significant development associated with the Spring Mobilization was the burning of almost 200 draft cards in the Sheep Meadow section of Central Park. Twenty-three-year-old Gary Rader, an American reservist, was one of those lighting his draft card on fire; what was noteworthy was that Rader appeared in uniform and with his Green Beret visible. Cries of "Resist, Resist" rang out as the illicit torching of draft cards took place. Recent federal court rulings had split regarding the constitutionality of the 1965 law prohibiting the burning of draft cards and establishing a five-year maximum prison sentence along with a $10,000 fine.

The mass protest occurring on the other side of the country, at San Francisco's Kezar Stadium, saw the public emergence of a new antiwar organization, designed to battle the Selective Service System. Its founders included Dennis Sweeney, Lennie Heller, Steve Hamilton, and David Harris, a civil rights and antiwar activist who had been elected student body president at Stanford and was Joan Baez's boyfriend. They called themselves the Resistance, deliberately, even provocatively invoking analogies to the wartime fight against Nazi hegemony in Europe. They rode around on motorcycles, devoured existentialist writers, lived in an urban commune in East Palo Alto, grew their hair long, smoked dope, and identified with a "virile" kind of nonviolence. They issued a leaflet, "We Refuse," discussing the Resistance and a projected mass turn-in of draft cards in mid-October. Members of the Resistance did not want to go to jail, but knew "of no justifiable alternative," and hoped that many others would, eventually, "also choose to resist the crimes done in their names."

The question now arose within the leading New Left organization about how to cultivate "revolutionary consciousness." SDS National Secretary Gregory Calvert had recently applauded SNCC for having instructed white radicals, "Go home and organize in white America which is your reality and which only you are equipped to engage." SDS's vice-president, Carl Davidson, reflected on the dilemma of what young radicals had to do: "We need to move from protest to resistance, to dig in for the long haul, to become full-time, radical, sustained, relevant. In short, we need to build a revolution. But again, how do we go about it?" One approach involved acquiring an ideological framework, with the idea of "the new working class," something of an ironic reference to most middle-class job holders, acquiring support.

On April 28, heavyweight boxing champion Muhammad Ali—whom the *New York Times* continued to refer to as Cassius Clay—refused induction. His conscience and religious beliefs compelled him to do so, Ali explained in a prepared statement. Boxing authorities quickly moved to strip Ali's title, and brickbats continued to come his way.

A new antiwar organization, Vietnam Veterans Against the War (VVAW), emerged in June. Twenty-four-year-old Jan Barry, a Spring Mobilization participant, met with five other veterans in New York City to found VVAW. After gathering signatures from Vietnam vets, Barry, soon to be VVAW's first president, had placed a statement that appeared in the *New York Times*.

> We believe that the conflict in which the United States is engaged in Vietnam is wrong, unjustifiable and contrary to the principles on which this country was founded. We join the dissent of the millions of Americans against this war. We support our buddies still in Vietnam. We want them home alive. We want them home now. We want to prevent any other young men from being sent to Vietnam. We want to end the war now. We believe this is the highest form of patriotism.

At the end of June, SDS held its sixth annual convention in Ann Arbor, where the organization had been founded seven summers earlier. As many as 300 people attended the conclave, with a more pronounced countercultural presence given the longer hair sported by many men and women alike and their attire. Many delegates were new or relatively new members, underscoring the continued shift away from the founders and in a more radical direction. Analyzing the convention for the *National Guardian*, Jack A. Smith predicted that SDS was deliberately headed toward "a collision course with the United States government," as indicated by an overwhelmingly passed resolution supporting soldiers ready to head underground. SDS identified, Smith wrote, "more with Che than Fidel; more with Fidel than Mao; and certainly more with Mao, at least as a revolutionary figure, than Kosygin. As far as identity goes, a combination Gene Debs, Joe Hill and Rosa Luxemburg might beat them all."

The National Black Power Conference was held in July in Newark, the scene of recent terrible racial disturbances, both just before and then during the initial stages of an inferno in Detroit. H. Rap Brown, newly named SNCC chair, warned in a session, "If this country doesn't come around, then black people are going to burn it down." The plenary applauded Brown, black nationalist Robert Williams, now ex-heavyweight champ Muhammad Ali, and the poet Amiri Baraka, who deemed the Newark explosion "a rebellion of black people for self-determination."

The National Mobilization Committee prepared for a planned Washington protest in October, declaring a readiness to "obstruct the war machine." The antiwar coalition also expressed support for urban eruptions, affirming there was but "one struggle—for self-determination—and we support it in Vietnam and in black America." Mobe leaders Dave Dellinger, Jim Peck, and Robert Greenblatt favored direct action tactics in Washington, hoping to bring about "structure confrontation" and predicting, "LBJ isn't going to know what's hitting him." Contacted by Dellinger, Berkeley activist Jerry Rubin began to plan protests centering on the Pentagon. Rubin in turn got ahold of Abbie Hoffman, who had been involved with both SNCC and the New York anarchist Diggers and had triggered a stunt at the New York Stock Exchange, where protestors tossed dollar bills at traders, who scrambled to grab what they could. Protestors would levitate the Pentagon, Hoffman informed the media, and he insisted that old-styled protest was done. "The time has come for resistance." Rubin seconded that notion. "We are now in the business of wholesale and widespread resistance and dislocation of American society." Even longtime pacifist Dellinger discussed the need to move "from dissent to resistance." Additionally, Dellinger was "thrilled and excited that this whole new element of humor and creativity and youthful zest was coming into things."

The passions engendered by the Vietnam War and civil rights convinced President Johnson and intelligence agencies of the need to track peace, New Left, and civil rights activists. During the late summer of 1967, Operation CHAOS began, and was intended to ascertain how much "hostile foreign influence" impacted domestic unrest. Events earlier that year, including the Spring Mobilization rallies, the Resistance's emergence, and the Newark and Detroit riots, fed fears regarding a possible unraveling of America's domestic fabric. An FBI memo reported that the White House had instructed CIA Director Richard Helms to "exert every possible effort to collect information concerning U.S. radical agitators who might travel abroad." During its six-year life span, Operation Chaos resulted in the compiling of thousands of files on U.S. citizens.

RESIST, an intellectual collective based in Somerville, Massachusetts, just outside of Boston, was established to provide support for the antiwar movement, and particularly for those battling the Selective Service System. Early participants included Paul Lauter, Noam Chomsky, Mitchell Goodman, Denise Levertov, Robert Lowell, Dwight Macdonald, and Norman Mailer. They issued "A Call to Resist Illegitimate Authority," on September 27, expressing agreement with young men outraged by the Vietnam War, which they deemed "unconstitutional," "illegal," and contradicting the Charter of the United Nations, the 1949 Geneva Conventions, and the 1954 Geneva Accords. More than 300 individuals signed the call, largely drafted by Arthur Waskow and Marcus Raskin of the leftwing Washington think tank, the Institute for Policy Studies. It appeared as an advertisement in both *The New York Review of Books* and *The New Republic*. Signatories included something of a Who's Who of the American left: Gar Alperovitz, Philip Berrigan, James Bevel, Robert McAfee Brown, Noam Chomsky, William Sloane Coffin, Lawrence Ferlinghetti, Allen Ginsberg, Paul Goodman, Nat

Hentoff, Leo Huberman, Gabriel Kolko, Christopher Lasch, Staughton Lynd, Dwight Macdonald, Herbert Marcuse, Seymour Melman, Thomas Merton, Barrington Moore Jr., Jack Newfield, Carl Oglesby, Philip Rahv, Marc Raskin, Philip Roth, Susan Sontag, Benjamin Spock, Paul Sweezy, Immanuel Wallerstein, Arthur Waskow, and Howard Zinn. Eventually, 28,000 others signed the pronouncement.

As if goaded by the killing of New Left icon Ernest "Che" Guevara, the Argentine physician turned revolutionary, by Bolivian troops, who had been aided by the CIA, antiwar activists geared up for more militant action, including Stop the Draft Week, which started on October 16 in a number of American cities. The most notable protests, perhaps, took place in Boston and Oakland, with different brands of militancy displayed. Members of the New England Resistance were at the forefront of the Boston protest, which centered on the turning in of draft cards at the Arlington Street Church, where abolitionists had once condemned slavery. Michael Ferber delivered a sermon, "A Time to Say No," in which he admitted, "The sun will rise tomorrow as it does every day, and when we get out of bed the world will be in pretty much the same mess it is in today." The United States would continue dropping incendiary bombs and pacification campaigns would take place. American ghettoes would remain "rotten places to live." Farm workers would be exploited. American educational institutions would "continue to cripple the minds and hearts of its pupils." The U.S. Selective Service System would keep sending draftees "out to slaughter." Thus, "today is not the End. Today is the Beginning," Ferber said. It was time "to dig in for the long haul." Calling for those gathered to assert "No" to their government, Ferber urged that it be "the loudest No the government ever heard."

A different ambiance characterized the anti-draft protest that took place on the opposite side of the country, in Oakland, California. Militant antiwar activists had been seeking "to 'do something' about the draft," since midsummer. They felt it necessary "to go beyond the Resistance," and that usual protest techniques were insufficient. They even viewed draft card burning as "no more than a symbolic act of moral indignation." The architects of Stop the Draft Week agreed on new tactics: they wouldn't compel others to pledge adherence to nonviolence, and they intended to "shut the mother down," referring to the induction center. In the early morning of October 16, 3,000–4,000 protestors amassed at the Oakland Induction Center; 123 people would be arrested. Protests continued the next day, which would be called "Bloody Tuesday." Wielding mace and nightsticks, police waded in, injuring twenty. One hundred and twenty individuals, including Joan Baez and her sister, Mimi Farina, also a singer and the widow of the writer Richard Farina, were arrested. Some 10,000—many sporting helmets, protective equipment, and heavy coats—appeared on the third day of protests. By October 20, some protestors, using "mobile tactics," battled the police. Thousands of demonstrators sought to obstruct a series of intersections, managing to delay for a couple of hours buses transporting inductees. Despite arrests, the latest protests remained nonviolent.

Berkeley activist Frank Bardacke believed that Stop the Draft Week reshaped the Movement. "We went through a change—we became a more serious and more radical movement. . . . We did not loot or shoot." However, in their own way, many radicals no longer viewed American political leaders as legitimate, and saw themselves as "political outlaws."

The culmination of anti-draft activity, which occurred across the country, was the March on the Pentagon, which some would refer to as "the March on Washington," slated for October 21. The National Mobilization Committee to End the War in Vietnam or "the Mobe" initiated the protest, led by David Dellinger and Jerry Rubin. Weeks earlier, Rubin had informed the media, "We are going to close down the Pentagon." President Johnson purportedly responded, "I will not allow the peace movement to close down the Pentagon." As Rubin reflected, "By saying he wasn't going to allow us to close it down, he gave us the power to have that possibility. So in a way, just by announcing it, we created a victory." The other key organizer of the October rally, the "militant pacifist" Dellinger, had assumed the Mobe's key leadership role following A. J. Muste's death. The Mobe served as an umbrella for a wide array of groups, from religious organizations to Progressive Labor, which championed China's Cultural Revolution. Pacifists joined in the planned demonstration, along with those determined to "offer themselves" as they moved "from dissent to resistance."

On Friday, October 20, after speeches by Yale chaplain William Sloane Coffin and the poet Robert Lowell, several antiwar figures went to the Justice Department, carrying a briefcase with nearly a thousand draft cards. Coffin, Benjamin Spock, Mitchell Goodman, and Marcus Raskin were among those who saw Deputy Assistant Attorney General John McDonough, Attorney General Ramsey Clark having refused to meet the antiwar group. McDonough declined to accept the cards, advising that they be turned in at local draft boards. As the White House awaited the mass demonstration at the Pentagon, Lady Bird Johnson, the First Lady, recorded her impressions: "There is a ripple of grim excitement in the air, almost a feeling of being under siege."

By the following day, as many as 100,000 people congregated in Washington, D.C., determined to "confront the warmakers." The counterculture's influence was obvious, with one sign reading "LBJ, Pull Out Now, Like Your Father Should Have Done." Jerry Rubin, Abbie Hoffman, Allen Ginsberg, and Ed Sanders envisioned an exorcizing and levitating of the Pentagon. They gathered at the Lincoln Memorial to listen to speeches by Dellinger, Spock, and Dagmar Wilson, as well as musical performances by Phil Ochs, who sang "I Declare the War Is Over," and Peter, Paul, and Mary. In the early afternoon, Dellinger talked about the event evolving into a "gigantic teach-in" that could "educate" the soldiers guarding the Pentagon about the Vietnam War. The march, Dellinger declared, would terminate peaceful protest, and set the stage for civil disobedience, confrontation, and "active resistance." Dellinger envisioned a melding of "Gandhi and Guerilla," which would involve "a 'creative synthesis' of 'nonviolent militancy.'"

During the early afternoon, with a gigantic "Support Our GIs, Bring Them Home Now!" banner in front, about 50,000 of those in attendance passed over the Memorial Bridge on the way to the Pentagon. Deputy federal marshals and soldiers stood ready to safeguard that symbol of the American military establishment. Arriving at the Pentagon, a sizable New York group, which called itself the SDS Revolutionary Contingent, rushed toward the gigantic building, with several members attempting to land on service ramps. Some held North Vietnam flags. Military police and federal marshals repelled them. A number of prominent figures invited arrest, including Noam Chomsky, David Dellinger, Norman Mailer, and Gary Rader. Nearly 700 protestors were arrested, along with a pair of UPI reporters, while forty-seven individuals, some of them police, suffered injuries.

On October 27, four radical pacifists, including Father Philip Berrigan— all participants in what the writer, Francine du Plessix Gray, would later call the Ultra-Resistance—strode into Baltimore Customs House and poured blood onto draft files. They issued a prepared statement that indicated, "We shed our blood willing and gratefully in what we hope is a sacrificial and constructive act. We pour it upon these files to illustrate that with them and with these offices begins the pitiful waste of American and Vietnamese blood, 10,000 miles away." They charged that the United States preferred to "protect its empire of overseas profits than welcome its black people, rebuild its slums and cleanse its air and water." The demonstrators condemned "the idolatry of property," which they deemed "often an instrument of massive injustice—like these files. Thus, we feel this discriminate destruction for human life is warranted." They urged others "to continue moving with us from dissent to resistance."

* * *

The Movement catapulted into the national consciousness as the decade of the 1960s began, with the sit-ins and freedom rides. The long envisioned New Left appeared, bolstered by both SNCC and SDS. As the progressives and the New Dealers had for the early twentieth century left and the Old Left, the liberal administrations of John F. Kennedy and Lyndon B. Johnson proved somewhat supportive, but also critical of the young radicals who aspired to the beloved community and participatory democracy during the Sixties. A loss of faith, of hope, of belief occurred too, including that engen-

dered by the politics of assassination, disillusionment regarding liberal programs, and dismay about U.S. engagement in Southeast Asia. The Movement
grew and shifted course as civil rights activists tired of beatings and deaths,
student protestors appeared on college and university campuses, critics of
American operations in Vietnam became increasingly frustrated, and both
SNCC and SDS underwent radical shifts of their own. Talk of black power,
prairie power, student syndicalism, and resistance wended their way through
the Movement. Figures like Martin Luther King Jr., Bob Moses, David Dellinger, and other practitioners of nonviolent direct action adopted more militant postures, while other Movement figures insisting on what they deemed
still sharper challenges to U.S. policies, both foreign and domestic.

Chapter 6

The Year of Revolution and Beyond

1968 is viewed as the *annus mirabilis*, when talk of revolution was in the air, not only in the United States but around the globe. Such discussion had begun the previous year, if not a bit earlier than that, with SDS, black power proponents, the Resistance, the Ultra-Resistance, and the Mobe not hesitant to employ the word. Additionally, incandescent figures like Martin Luther King Jr. and Benjamin Spock delivered more openly radical rhetoric of their own, supporting the idea of moving beyond reform to resistance in various instances. Both foresaw the need for mass civil disobedience, while others were less inclined to adhere to nonviolence.

The year opened with a welter of events of a radical, even potentially revolutionary nature. A band of political activists, heavily influenced by the counterculture, gathered on New Year's Eve at an East Village apartment to discuss the American political scene. Among those present were new friends Abbie Hoffman and Jerry Rubin, both civil rights and antiwar veterans, but also having adopted the shaggy hair, hip clothing, and fascination with the counterculture's holy trinity of sex, drugs, and rock 'n' roll. Hoffman wanted to harass President Johnson during his reelection bid through "armies of protestors" determined to confront "the policy makers with their own madness." Allen Ginsberg later recalled Hoffman's declaring "that politics had become theater and magic, basically, that it was the manipulation of imagery through the mass media that was confusing and hypnotizing the people in the United States, making them accept a war which they really didn't believe in."

Looking back to the March on the Pentagon, which Rubin had helped to plan, and his own guerrilla theater at the New York Stock Exchange, Hoffman envisioned days of protest paired with hippie-laden events during the Democratic Party National Convention, scheduled for Chicago in August. Recently, he had talked about the possibility of 100,000 protestors ready to engage in "disruption or sabotage" in the great Midwestern metropolis. As Paul Krassner, founding editor of the irreverent magazine, *The Realist*, worried that a "convention of death" beckoned, Rubin tossed out the notion of a Festival of Life in Chicago. When Hoffman emphasized the need to move beyond boring, stale protest tactics and to reach out to America's young through "weirdness, absurdity, and colorfulness," Krassner cried out, "Yippie! Yippie." Soon, someone came up with the notion of a Youth International Party, in keeping with the global ferment that was bubbling to the surface.

Over the next several months, the Yippies, led by Rubin and Hoffman, but also including Allen Ginsberg and a colorful cast of characters, grabbed media attention through a variety of outlandish stunts, predictions, and declarations. Rubin lauded "freaky, crazy, irrational, sexy, angry, irreligious, childish, and mad" individuals, including those who burned draft cards, partook of drugs, waved Vietcong flags, considered property theft, and spat out "fuck" on public airwaves. Viewing the Movement as "a school," he considered its teachers "the Fugs/Dylan/Beatles/Ginsberg/mass media/hippies/students fighting cops in Berkeley/blood on draft records/sit-ins/jail." He extolled "the heroic romantic fidel che Vietcong." And looking ahead to Chicago, Rubin predicted that the president would be renominated amid "tear gas and bayonets." There, the Yippies believed, "FREE AMERICA" would do battle with "the NATIONAL DEATH PARTY," and not be intimated by LBJ, Mayor Richard Daley, or "J. Edgar Freako." *Time* magazine termed the Yippies "1968's version of the hippies," offering a "special kind of antic political protest." The Yippies, Ed Sanders of the Fugs indicated, were enmeshed in "the politics of ecstasy." They talked about nominating a piglet, Lyndon Pigasus Pig, for the presidency, spiking Chicago's water supply with LSD (lysergic acid diethylamide), and seducing delegates.

Berkeley activist Michael Rossman worried that his friend Jerry Rubin was behaving irresponsibly, acting like "a politico who dropped acid" and was "surrounded by death." Peter Coyote of the San Francisco Diggers thought the Yippies were involved with "chicanery," tricking "kids from all over the United States to come and get their fucking heads cracked." *The Seed*, a leading underground paper in Chicago, warned that the city might "host a festival of blood." By contrast, Up Against the Wall Motherfucker, an anarchist group situated in New York's Lower East Side, cheered on the Yippies. But then the Motherfuckers, who saw themselves as "flower children with thorns," favored a "total break: cultural, political, social, everything."

* * *

A group with a distinctly different approach than the Yippies, the Boston Five also landed in the news shortly after the New Year began. On January 5,

1968, indictments were handed down against Dr. Benjamin Spock, the nation's most renowned pediatrician; Yale University chaplain and ex-CIA operative William Sloane Coffin Jr.; Marcus Raskin, former State Department official and cofounder of the Institute for Policy Studies, the progressive think tank located in Washington, D.C.; author Mitchell Goodman; and Harvard graduate student Michael Ferber. In the first of the era's conspiracy trials, the Justice Department intentionally selected high-profile individuals, all of whom had become antiwar activists involved with the draft resistance movement. They were charged with having violated the University Military Training and Service Act, which criminalized "knowingly" counseling or assisting another's refusal or evasion of military registration or service. Conviction carried a possible sentence of five years behind bars and a $10,000 fine.

The prosecution occurred as American troop deployment in Vietnam surpassed half-a-million, and the Selective Service was drafting 25,000 young men or more monthly. Concerns within the White House about draft resistance were hardly surprising as the Movement had grown the previous year, with the appearance of both the Resistance and the Ultra-Resistance. "A Call to Resist Illegitimate Authority" proved all but irresistible in left-of-center intellectual circles and the March on Pentagon had already acquired virtually mythical stature. The actions of Father Philip Berrigan and his three compatriots at the Baltimore Customs House were, if anything, still more worrisome.

The willingness of the Justice Department to prosecute individuals as distinguished as Spock and Coffin was, nevertheless, remarkable. Also significant was the readiness to resort to conspiracy law, which had been employed against radical organizations and individuals in the past. But the Johnson administration obviously feared the possibility of mass civil disobedience, as well as a breakdown of the Selective Service apparatus. General Lewis B. Hershey, director of the Selective Service system, wanted to punish anyone who contested it, and thus clearly welcomed prosecution of the Boston Five. Although less ill-disposed to anti-draft activists, Attorney General Ramsey Clark actually favored selective targeting of such thoughtful and committed individuals, reasoning that otherwise his department "could have ground up thousands of youngsters and nobody would ever notice it."

The *New York Times*' front-page headline on January 6 read, "Spock and Coffin Indicted for Activity Against Draft." Spock was quoted as expressing hope that as many as half-a-million young men would refuse conscription or disobey military orders. The paper's legal correspondent, Fred P. Graham, indicated that the indictment served as the strongest government "countermove" against the anti-draft movement. A companion piece by Edward C. Burks had Spock stating, "I certainly don't feel myself guilty," and talking about the "higher law" examined during the Nuremberg Trials, which required one to refuse to go along if "your government is up to crimes against humanity." Goodman wondered why the Johnson administration was so selective in its prosecution of those who signed "A Call to Resist Illegitimate Authority."

Appearing on January 12 next to Martin Luther King Jr. at a CALCAV-sponsored news conference, Reverend Coffin conveyed his readiness to go to jail, while refuting the notion of a conspiracy. "Everything we did," he declared, "we did as publicly as possible." Both ministers pledged to continue urging young men to heed "their consciences" regarding the draft. An editorial in *Ramparts* soon warned that if the Boston Five were "conspirators, then we must become a nation of conspirators" to ward off repression. Raskin expressed fears of his own, that the federal government was about to go after the American "intelligentsia," including possibly Chomsky, Paul Goodman, King, and Mailer.

The anti-draft movement remained in the news during the spring, as high-profile cases, all resulting in guilty verdicts, transpired. The first involved the Baltimore Four, who had carried out the initial attack on a draft board associated with the Ultra-Resistance. Believing the Catholic Church had to support revolution and enraged by the Vietnam War, Father Philip Berrigan expressed no remorse, quickly plotting another action. The case of the *United States v. Benjamin Spock* and his purported co-conspirators ensued, with the defense attorneys underscoring the Vietnam War's illegality and their clients' protection under the First Amendment for prosecution involving anti-war activities. Only Marcus Raskin failed to be convicted.

While that trial was starting and before the sentencing of the Baltimore Four, the Ultra-Resistance struck yet again, when Philip Berrigan, his brother Daniel, and seven other Catholic opponents of the war and conscription converged on the Selective Service offices in Catonsville, Maryland. They burned draft card files in an adjacent parking lot, while praying for peace and awaiting arrest. Father Daniel Berrigan subsequently offered, "Our apologies, good friends, for the fracture of good order, the burning of paper instead of children, the angering of the orderlies in the front parlor of the charnel house. We could not, so help us God, do otherwise. For we are sick at heart, our hearts give us no rest for thinking of the Land of Burning Children."

The trial of David Harris, who had recently married Joan Baez, quickly followed in a federal court in the Bay Area. Refusing to ask for mercy, Harris instead indicated that his "only crime had been not to commit an even greater crime." In delivering a harsh sentence, the presiding judge expressed belief in and respect for the defendant's sincerity. But he also lectured Harris, who was clearly determined "to be here or in some other court in this kind of situation, if I may use the term, come hell or high water." Indicating that rehabilitation made no sense in Harris's case, the judge said the sentence "has to be stark and real and just as hard and tough as you are."

Grabbing far more attention, the case of the Boston Five proceeded, with Federal Judge Francis J. W. Ford denying that the jury could consider the Vietnam War's "legality, morality, or constitutionality . . . or the rights of a citizen to protest." Rather, the issue involved whether Spock, Coffin, Goodman, Raskin, and Ferber had "knowingly and willingly" engaged in a conspiracy to violate the Selective Service Act. In imposing two-year sentences for the convicted defendants, and $5,000 fines against all, except for Ferber, who was fined $1,000, Judge Ford bristled, "Where law and order stops, obviously anarchy begins." He continued, "Be they high or low, intellectuals as well as others must be deterred from violating the law. These defendants should not escape under the guise of free speech." Ferber pledged to continue working with the anti-draft movement, while Coffin, Goodman, and Spock promised to keep supporting young resisters.

The trial of the Catonsville Nine occurred later in the year, with defense attorney William Kunstler likening the prosecution to the ways in which Socrates and Jesus had been persecuted. When guilty verdicts were handed down, a spectator charged, "Members of the jury, you have just found Jesus guilty." The presiding federal judge declared, "People can't take the law into their own hands." Speaking for his codefendants, Daniel Berrigan affirmed, "For the nine of us, it was an opportunity without parallel; to 'give evidence' for our lives, to unite with the hundreds in the streets and the millions across the world who are also saying 'no' to death as a social model."

Many of the more spectacular events involving the Ultra-Resistance occurred after the death of Martin Luther King Jr., who had demonstrated unwavering support for Benjamin Spock and his codefendants. Following the announcement regarding indictments of the Boston Five, King had immediately declared, "I wish I did not have my ministerial exemption. And I say to the federal government, or anybody else, they can do to me what they did to Dr. Spock, and William Sloane Coffin, my good friend the chaplain of Yale. They can just as well get ready to convict me."

* * *

While terribly distressed by the war, King had continued his Poor People's Campaign to demand Congress initiate an extensive jobs program or provide guaranteed income for the American people. During the last months of his life, King openly advocated the democratic socialism he had long favored. Amid his courting of Coretta Scott, the then twenty-three-year-old King had revealed in 1952, "I am much more socialistic in my economic theory than capitalistic." Assailing capitalism, King charged that it took "necessities from the masses to give luxuries to the classes." Talking to the Negro American Labor Council in 1961, King declared, "Call it democracy, or call it democratic socialism, but there must be a better distribution of wealth within this country for all God's children." In his acceptance speech for the Nobel Peace Prize in late 1964, he acknowledged that Scandinavian democratic socialism had much to offer. Capitalism he saw as linking racism, militarism, and materialism. Talking at a SCLC retreat in the spring of 1967, King indicated, "I think it is necessary for us to realize that we have moved from the era of civil rights to the era of human rights." He also stated, "We see that there must be a radical redistribution of economic and political power."

Speaking with the journalist David Halberstam in mid-1967, King conceded, "For years I labored with the idea of reforming the existing institutions of the society, a little change here, a little change there. Now I feel differently. I think you've got to have a reconstruction of the entire society, a revolution of values." Emphasizing the need for improved distribution of wealth, King suggested to his staff, "Maybe America must move toward a democratic socialism." In his final book, *Where Do We Go From Here: Chaos or Community?*, published during the summer of 1967, King wrote, "The time has come for us," he asserted, "to civilize ourselves by the total, direct and immediate abolition of poverty."

Discussing the Poor People's Campaign at a SCLC gathering in early December, King indicated his organization would "lead waves of the nation's poor and disinherited to" the nation's capital the following spring to demand "jobs or income for all." The demonstrators would insist on being heard and remain in Washington, D.C., "until American responds." They would confront, even embrace "scorn or ridicule," if necessary, for that was what the poor faced. They would willingly accept jail, for that too was something the indigent experienced. However, SCLC hoped that the Washington action and subsequent militant nonviolent protests across the country would be sympathetically received. Staff members would farm out to key cities and rural communities to elicit volunteers for the Poor People's Campaign. "Our nation is at a crossroads of history," King warned. He genuinely feared this amounted to a "last chance" to head in the direction of "constructive democratic change."

As King planned his Poor People's Campaign, FBI director J. Edgar Hoover added SCLC as a target under COINTELPRO. Orders went out to FBI offices "to expose, disrupt, misdirect, discredit, or otherwise neutralize the activities of Black Nationalist hate-type organizations." President Johnson, for his part, pledged not "to preside over the liquidation of the American nation or sit fiddling in the White House while Washington burns." Both the agency and the president worried about the possibility of a "massive bloodbath." Consequently, Hoover initiated another clandestine program, POCAM ("poverty campaign"), to be embedded in COINTELPRO. In early March 1968, Hoover undertook yet another COINTELPRO operation to "prevent the rise of a 'messiah' who could unify and electrify the militant black nationalist movement." Among those singled out as a possible "messiah" were Stokely Carmichael, Elijah Muhammad, and Dr. King.

Johnson was equally displeased that his former ally, Martin Luther King Jr., had become such a vocal, impassioned critic of the Vietnam War. He certainly wasn't happy when King applauded Eartha Kitt, the African American actress and singer, for telling Lady Bird Johnson as the First Lady hosted a panel at the White House on urban crime, "Vietnam is the main reason we are having trouble with the youth of America." King went further in a speech delivered at Ebenezer Baptist Church in Atlanta on February 4, not only condemning the "senseless, unjust war . . . in Vietnam," but charging, "We are criminals in that war." He surmised that the American people failed to stop the war due to "our pride and our arrogance." Then, in one of the many remarkable moments during his public addresses, King foreshadowed his own death, hoping that somebody would indicate he had attempted "to give his life serving others . . . to love somebody . . . to be right on the war question . . . to feed the hungry . . . to clothe those who were naked . . . to visit those who were in prison . . . to love and serve humanity." He wanted to be viewed as "a drum major for justice . . . peace . . . righteousness." King declared, "I just want to leave a committed life behind."

Many believed that King's leadership of the civil rights movement had ebbed, and that his fervent commitment to nonviolence was wrongheaded. But more individuals than ever were drawn to his preachments, as attested by those participating in the Resistance, including the Boston Five, and the Ultra-Resistance as well. Some like John Lewis and Cesar Chavez never questioned the worth of King's approach. Chavez, cofounder of the United Farm Workers (UFW), employed nonviolent tactics in his difficult struggle to improve the condition of migrant farm laborers. Welcome publicity came the UFW's way during the early winter of 1968 as Chavez conducted a twenty-five-day hunger strike. The UFW chieftain broke bread with New York Senator Robert F. Kennedy, as the latter readied for a presidential run. In the midst of the hunger strike, King fired off a telegram to Chavez, stating, "Our separate struggles are really one. A struggle for freedom, for dignity, and for humanity."

Nevertheless, the fight against racially discriminatory practices was, in some ways, more divided than ever. Not only was there talk of Brown Power and Red Power, referring to Latinos and Native Americans, but African Americans, especially young people, were of contrasting minds regarding what path to take. A new group had appeared in Oakland, California, during the fall of 1966, the Black Panther Party, headed by a couple of young men, Bobby Seale and Eldridge Cleaver. Their Ten-Point Program demanded self-determination within the black community, full employment, economic empowerment, decent housing, better education, exemption from military service, termination of police brutality, release of all black prisoners, jury trials with black peers, "Land, Bread . . . Clothing, Justice and Peace." The Panthers became known for following police vehicles passing through African American communities in cars of their own, with rifles visible and copies of the U.S. Constitution in hand.

The group achieved greater notoriety in May 1967 when Seale led a group of about thirty gun-wielding Panthers to the California state legislature in Sacramento, after a bill was proposed to prevent loaded weapons from being carried inside incorporated areas. By early 1968, Eldridge Cleaver, an ex-convict and former black separatist turned acclaimed writer, served as the Panthers' Minister of Information. Cleaver's autobiographical book, *Soul on Ice*, became a best seller, notwithstanding its characterization of rape of white women by black men as a political act. In keeping with the era's ambiance, *Soul on Ice* viewed the black struggle in the United States as tied to anti-colonial battles elsewhere. Cleaver also set up a number of "Free Huey Newton" rallies, with many activists, both blacks and whites, contending Newton had been wrongly accused of the murder of John Frey, a white Oakland police officer, killed in a shootout the previous October.

While assailed by black power advocates, including the Panthers, and the target of an untold number of assassination plots, King continued planning the Poor People's Campaign. The necessity and timeliness of that effort appeared borne out by the warnings delivered on February 29, 1968, by the President's National Advisory Commission on Civil Disorders, headed by Illinois Governor Otto Kerner Jr. The commission charged that absent immediate drastic and expensive reforms, the nation would experience a "continuing polarization of the American community and, ultimately, the destruction of basic democratic values." Concerned about both "white racism" and black separatism, the commission warned that the United States was "moving toward two societies, one black, one white—separate and unequal." The report's findings, King believed, underscored early admonitions of his. "Chaos and disintegration" would follow, he worried, unless blacks were wholly welcomed into the larger American society.

Over the next few weeks, King also became ensnared in an embittered labor conflict involving Memphis sanitation workers. Refusing to negotiate, Mayor Henry Loeb declined to approve of a city council-approved wage increase, leading to nonviolent marches, mace and tear being employed against demonstrators, and a mass rally that Reverend James Lawson led and King joined. On March 18, King spoke of people being "tired of being at the bottom . . . being trampled over," their children attending inferior schools, their families residing in slums, enduring poverty, and "being emasculated." He also referred to his Poor People's Campaign, which King indicated would act "nonviolently but militantly . . . to plague Congress." Another scheduled march turned violent, leading King to meet with the Invaders, young black militants, during the period when black power was extracting more attention.

H. Rap Brown had recently spoken of the need to "move from resistance to aggression, from revolt to revolution."

Talking to the *New York Times*, King declared, "In a sense you could say we are engaged in a class struggle." The fight to end poverty and inequality in America would prove "long and difficult," and required "a redistribution of economic power," he admitted. It was clear that the country could not undertake such an endeavor and wage war in Vietnam simultaneously.

Depressed by the resort to violence, King nevertheless returned to Memphis on April 3, delivering a speech that evening in which he again foresaw his own death. Pleased that he had been allowed "to do God's will" and "go up to the mountain," King had "seen the Promised Land." Acknowledging that he might "not get there with you," he declared, "We, as a people, will get to the promised land!"

King was shot early the next evening as he stood on a balcony outside his motel room. Just over an hour later, the American apostle of nonviolence was pronounced dead. More than 100 American cities erupted, with some of the worst violence occurring in Washington, D.C. Army soldiers and Marines helped quell disorder there, and in both Chicago and Baltimore. The death toll stood at thirty-nine, with over 2,600 people injured, and 21,000 arrested. The civil rights movement suffered a near fatal blow, from which it never really recovered. King had believed that a "nonviolent army of the poor, a freedom of the church" could transform the American nation.

* * *

That same spring saw anger spew forth in a locale where that would have largely unimaginable a short while before. Part of the famed Ivy League, Columbia University, located at 116th Street and Broadway on Manhattan's Upper West Side, became the scene of the most prolonged student unrest since the Berkeley Free Speech Movement. Fueled by dismay over the university's involvement with defense research and its attempt to construct a gymnasium in Morningside Park, which traversed Harlem neighborhoods, students occupied campus properties. University administrators eventually called on the police to remove demonstrators, who had largely been divided into white and black, when African American students compelled white counterparts to leave Hamilton Hall, the first building occupied. That enabled the police to tread lightly with black students, owing to concerns about a possible incendiary response by neighboring Harlem, while treating white occupiers brutally.

The Columbia revolt was part of a global phenomenon, as the English poet Stephen Spender would indicate. 1968 proved to be "The Year of the Young Rebels," with revolts occurring around the globe. Guerrilla forces were on the march in what was increasingly referred to as the Third World, as indicated by the Tet Offensive that began early in the year in Vietnam. But more surprisingly, talk of revolution arose in Europe and the United States. The Prague Spring, until Warsaw Pact nations poured in soldiers and tanks, offered the possibility of a melding of socialism and democracy. In France, and especially in the capital city, anarchist-flavored rebellion attempted to bring together students and workers as imaginative slogans took hold: *Il est interdit d'interdire.* (It is forbidden to forbid.) *Le patron a besoin de toi, tu n'as pas besoin de lui.* (The boss needs you, you don't need him.) *La barricade ferme la rue mais ouvre la voie.* (Barricades shut down the street but open the way). *Imagine: c'est la guerre et personne n'y va!* (Imagine: there was a war and no one turned up!) *Je suis marxiste, tendance Groucho.* (I am a Marxist, Groucho tendency.)

As the Parisian near-revolution collapsed, Senator Robert F. Kennedy, running an insurgent candidacy associated with the short-lived New Politics that was tied to the New Left's idea of participatory democracy, became yet another victim of the politics of assassination. Dispirited antiwar forces headed to Chicago for the Democratic National Convention in late August, many aware that Soviet and other Warsaw Pact forces had crushed the Prague Spring. The anticipated 100,000 young people that the Yippies and New Left leaders had envisioned demonstrating in the streets of Chicago never showed up, with only about a tenth that number congregating in city parks.

Establishment forces tied to the Johnson administration controlled the convention, even though LBJ had declined to run for reelection, ensuring Vice-President Hubert Humphrey's nomination. With the defeat of an antiwar plank offered by forces tied to Minnesotan Eugene McCarthy, who was also connected to the year's New Politics, the Democratic Party's hawkish stance on the Vietnam conflict only further enraged demonstrators. Over the course of several days, they battled with police, the latter at times appearing unleashed, leading to a post-convention report charging that a police riot had ensued. Perversely, the Yippies and various SDS leaders considered the beatings and arrests of young protestors another step on the path toward the revolution, reasoning that such treatment radicalized many.

* * *

Responding to the events in Chicago, the poet and political activist John Sinclair, long involved in bohemian and radical circles in Detroit, established the tiny White Panther Party (WPP), issuing, in the fall of 1968, a 10-Point Program. Consciously drawing on both the experiences of the Black Panthers and the counterculture, the WPP's party statement demanded "FREEDOM!," "total freedom for everybody!" Promising not to stop until that was achieved, Sinclair referred to the need for "Cultural Revolution through a total assault on the culture," pertaining to "our culture, our art, the music, newspapers, books, posters, our clothing, our homes, the way we walk and talk, the way our hair grows, the way we smoke dope and fuck and eat and sleep." Spearheading the assault was "ROCK AND ROLL music," along with "direct access to millions of teenagers." Insisting that "everything" be "free for everybody!," Sinclair demanded "the end of money!," "free access to information media," emancipation of all schools and institutions from corporate dominance, liberation of all prisoners and soldiers, and the handing of "all power to all the people!"

As the presidential race wound down to an inglorious close, with the seemingly inevitable election of Richard M. Nixon, the issue of human rights remained prominent as attested by the response to protests involving the Mexico City Olympics, held in October 1968. A young African American sociologist, Harry Edwards, had devised the Olympic Project for Human Rights (OPHR), to spark a boycott of the Games. The OPHR's founding statement the previous year urged African Americans to "no longer allow the Sports World to pat itself on the back as a citadel of racial justice when the racial injustices of the sports industry are infamously legendary." Three members of UCLA's NCAA-championship basketball team—Lew Alcindor, Lucius Allen, and Mike Warren—refused to participate in Olympic Games Trials, while the International Olympic Committee banned apartheid South Africa from sending a team to Mexico City. Protest followed the 200-meter dash, when barefooted gold-medal winner Tommie Smith and bronze-medal recipient John Carlos, two other young African Americans, delivered gloved, single-fisted black power salutes with heads bowed as the National Anthem played during the award ceremony. The U.S. Olympic Committee suspended the pair, sending them home.

Black power was also at the forefront of the most sustained student strike in American educational history. Beginning in November and lasting until the following March, students at San Francisco State went on strike, demanding more black students, additional black faculty, and a Black Studies Department. Having been involved in a pair of fatal shootouts with the police, the Black Panther Party was finally targeted by the FBI, which deemed it "extremist," warned that it was "rapidly expanding," and supported counterintelligence efforts to disrupt it. Huey Newton was convicted of voluntary manslaughter, leading to threats of war "until black people are free." Declaring that her husband Eldridge refused to return to jail, despite having broken his parole agreement, Kathleen Cleaver warned that the Panthers would employ "any means necessary" to ensure that didn't happen. Publicity surrounding the Panthers enabled their party to experience a growth spurt, which allowed for a Free Breakfast Program, free medical clinics, and a party newspaper.

* * *

Like both Columbia and San Francisco State, the 1968–1969 academic year saw the number of sit-ins, occupations, classroom disturbances, and politically-motivated violence on American colleges and universities attain record levels. Membership in SDS skyrocketed, possibly reaching 100,000 in as many as 400 chapters around the country. This came on the heels of the organization's national convention where Bernadine Dohrn, a University of Chicago School of Law graduate, nominated as Inter-organization Secretary, responded to a query if she were a socialist, "I'm a revolutionary communist." She was elected without opposition. As rhetoric included more easy talk of revolution, SDS was increasingly riven by sectarian divisions, the kinds that had maimed the Old Left and which the early New Left sought to avoid. But then that edition of the New Left was drawn to the SNCC vision of the beloved community and SDS's own lauding of participatory democracy. This version wrestled over Marxism, imperialism, and revolutionary tactics. It also increasingly felt the need to stay abreast of ongoing events, and to not lag behind the pace seemingly set by local chapters, unaffiliated radicals, and black militants. A doctrinaire quality set in, with a greater turn toward "the pseudo-scientific language of Marxism-Leninism," acknowledge SDS veterans Greg Calvert and Carol Neiman. Burnings and bombings increased too, with ROTC buildings frequently targeted. SDS emphasized more and more the need to support "a revolutionary youth movement." The bombings during 1969, historian Jeremy Varon contends, "were an expression, an act of, if not foolhardy, optimism. . . . [The bombers] were desperadoes. They had the belief that they could bomb old ideologies out of existence."

The wit and panache displayed by the Yippies with their zap-ins were less frequently displayed, although the new women's liberation and gay liberation movements were not completely ill-disposed to emphasize humor, irony, and satire. However, the new Nixon administration, the seemingly relentless nature of American operations in Vietnam, and the greater reliance on conspiracy trials only ensured a radical turn by many activists. By the spring of 1969, black students at Cornell, ending an occupation, walked out with guns at the ready. Harvard was rocked by a strike. A bomb at the University of California at Santa Barbara killed a custodian working at the faculty club. In Berkeley, protestors battled with police and highway patrolmen ordered in by Governor Ronald Reagan to remove them from a plot of land close to the UC campus, which had been nurtured by community members into what they tagged People's Park. On Bloody Thursday in mid-April, a police assault resulted in tear gassing and the shooting of several people, one fatally.

That summer, SDS imploded, as a Maoist Progressive Labor faction battled with one sporting the label of Revolutionary Youth Movement, out of which emerged Weatherman, a small band of self-proclaimed revolutionaries. The largest New Left organization was soon reduced to a shell of its former self, while Weatherman claimed about 300 members. In early October, Weatherman carried out the Days of Rage in the streets of Chicago, deliberately vandalizing property and confronting police, leading to mass arrests and the eventual decision by several members to go underground. A group not associated with Weatherman, one guided by Samuel J. Melville, carried out a series of bombings in New York City, hitting corporate and government offices, including the Armed Forces Induction Center at 39 Whitehall Street. All of this occurred in the very period when the antiwar movement was surging, able to conduct a nation-wide Moratorium in mid-October, led by Sam Brown and David Hawk, former McCarthy campaign workers, who supported the idea of a one-day halt to business-as-usual. The Moratorium gave way to a March Against Death on November 13 and the New Mobilization Committee to End the War in Vietnam's mammoth rally of 500,000 in Washington, D.C., two days later. In late December, Weatherman's last public gathering occurred in Flint, Michigan, which included a "wargasm" with rants praising mass murderer Charles Manson and a decision to engage in revolutionary action involving guerrilla warfare and armed struggle.

As the historian Arthur M. Eckstein reveals, members of the Weather Underground envisioned something darker still as they intended to take matters to the next level and thereby display true revolutionary colors. The newest crop of SDS leaders—Bernadine Dohrn, Mark Rudd, Bill Ayers, John Jacobs, and Jeff Jones, among others—identified more openly with revolutionary regimes and the possibility of revolution in the United States. They planned to commit acts of revolutionary violence, recently employed in Algeria, South Africa, Cuba, Jordan, France, Vietnam, Israel, Colombia, South Africa, Rhodesia, Guatemala, Brazil, Switzerland, Italy, and elsewhere. Thus, an organization that had been rooted in the American grain and core liberal values, albeit ones of a radical cast, devolved into a sectarian, violence-enthralled cult with no mass following, notwithstanding the certain revolutionary cachet it held among various portions of the New Left.

Egomaniacal to a fault, members of Weatherman alienated the vast majority of the growing number of Americans opposed to the war, even those who had identified with SDS's earlier tenets of participatory democracy, community organizing, student power, resistance, or utopian-flavored revolution. What Weatherman offered was precisely opposite to that which SDS had long stood for, replacing an indigenous radicalism with an infantile leftism veering in the direction of dystopia. Thus, the dreams of the 1960s turned and transmuted into something different than the ones that had guided a number of the most idealistic and determined young people of their generation to participate in campaigns to improve the lot of the indigent, the exploited, and the disfranchised. Idealism and good works gave way to a demand for instant transformation, a type of temper tantrum run amuck. Jacobs later reflected, "We were going to bring the war home. 'Turn the imperialists' war into a civil war,' in Lenin's words. And we were going to kick ass."

At the beginning of 1970, Weatherman shut down SDS' National Office, which had been located in Chicago, and sold the organization's files to the Wisconsin Historical Society. According to Jeremy Varon, the group's leaders adopted a plan referred to as "consolidation," through which collectives undertook "purges" of those deemed suspect, weak, too bourgeois, or less than fully committed to the cause. It was also the time, the journalist Bryan Burrough charges, when Weathermen "set out to kill people."

Members of Weatherman began heading underground, which Burrough deems more "a fugitive lifestyle," but one that benefited from large numbers of "aboveground" backers, the most important of whom were committed radical attorneys, especially Michael Kennedy. There existed "a loose network of service providers," with false IDs and safe havens provided. Weathermen constructed new identities, sometimes relying on stolen documents. Underground collectives or "tribes" appeared in Buffalo, Chicago, Cleveland, Detroit, New York City, Pittsburgh, and San Francisco. The next step for Weatherman, however, remained very much in question. Bombings were anticipated and would certainly take place. But as Burrough reflects, the issue involved "what kind." He insists that many believed "Weathermen would become revolutionary murderers." Jon Lerner told him about a discussion with Ted Gold involving the placing of "a bomb on the [Chicago railroad] tracts at rush hour, to blow up people coming home from work."

The leaders of Weatherman particularly wanted to target policemen, considering them "legitimate targets," in part to display solidarity with the Black Panthers. On February 12, Weathermen placed a pair of bombs near a police station in Berkeley. Plate-glass windows subsequently shattered, along with the arm of patrolman Paul Morgan. One Weatherman later acknowledged, "We wanted to do it at a shift change, frankly, to maximize deaths." No cadre opposed the action, with some upset that no police officers were killed. One incident proved newsworthy, a bombing just outside the Park Police Station in the Haight on February 16 that led to the death of forty-four-year-old Brian McConnell, a police sergeant, and injuries to other police officers. Both Weatherman and the Black Panthers would be accused of setting the blast.

Across the country, Weatherman planted three gasoline-loaded firebombs at the home of New York State Supreme Court Justice John M. Murtagh, who was presiding over the trial of the Panther 21, charged with having plotted to bomb landmarks and department stores in New York City. The bombs went off at the Murtagh residence, a semidetached brownstone, on 217th Street, one underneath the family car. Additional bombs were hurled that evening at a police vehicle in Manhattan and at a pair of military recruiting stations in Brooklyn. The day following the bombing, New York City police arrested a dozen members of the Young Patriots Organization, including William "Preacherman" Fesperman, charging them with the illegal holding of dangerous weapons. The Young Patriots, a group largely made up of white Southerners, first appeared in Chicago, where they had formed a coalition with Fred Hampton and the Black Panther Party.

Weatherman delivered a statement supporting the Panthers, but Terry Robbins insisted more needed to be done. He told other Weathermen, "We've got to up the ante. The bomb at Judge Murtagh's house didn't do anything. Now we've got to do something." The New York Collective began meeting at Cathy Wilkerson's family townhouse, situated on Eleventh Street in Greenwich Village. Disappointed about the impact of firebombs and believing ROTC buildings had already been struck by Molotov cocktails, five Weathermen discussed using other devices. Robbins proposed dynamite, and the group mentioned possible targets, including "universities, police stations, ROTC buildings." Someone suggested planting "three anti-personnel bombs . . . dynamite pipe bombs in them" at a dance for noncommissioned officers at Fort Dix, Mark Rudd remembers. Ted Gold confronted the only individual who questioned the plan, threatening him, "You have been my best friend for ten years. But you gotta calm down. I wouldn't want to have to kill you."

In the meantime, Bill Ayers, according to Bryan Burrough, took over more of the planning for future Weathermen actions. At "a criticism session" in Buffalo, Ayers attacked those in attendance "for having spent too much time preparing for actions (bombings) and not doing anything," recalls FBI informant Larry Grathwohl. Meeting in Detroit, Weathermen led by Ayers explored potential kidnapping and bombing targets. Participants talked about Vice-President Spiro Agnew, Detroit Democratic mayor Roman Gribbs, and Detroit police officers. Ayers proposed hitting the downtown headquarters of the Police Officers Association. "We blast that fucking building to hell . . . when the place is crowded. We wait for them to have a meeting, or a social event. Then we strike." The bombing would occur, Ayers reported, as the 13th Precinct house was being struck by another Weather group. When Grathwohl, who infiltrated Weatherman, worried that customers, most of them black, would be killed at a nearby restaurant, Ayers expressed little concern about "collateral damage." Ayers later insisted that Weatherman never sought to kill anyone, but Howie Machtinger refuted that. "You know, policemen were fair game," he told Burrough.

On March 6, five members of Weatherman were staying at the Wilkerson townhouse at 18 West 11th Street in Greenwich Village, only three blocks from Washington Square Park. All kinds of luminaries had once lived there or nearby, including Edgar Allen Poe, Herman Melville, Walt Whitman, longtime ACLU chair Roger Nash Baldwin, and the actor Dustin Hoffman, currently residing next door. Three Weathermen—Ted Gold, Diana Oughton, and Terry Robbins—were in the Wilkerson basement, evidently building nail bombs to attack Fort Dix. Gold had recently told a friend, "We've got to turn New York into Saigon," referring to the Tet Offensive. Kathy Boudin and Cathy Wilkerson were upstairs, the one showering, the other working in the kitchen. The pipe bombs exploded, setting off three cases of dynamite, blowing up Gold, Oughton, and Robbins, along with the townhouse, then appraised at a pricey $275,000. Stunned, the lightly clad Boudin and Wilkerson managed to collect themselves, obtained clothes from a neighbor, took the subway located on Sixth Avenue, and fled into the underground. Like other leading members of Weatherman, neither would surface for several years, and when Boudin did, it would be to calamitous ends. For now, the bombings continued.

In fact, notwithstanding earlier suggestions by the Nixon administration that the pace of violence on college and university campuses would dampen, the 1969–1970 academic year proved the most violent yet. A purported 174 bombing incidents occurred on campuses, but scores of additional explosions were carried out against corporations, military facilities, police stations, military centers, federal offices, and other buildings. Weatherman was involved in an untold number of those bombings, as were Weather-affiliated or sympathetic groups, the Black Panthers, the Puerto Rican Armed Forces of National Liberation (FALN), and other radical organizations.

The decision by President Nixon to send American troops into Cambodia in the spring of 1970 ignited some of the fury that led to more bombings, student strikes, and demonstrations across the country. It also resulted in tragedy on the home front, with four students at Kent State University in Ohio killed by National Guardsmen and two more slain by police who repeatedly fired into a dormitory on the largely African American campus of Jackson State College in Jackson, Mississippi. The largest wave yet of student protest followed the Kent State shootings, but there was little response to the Jackson State tragedies.

Throughout the duration of U.S. involvement in Vietnam, which involved a dramatic reduction of American troops and also an invasion of Laos and massive bombing raids, protest of both the violent and nonviolent sort ebbed and flowed. The Weather Underground, who helped spring LSD guru Timothy Leary from prison before smuggling him to Algeria, continued to place bombs, albeit selectively, and affinity groups did as well. The results could prove dire, as when the Army Mathematics Research Center at the University of Wisconsin was bombed on August 24, 1970, killing a young graduate student, who was himself a war opponent. The Weather Underground claimed credit for having bombed the Harvard Center for International Affairs, the U.S. Capitol, corrections' offices, the Pentagon, police stations, corporate facilities, and various government buildings.

During the 1970s, Bryan Burrough claims, "protest bombings" in the United States proved "commonplace," particularly in New York, Chicago, and San Francisco. Almost "a dozen radical underground groups" like the Weather Underground, and later the Symbionese Liberation Army (SLA) placed "hundreds of bombs." Over an eighteen-month stretch of time in 1971 and the following year, the FBI traced "2,500 bombings on American soil." A Puerto Rican separatist group, Fuerzas Armadas de Liberacion Nacional, carried out eighty-two bombings, most affecting civilians in New York City and Chicago. Involved in a series of bombings, the Maoist Black Liberation Army (BLA) was an underground Black Nationalist group established by former Panthers who, like Eldridge Cleaver, came to view Huey Newton as a "sellout." Favoring armed struggle and intending to "take up arms for the liberation and self-determination of black people in the United States," BLA would be accused of at least twenty murders, including of several police officers. The New World Liberation Front, a militant urban guerrilla collective, would be associated with a series of bombings from San Jose and San Francisco to Boston. Also engaging in acts of violence, the SLA, a miniscule group of Berkeley radicals, nevertheless briefly acquired high-profile status through the murder of the African American educator Marcus Foster, who headed the Oakland Unified School District, and the kidnapping of the heiress Patricia Hearst. The United Freedom Front purportedly participated in both bombings and bank robberies, well into the 1980s.

The U.S. government adopted different tactics to weaken or break many of these organizations, which proved more or less successful in various instances. The assault on the Black Panther Party, considered by FBI Director Hoover "the greatest threat to the internal security of the country," appeared systematic and far-flung, ranging from public relations efforts to vilify and delegitimize the organization to legal and possibly extra-legal efforts. Prosecutors singled out the Panthers, particularly leaders, but then the charged rhetoric and activities of particular individuals, including Huey Newton, Bobby Seale, and Eldridge Cleaver, made attainment of indictments relatively easy. Panthers were harassed, pulled over, and interrogated in their homes and offices. An untold number of Panthers were killed, including seventeen-year-old Bobby Hutton during a 1968 shootout involving Cleaver and the Oakland police, and twenty-one-year-old Fred Hampton and Mark Clark, but a year older, fatally shot in the early morning of December 4, 1969, as fourteen Chicago officers fired approximately 100 bullets into a West Side apartment. Internal battles and squabbles with rival groups, many of the divisions sown by agent provocateurs and government disinformation efforts, led to other deaths, including the killing of twenty-six-year-old Bunchy Carter and twenty-three-year-old John Huggins Jr., gunned down in mid-January 1969 by members of the rival black nationalist U.S. Organization on the UCLA campus.

The Panthers, like various radical organizations and individuals, went through a conspiracy trial, that involving the Panther 21, charged in early 1969 with plotting to bomb the New York Botanical Gardens, police stations, schools, and a railroad yard. Following a lengthy trial, "not guilty" verdicts were delivered, after it was revealed that New York City police undercover operatives had provoked much of the conspiracy. The state spent approximately $1.2 million, at a minimum, to conduct the trial. In the process, it compelled the Panthers to expend resources that were far more limited than what were available to the government. Other Panthers proved still less fortunate, with several incarcerated for decades. A much-decorated combat veteran of the Vietnam War, Elmer "Geronimo" Pratt, was charged with killing Carolina Olsen, a teacher, and her husband Kenneth, in Santa Monica in late 1968. Unfortunately for Pratt, Panthers in Northern California, following Huey Newton's directives, refused to corroborate his alibi, and he served twenty-seven years in prison before the conviction was overturned on grounds that the prosecution had concealed exculpatory information. Caught up in the COINTELPRO web, Pratt was singled out by the FBI as one to "neutralize . . . as an effective BPP functionary."

According to J. Soffiyah Elijah from Harvard Law School, COINTEL-PRO resulted in "maiming, murdering, false prosecutions and frame-ups, destruction, and mayhem throughout the country." Municipal red squads, military intelligence services, the FBI, and the CIA, in violation of its statutory charter, gathered information on thousands of American citizens, pinpointing "dissident elements" and purported "subversives." Drug busts were used to rein in political activists ranging from Houston civil rights activist Lee Otis Johnson to White Panther Party founder John Sinclair, both receiving lengthy prison sentences for a purported marijuana sale or usage.

The Nixon Justice Department obtained indictments against New Left and antiwar activists, Weather Underground leaders, the Ultra-Resistance, and the VVAW. Although Johnson's last Attorney General, Ramsey Clark, had refused to bring conspiracy charges regarding the street disturbances amid the 1968 Democratic Party National Convention, his successor, John Mitchell, proceeded to do so. Indicted for having conspired to create a riot, the Chicago Eight included Black Panther cofounder Bobby Seale, former SDS leaders Tom Hayden and Rennie Davis; Yippies Abbie Hoffman and Jerry Rubin; radical pacifist David Dellinger; and a pair of academics, John Froines and Lee Weiner. Judge Julius Hoffman eventually ordered Seale bound and gagged, before severing his case. The jury acquitted the remaining defendants of conspiracy charges, and fully acquitted Froines and Weiner. Hayden, Davis, Hoffman, Rubin, and Dellinger were declared guilty of having crossed state lines while intending to incite a riot, leading to five-year prison sentences and $5,000 fines. Judge Hoffman also cited the defendants and their attorneys, William Kunstler and Lee Weinglass, for contempt, tacking on additional sentences of up to four years. An appellate court later overturned the convictions, on the grounds of judicial prejudice. Later, some of the contempt charges were sustained but resulted in no prison time or fines. Several Weather members, including Mark Rudd, Cathy Wilkerson, and Bernadine Dohrn, only resurfaced after years in the underground, generally facing little (if any) prison time.

The Catholic Left achieved even greater notoriety following charges in 1971 that the Harrisburg Seven, whose six priests or nuns included soon-to-be spouses Philip Berrigan and Elizabeth McAlister, conspired to kidnap National Security Advisor Henry Kissinger and to blow up underground tunnels in the nation's capital. Defense counsel Ramsay Clark, the former Attorney General, called on no defendants to testify, merely stating, "Your Honor, the defendants shall always seek peace. They continue to proclaim their innocence. The defense rests." A hung jury led to the eventual release of the Harrisburg Seven, who pledged to keep opposing the war "all over the country."

More than 7,000 demonstrators were arrested in early May 1971 during protests in Washington, D.C., intended to shut down the Nixon administration. The slogan of Mayday Tribe was "if the government won't stop the war, we'll stop the government." Antiwar activists sought to block significant bridges and traffic circles to prevent traffic flow, in order "to create the specter of social chaos while maintaining the support or at least toleration of the broad masses of American people." National Guardsmen, along with Army and Marine troops, rounded up suspects during "qualified martial law," as Assistant Attorney General William H. Rehnquist offered. The Peoples Coalition for Peace and Justice supported civil disobedience, Movement strategist L. A. Kauffman explains, but the Mayday Tribe was intended to "bring the most politicized hippies . . . together with the hippest of the hardcore radicals." Mayday organizer Rennie Davis favored "action rather than congregation, disruption rather than display." In the face of over 200,000 protestors, including embittered Vietnam vets, the Nixon administration chose to allow for mass arrests that resulted in 14,500 being held at various sites, including Robert F. Kennedy Stadium, home of the Washington Redskins. One of those detained, Dr. Benjamin Spock, declared, "Calling this a concentration camp would be a very appropriate description." But the Mayday protest also ushered in "a new style and structure of radical organizing," including the use of "affinity groups," subsequently adopted by many movements. The Mayday radicals proved to be "decentralized, multi-vocal, ideologically diverse, and propelled by direct action."

The Gainesville Eight, members of the VVAW, were accused of conspiring to disrupt the 1972 Republican National Convention held in Miami Beach, Florida. The VVAW's Winter Soldier hearings in Detroit early the previous year first garnered considerable attention for the antiwar veterans' group. There, soldiers delivered personal testimony regarding atrocities they had witnessed or carried out in Vietnam. That spring as massive antiwar protests occurred, veterans hurled back commendation medals and discharge documents at the Capitol as part of their "limited incursion into the country of Congress." One veteran declared, "If we have to fight again, it will be to take these steps." Naval veteran John F. Kerry spoke to the Senate Foreign Relations Committee about the Winter Soldier Hearings. He referred to soldiers recalling having "personally raped, cut off ears, cut off heads, taped wires from portable telephones to human genitals and turned up the power, cut off limbs, blown up bodies, randomly shot at civilians, razed villages in fashion reminiscent of Ghengis Khan, shot cattle and dogs for fun, poisoned food stocks, and generally ravaged the countryside of South Vietnam in addition to the normal ravage of war and the normal and very particular ravaging which is done by the applied bombing power of this country." Poignantly, Kerry indicated that the VVAW wanted their fellow citizens "to think about that because how do you ask a man to be the last man to die in Vietnam? How do you ask a man to be the last man to die for a mistake?" The jury in the case of the Gainesville Eight case quickly turned in not guilty verdicts, but one defendant recalled, "I can't forget the government put me through fourteen months of hell."

* * *

The year 1968 was a time of tremendous highs and lows for American radicals, as it was for the nation as a whole. The possibility of a New Politics beckoned, however briefly, before being extinguished through assassinations, continued control of the Democratic Party by Establishment politicians, and the willingness of the American people to vote Richard Nixon into the White House. The deaths of Martin Luther King Jr. and Robert F. Kennedy were simply crushing, no matter that each was viewed unfavorably by many who considered themselves more radical. That was somewhat ironic as King was radical to the core and was engaged in a quest to demand Congress address the plight of the economically disfranchised, while Bobby flirted with a new brand of political radicalism, before each was murdered, resulting in the killing of both the men and the dreams associated with them.

Revolution seemed to be in the air both at home and overseas, whether that involved the Tet Offensive in Vietnam, the Prague Spring, occupation of buildings at Columbia University, student-worker protests in Paris, the challenge to one-party monopoly in Mexico, the beginning of a sustained strike at San Francisco State, the Black Panthers' greater notoriety, and SDS's increased support of heightened militancy. Ultimately, most of those revolutionary surges would be halted or smashed, but the revolutionary dreams endured for some time longer. That led to attempts in the United States to bring the war home, resulting in SDS's splintering, the emergence of Weatherman, slipping underground, and a cascade of bombings, not all mortality-free. The federal, state, and local governments responded accordingly, carrying out both barely legal and illicit operations and using the arm of the law to target Movement leaders.

Chapter 7

One, Two, Many Movements

The Movement that began in the 1950s, and eventually included the civil rights, student, New Left, and antiwar campaigns, became even more fractured during its zenith, the 1960s. Beats, hippies, women, gays, Latinos, Native Americans, Asian Americans, environmentalists, the elderly, consumers, the disabled, prisoners, and welfare recipients demanded that attention be paid to issues of particular concern to them. Each is well deserving of far more space than can be afforded in a book of this length. Together, like the broader Movement, they strove for empowerment of often disfranchised, neglected, and sometimes terribly exploited groups. Virtually all acquired greater appeal, at least bordering on respectability, during the 1970s and beyond. Other progressive organizations sprouted throughout the same period, making for a complex cauldron of left-of-center forces, notwithstanding the typical media representation that the American left was in retreat. Moving beyond and outside the Movement, in various instances, these drives helped lay the foundation for the Untethered Left that would dominate until the near end of the century. Its emergence, such as it was, unfolded in response to the failings of previous lefts in the United States: an all too unfortunate propensity toward sectarianism, doctrinal fixations seemingly alien to the American experience, and an equally misguided looking to revolutionary actors elsewhere.

A small circle of friends, including a number of Columbia University students at one point, sparked the latest version of an American counterculture to emerge during and immediately after World War II. Led by Allen Ginsberg and Jack Kerouac, this group, which came to be known as the beats, challenged the conformity, complacency, and conservatism that increasingly appeared to dominate much of American society as the Cold War uncoiled. Some, like Ginsberg, Kerouac, and the poet Gary Snyder, looked to the East, immersing themselves in Zen Buddhism and "beatific" spirituality. Congregating in welcoming enclaves in Greenwich Village, San Francisco's North Beach, and Venice, California, just north of Los Angeles, the beats partook of marijuana, hashish, and eventually, psychedelics. In the summer of 1955, Ginsberg delivering an initial reading of his epic poem, "Howl," with its electric opening, "I saw the best minds of my generation destroyed by madness, starving hysterical naked,/dragging themselves through the negro streets at dawn looking for an angry fix,/angelheaded hipsters burning for the ancient heavenly connection to the starry dynamo in the machinery of night." The publication of Kerouac's *On the Road*, an account of the frenetic journeys of the beat leaders, came two years later, while Ginsberg's own peripatetic makeup ensured that ideals associated with the beats would spread internationally.

The beats gave way during the 1960s to the very spectacle Kerouac had predicted in his novel, *The Dharma Bums*: the appearance "of a great rucksack revolution thousands or even millions of young Americans wandering around with rucksacks, going up to mountains to pray, making children laugh and old men glad, making young girls happy and old girls happier, all of 'em Zen Lunatics who go about writing poems that happen to appear in their heads for no reason and also by being kind and also by strange unexpected acts keep giving visions of eternal freedom to everybody and to all living creatures."

Encouraged by the great English writer, Aldous Huxley, author of the dystopian classic, *Brave New World*, but also *The Doors of Perception* and *Heaven and Hell*, about mescaline trips, Ginsberg attempted to spread the gospel of psychedelia. Eager to do so were a pair of psychologists, Timothy Leary and Richard Alpert, involved with the Harvard Psilocybin Project, and a young graduate student, Ken Kesey, enrolled in Stanford's Creative Writing Program. While Leary and Alpert emphasized the importance of controlled settings for psychedelic experiences, Kesey and his band of like-minded misfits, the Merry Pranksters, carried out Acid Trips, during which attendees at mass parties might not know their drinks were spiked with LSD. As members of the American intelligentsia dabbled in the world of psychedelia, something Huxley had hoped for, young people increasingly became drawn to the counterculture. They grew their hair long, were viewed as part of "a love generation," and proved enamored with the music, itself often drug-inflected, of Bob Dylan, the Beatles, Jefferson Airplane, Country Joe & the Fish, Jimi Hendrix, and an array of acid rock groups. The hippies, as the newest countercultural participants were called, gravitated to Greenwich Village and San Francisco's Haight-Ashbury, where a Summer of Love was supposed to take place in 1967, and musical venues like the Fillmore West in San Francisco and the Fillmore East in New York City's Lower East Side. Large "happenings" also appeared, including the Human Be-In in San Francisco's Golden Gate Park in January 1967, Monterey Pop that summer, and the Woodstock Festival, where 400,000 gathered on a dairy farm among New York's Catskill Mountains during August 1969, amid mud, rain, and sun.

At its purest, the counterculture, as exemplified by beats and hippies, fit within the pantheon of American radicalism. Commercialism ensnared the counterculture of the 1960s and later, and yet, for a time at least, it possessed radical, arguably even revolutionary potential, as the Yippies and members of the Establishment recognized. Before falling prey to it, the counterculture challenged that very commercialism, along with capitalism itself, through communes, collectives, cooperatives, and groups like the San Francisco Diggers, who gave away food and clothing, and symbolized the counterculture at its essence. Publicized by underground newspapers that threaded the counterculture, free concerts and hip stores demonstrated the possibility of an alternative mode of operating. The underground press, initially including the *Los Angeles Free Press*, *Fifth Estate* (Detroit), the *East Village Other*, the *Berkeley Barb*, the *San Francisco Oracle*, and *The Rag* (Austin), sought to evangelize for both the counterculture and the Movement. Eventually, hundreds of underground publications cropped up, some lasting for only a few issues but others, like *The Rag*, serving as both a fulcrum for radical ideas and something of a community, notwithstanding often hostile and sometimes dangerous, even deadly, environments. Founded by Raymond Mungo and Marshall Bloom, Liberation News Service strove to weave together antiestablishment papers and offer "hard information" to Movement activists.

But the counterculture possessed fatal flaws of its own, including rampant sexism, even misogyny, degrees of racism, and a too ready attraction for the very material objects it supposedly reviled. And drugs both connected first the beats and then the much larger group of hippies, but also left in their wake ruined lives and ravaged minds. The young, with not wholly formed psyches, were especially prone to becoming casualties of the resort to illicit pharmacology.

On a more positive note, the counterculture proved emancipatory for many and spurred incredible visual artistry, in addition to the musical brilliance displayed by Dylan's *Highway 61 Revisited*, Beatles' offerings from *Rubber Soul* through *Let It Be*, the Airplane's *Surrealistic Pillow*, Country Joe's *Electric Music for the Mind and Body*, Hendrix's *Are You Experienced*, and numerous other albums. There were, for example, the poster and album covers designed by Rick Griffin, Alton Kelley, Victor Moscoso, Stanley Mouse, and Wes Wilson, and the underground cartoonist sketches of Ron Cobb, Robert Crumb, and Gilbert Shelton.

* * *

The counterculture's less than ideal treatment of women, which matched that of the Movement in general, was yet another reason why so many activists were drawn to second-wave feminism during the 1960s and 1970s. Like their antebellum sisters, New Left activists came to view SDS and SNCC, by the mid-60s, as riddled with sexism. The modern American women's movement was surfacing, despite the latest version of a cult of domesticity that took place following World War II. As had occurred a generation earlier, gender roles underwent alterations during the war, with women entering both industrial plants, resulting in the iconic image of "Rosie the Riveter," and the U.S. Armed Forces. At war's end, concerns about a possible return to the depression and desires for security led to the extolling of the male-dominated nuclear family.

And yet, contrasting, even contradictory developments were in the offing. Published in 1953, the second book-length report by the Institute for Sex Research, headed by Alfred Kinsey, revealed that almost half of the women sampled had sexual intercourse before marriage and that a quarter of married women had extramarital affairs by the time they turned forty. New images of women flitted through the lens of popular culture, with characters like *I Love Lucy*'s Lucy Ricardo and *The Honeymooners*' Alice Kramden challenging gender constraints. In 1955, the Daughters of Bilitis, initially a group of eight women based in San Francisco, was established as a social club by Phyllis Lyon and Del Martin, who reasoned that "women needed privacy . . . not only from the watchful eye of the police, but from gaping tourists in the bars and from inquisitive parents and families."

The Food and Drug Administration's approval on May 9, 1960, of Enovid-10, a birth control pill, soon reshaped American sexual relations, despite fierce opposition, particularly emanating from the Catholic Church. The Kennedy administration provided additional backing for the alteration of gender relations though the President's Commission on the Status of Women, originally headed by Eleanor Roosevelt and later, Esther Peterson. Its report, issued on October 11, 1963, prohibited sex-based wage discrimination, and called for paid maternity leave, universal child care, and judicial acknowledgment of women's equality under the Fourteenth Amendment. That came on the heels of publication of Betty Friedan's book, *The Feminine Mystique*, and the recent passage of the Equal Pay Act, designed to prevent sex-based wage disparities. A woman with Old Left political ties, Friedan highlighted the anxiety and unhappiness that afflicted so many women distressed about "the problem that has no name." Title VII of the Civil Rights Act of 1964 prohibited job discrimination based on "race, color, religion, sex, or national origin." Even the U.S. Supreme Court was shifting course, as exemplified by its 7–2 ruling in the case of *Griswold v. Connecticut* (1965) involving statutory prohibitions regarding the providing of contraception information. Justice William O. Douglas's opinion articulated a "right to marital privacy," deeming it "of such a character that it cannot be denied without violating those fundamental principles of liberty and justice which lie at the base of our civil and political institutions."

In the mid-1960s, Mary King and Sandra Cason Hayden delivered a pair of papers, one untitled and the other titled "A Kind of Memo," bemoaning the rampant sexism that afflicted the Movement. They complained about the patriarchal nature of their fellow male activists, the assignment of women to menial tasks, and the refusal to take seriously concerns about "gender contradictions." King and Hayden admitted that "objectively, the chances seem nil that we could start a movement based on anything as distant to general American thought as a sex-caste system." Seemingly proving their point, the early response by male SDS members to charges of sexism was largely hostile or, at best, dismissive.

Friedan and Pauli Murray, the African American attorney and civil rights activist, were among the founders of the National Organization for Women (NOW), established in 1966. Its statement of purpose affirmed the need "for a new movement toward true equality for all women in America, and toward a fully equal partnership of the sexes, as part of the world-wide revolution of human rights now taking place within and beyond our national borders." The organization subsequently proposed a Bill of Rights for Women, which urged passage of the Equal Rights Amendment, enforcement of legally mandated equal employment opportunities, paid maternity leave, and tax deductions related to "home and child care expenses for working parents." NOW called for child care day centers, unrestricted "access to contraceptive information and devices," legalization of abortion, job training, and equal educational opportunities.

The women's movement, like the other left-oriented movements of the period, continued to display various strands, some more radical than others. In January 1967, *New Left Notes* included SNCC veteran Jane Adams's article, "People's Power: On Equality for Women," which indicated that relationships in American society were inherently unequal, rooted in dominant-submissive relationships. The cover of the June 26, 1967, issue of *New Left Notes*, which highlighted the SDS National Convention in Ann Arbor, featured a smiling blond woman, sporting a rifle, and the heading, "The New American Woman." The convention included a workshop that urged greater autonomy for women and a challenge to "male chauvinism." Radical feminists began forming new political groups, generally with both a feminist and a socialist orientation, and they began to congregate in small gatherings, constructing consciousness-raising groups. Each individual was encouraged to participate, expected only to speak truthfully and to maintain everything related during the sessions in confidence.

No group was initially more instrumental in exploring consciousness-raising than New York Radical Women (NYRW). Pam Allen and Shulamith

Firestone created NYRW in the fall of 1967, soon joined by Carol Hanish, Robin Morgan, and Kathie Sarachild. By the following spring, Firestone pulled together *Notes from the First Year*, which contained some remarkable pieces, including her own "When Women Rap About Sex" and "On Abortion," Anne Koedt's "The Myth of the Vaginal Orgasm," and Kathy Amatniek's "Funeral Oration for the Birth of Traditional Womanhood." Cell 16, a radical feminist organization based in Boston, delved into Valerie Solanas's *SCUM Manifesto*, which decried men's "pussy envy," worthlessness, conformity, "subhuman" quality, and wholly self-centered nature. One of the first women's groups to demand separation from men, Cell 16, in historian Alice Echols's estimation, set the stage, at least theoretically, for lesbian separatism.

The protest NYRW undertook at the Miss America Pageant in Atlantic City in September garnered greater attention for both the organization and radical feminism. NYRW conducted pickets on the Atlantic City boardwalk, holding signs that decried the objectified nature of the beauty contest, including "IF YOU WANT MEAT—GO TO THE BUTCHER SHOP," "WOMEN ARE ENSLAVED BY BEAUTY STANDARDS," "UP AGAINST THE WALL, MISS AMERICA," "MISS AMERICA IS A BIG FALSIE," "WELCOME TO THE MISS AMERICA CATTLE AUCTION," "CAN MAKE-UP COVER THE WOUNDS OF OUR OPPRESSION?" Tossing a shredded copy of *Playboy* into a trash can, dancing protestors shouted, "Liberation now!" As the show went on, demonstrators unfurled a banner reading "WOMEN'S LIBERATION."

During Halloween, the Women's International Terrorist Conspiracy from Hell (W.I.T.C.H.), a NYRW offshoot, made its initial public appearance, engaging in guerrilla theater or "zaps" down Wall Street. Directing its ire at Wall Street rather than men, W.I.T.C.H. termed itself "a total concept, a new dimension of women. It means breaking the bond of woman as a biologically and sexually defined creature. It implies the destruction of passivity, consumerism and commodity fetishism." It asked, "Who is the enemy?" and promised to "name names . . . trademarks and brand names." In mid-February, W.I.T.C.H. ridiculed Bridal Fairs in both New York City and San Francisco, having posted stickers that read "Confront the Whore-makers." Sporting black veils, they hectored women attending the fairs, singing, "Here come the slaves/Off to their graves." They released white mice in Madison Square Garden, and issued leaflets denouncing marriage as "dehumanizing," amounting to "legal whoredom for women."

Shulamith Firestone and Ellen Willis founded Redstockings, an avowedly radical feminist group that desired "a new left." Members of Redstockings were present during a legislative hearing on abortion in February 1969, when the only speakers were twelve men and a nun. In protest, Redstockings conducted an abortion speak-out the next month in the West Village, where hundreds listened as women talked about either having had illegal abortions or babies they gave up for adoption. Carol Hanisch, a key figure in both NYRW and Redstockings, and one of the instigators of the Miss America Pageant protest, produced a paper subsequently titled "The Personal Is Political," declaring that both facets of the movement needed to be intertwined. The Feminists, founded by Ti-Grace Atkinson, insisted "the male role . . . must be annihilated." Firestone, Koedt, Stanton-Anthony Brigade, and Cellestine Ware were instrumental in the founding of yet another group, New York Radical Feminists (NYRF), during the late fall of 1969. Its manifesto called for wiping away the "sex class system" that resulted in women being exploited. Emerging that same year, the National Association for the Repeal of Abortion Laws (later the National Abortion Rights Action League) championed reproductive freedom.

* * *

The issue of lesbianism rapidly became a point of contention within the women's movement. The notion of gay empowerment exploded into public consciousness during the summer of 1969, when homosexual men and women battled with police inside the Stonewall Inn, a gay bar, and out on the streets in Greenwich Village. The readiness of gays and lesbians to assert their rights and demand being treated with dignity thrilled many in the Movement and beyond it, while triggering new questions or igniting submerged ones into how homosexuals were perceived and kept apart from the American mainstream. The women's movement was hardly immune to the volcanic-like nature of what came to be known as gay liberation. Not all feminists were pleased, with Betty Friedan decrying "the lavender menace" inside the American women's movement.

The Stonewall riots demonstrated that the gay movement was itself divided, as leaders from the Daughters of Bilitis and the Mattachine Society confronted younger, more militant activists. Jim Fouratt, a Yippie founder and early proponent of gay liberation, recalled, "We wanted to end the homophile movement. We wanted them to join us in making the gay revolution." This was somewhat ironic as the Mattachine Society, established in 1950 at the height of the McCarthyite phase of the postwar red scare, and DOB had been condemning homophobia since their inception, demanding the discarding of laws prohibiting homosexuality and insisting on equal treatment for gay men and women. Various Mattachine founders, including Harry Hay, were CP members, who formed a cell, then set up discussion groups for both gay men and lesbians. Mattachine's Statement of Missions and Purposes compared the emerging "highly ethical homosexual culture" with that "of our fellow-minorities": Jews, blacks, and Latinos. Resulting red-baiting and the homophobia displayed by the Eisenhower administration proved crippling, but DOB soon appeared, and certain venues remained hospitable to gays, like portions of Greenwich Village, North Beach, and Venice, where the beats frequented.

Well before Stonewall, gays exhibited, on occasion, a readiness to fight back in different ways. In 1958, gays conducted something of a riot as police engaged in "routine harassment" at Cooper's Donuts, a popular hangout in downtown Los Angeles. Urging more measured media coverage, gay activists also saw one of their own, Jose Sarria, a waiter and drag performer, become the first avowed homosexual candidate in the country to run for public office, when he sought a seat on the San Francisco Board of Supervisors in 1961. Concerns about harassment of gay bars led to formation of the Tavern Guild in San Francisco and the Police Department named Elliot Blackstone to serve as a liaison to the "homophile community."

New York City and San Francisco provided much of the impetus for the early gay rights movement. Gay and lesbian activists in San Francisco joined with local liberal Protestant clergy, led by the Reverend Ted McIllvenna of Glide Memorial Methodist Church, to establish the Council on Religion and the Homosexual, seeking to educate and promote dialogue between religious leaders and gays. Also appearing in that coastal city, the Society for Individual Rights (SIR) demonstrated a new assertiveness and inclusiveness on the part of gay men and women, desirous of carving out a "community feeling." As the reporter Bill Brent recalls, SIR featured "parties, dances, and entertainment of all kinds," including "bowling leagues, bridge clubs, meditation groups, art classes, and more." It operated a gift shop, transmitted information regarding sexually transmitted diseases, and soon ran the nation's first gay community center. But gays also conducted pickets, including in front of the U.S. Army's induction center at 39 Whitehall Street in New York City, condemning the military's gay phobic approach, which resulted in witch hunts and release of homosexuals with less than honorable discharges. The picket signs read "'Homosexuals Died for US, Too,' 'Love and Let Love,' and 'Army Invades Sexual Privacy,'" reports the writer and activist Will Kohler. In April 1966, SIR set up the first gay community center, while Mattachine Society members Dick Leitsch, John Timmins, and Randy Wicker conducted a "Sip-In" in Greenwich Village. They entered a tavern, *Julius*, at Waverly Place and 10th Street, which sold beer for fifteen cents and hamburgers for half-a-buck, announced their sexual orientation, and ordered drinks. The bartender responded, "Hey, you're gay, I can't serve you," placing his hand over a glass.

That summer, a youth organization, Vanguard, emerged in San Francisco's Tenderloin district, urging "street power" to protect gay and transgender young people. The Street Orphans, a lesbian street group, also appeared. Members were involved in the Compton's Cafeteria riot in August at 101 Taylor Street in the Tenderloin. Although previously tolerated there, transgender youth, drag queens, and hustlers were suddenly no longer welcome, resulting in picketing. A drag queen tossed a cup of coffee in the face of a policeman, who had taken hold of her. The place "erupted," with tables turned over, silverware thrown, sugar shakers hurled into windows and doors, the historian Susan Stryker indicates. Heavy purses landed on policemen, while outside dozens battled efforts to corral them. A cop car was trashed and a newsstand set on fire, National Public Radio's Nicole Pasulka writes.

As harassment leading to violence continued, gays continued to push back. In early 1967, the recently established PRIDE, standing for Personal Rights in Defense and Education, called for members to "join Negroes, Mexicans, hippies" in demonstrating opposition to "the Establishment war on minorities." Hundreds turned out for the Black Cat Protest at the corner of Sunset and Hyperion in Los Angeles, the largest such gathering in American history, freelance journalist Ben Ehrenreich notes. Placards read "No More Abuse of Our Rights and Dignity," "Abolish Arbitrary Arrest," "Peace Officers—NOT Storm Troopers," "Blue Fascism Must Go!" and "Stop Illegal Search and Seizure." Out of the protest emerged *The Advocate*, published by PRIDE to highlight issues of concern to gays.

The matter of gay rights garnered greater attention than ever before following the Stonewall riots. The Mattachine Society led public forums and demonstrations to spur public engagement, but activists like New Left veteran Michael Brown, Bill Katzenberg, and Charles Pitt printed leaflets reading "Do You Think Homosexuals Are Revolting? You Bet Your Sweet Ass We Are" and terming Stonewall "the hairpin drop heard around the world." Inspired by a flyer from Brown, headed "GAY POWER" and calling for a "Homosexual Liberation Meeting," they soon spun off from Mattachine, forming the Gay Liberation Front (GLF). Chapters quickly sprang up in Los Angeles, New York City, San Francisco, and Washington, D.C. Members conducted "gay-ins," dances, protests, fundraisers, and consciousness-raising sessions, while employing the slogan "No revolution without us!" They proudly referred to themselves as "gay," a word often avoided by homosexuals earlier. Led by Brown, Lois Hart, Karla Jay, Bob Kohler, Bob Martin, Marty Robinson, and Martha Shelley, GLF protested at major media outlooks, ranging from *Time* to *The Village Voice*. They were angered by the *Village Voice*'s employment of such terms as "dyke" and "faggot," rather than "gay" and "lesbian." Asked what made them revolutionaries, GLF activists responded, "We identify ourselves with all the oppressed: the Vietnamese, the third world, the blacks, the workers . . . all those oppressed by this rotten, dirty, vile, fucked-up capitalist conspiracy."

Smaller groups like the Red Butterfly, which made up a Marxist group inside the GLF, appeared. Gay activist John Lauritsen helped to construct the small cell, which formed something of "a radical intelligentsia within GLF," desirous of exploring, as he recalls, a "developing theory of gay liberation and linking it to other movements for social change." Non-doctrinaire, Red Butterfly members read Marx and Engels, Marcuse, and Reich, among other radical theoreticians. They promoted gay pamphlets and attended antiwar and Black Panther sessions, delivering various critiques of "gay demands."

In December 1969, various GLF members, including Arthur Evans, Jim Owles, and Marty Robinson, established the Gay Activists Alliance (GAA), which determined to work within the existing political system but hardly meekly. Its constitution propounded an agenda "exclusively devoted to the liberation of homosexuals," while affirming "the right to make love with anyone, anyway, anytime," and "the right to treat and express our bodies as we will." Members carried out "zaps," public protests or confrontations designed to garner attention to various issues and helped to organize the first gay pride parade in Manhattan.

During a GLF session at the beginning of 1970, an unknown young author, Rita Mae Brown, stood on a chair and declared, "Enough already. We can't be out in NOW, the guys dominate this, we need a lesbian feminist civil rights movement." She was referring to the mean-spirited statement by Betty Friedan, warning about "the lavender menace"—lesbians—crippling the women's movement. Brown and a small number of like-minded women, including Karla Jay and Barbara Love, founded another organization, Radicalesbians.

On June 27 and June 28, the initial gay pride parades, intended to commemorate the Stonewall riots and to celebrate a new spirit in the fight for homosexual liberation, were conducted in Chicago, Los Angeles, New York City, and San Francisco. GLF's flyer announcing "Liberation Day" insisted "Freedom is never given—it must be taken," and indicated gay liberation was "for the homosexual who stands up, and fights back." Craig Rodwell, who had opened the nation's first gay bookstore, the Oscar Wilde Memorial Bookshop on Christopher Street in Greenwich Village, three years earlier, and Michael Brown helped to plan the rally in Manhattan that saw thousands march into Central Park and conduct a "gay-in' in the Sheep Meadow. A chant rang out, "Say it clear, say it loud. Gay is good, gay is proud."

* * *

The desire for empowerment that was derived from the civil rights crusade and fueled the women's movement and gay liberation also produced additional drives involving emancipation of little considered but often exploited or neglected groups. These include Latinos, Native Americans, and Asian Americans, all of whom participated in movements of their own by the 1960s and 1970s. The struggle by Latinos was both longstanding and of recent vintage. In parts of California, that effort dated back to the mid-nineteenth century, when non-Latinos arrived in large numbers, altering the demographic makeup of the new state and determining to create white-dominated communities. During the first several decades of the twentieth century, Latinos formed advocacy groups such as the League of United Latin American Citizens and the American G.I. Forum, to arrest ethnic discrimination.

Following the lead of community organizer Fred Ross, naval veteran Cesar Chavez, who had toiled alongside his family as a migrant field hand, joined with Dolores Huerta, whose migrant laborer father became a union organizer, in setting up, during 1962, the National Farmworkers Association, later part of the United Farm Workers of America (UFW). The UFW first attracted considerable attention with its support of grape pickers—many Filipino, Mexican, or Chicano—who, beginning in September 1965, went on strike against growers in Delano, a small central California town. Chavez led a 300-mile march from Delano to Sacramento, eliciting attention for the farm workers' struggle. By the third year of the strike, which now included a boycott of California table grapes, a number of young farm workers became increasingly frustrated at their mistreatment by large growers. Chavez insisted on adhering to nonviolence, along the lines of both Gandhi and Martin Luther King Jr. He conducted fasts at different points, as during a twenty-five-day period in early 1968, which he ended only after having lost thirty-five pounds and by breaking bread with Senator Robert F. Kennedy. The July 4 issue of *Time* displayed an artist's rendering of Chavez, with a banner to his right reading "The Grapes of Wrath, 1969: Mexican-Americans on the March."

Chavez and the farm workers movement sought to ameliorate the exploitative, abusive treatment many Mexican and Mexican-American laborers encountered. *La Causa* or *El Movimiento* spurred other protest efforts, ranging from direct action to demonstrations. A former highly ranked boxer who was also a poet, a playwright, and one-time director of Denver's War on Poverty, Rodolfo "Corky" Gonzales, founded *La Cruzada* or the Crusade for Justice (1966), which extolled Chicano nationalism. The organization hosted a series of National Chicano Youth Liberations conclaves, which issued the document, *Espiritual de Aztlan*, referring to Mexican land grabbed by the United States. Reies Lopez Tijerina, a former itinerant preacher called "the Malcolm X of the Chicano movement," initiated a land grant movement in northern New Mexico, *La Alianza Federal de Mercedes*, demanding compensatory treatment for the American takeover of Mexican territory. In June 1967, twenty La Alianza members, carrying rifles, semi-automatic weapons, and dynamite, raided the Rio Arriba County courthouse located in Tierra Amarilla, New Mexico. They were looking for District Attorney Alfonos Sanchez, who had ordered the arrest of several Alianza leaders. A gun battle unfolded in the shooting of two police officers, and the taking of two hostages. Two trials followed, the second resulting in Tijerina's conviction on kidnapping and aggravated assault charges.

Along with Chavez, Gonzales, and Tijerina, Jose Angel Gutierrez was seen as one of the "Four Horsemen of the Chicano Movement." Born in Crystal City, Texas, he was involved with the formation of the Mexican American Youth Organization (1967, MAYO) in San Antonio. MAYO preached cultural nationalism, political action, and mass protests, to 10,000 Latino public-school students, angered by discriminatory treatment, who were engaged in a mass walkout in Los Angeles. Attorneys established the Mexican American Legal Defense and Educational Fund (MALDEF, 1968) in San Antonio, drawing on a five-year, $2.2 million grant from the Ford Foundation, to safeguard Latino civil rights. Gutierrez elected to return to Crystal City, where, as the new decade opened, he founded La Raza Unida Party (LRUP), which quickly took control of the local school board.

Following the example set by the Black Panthers, the Brown Berets first appeared in East Los Angeles in late 1967, soon offering public condemnations of police brutality. They subsequently initiated that mass walkout by public school students in Los Angeles, protesting inadequate facilities. They adopted the term Chicano, long considered denigrating as representing Americanized Mexican-Americans and employed the motto, "To Serve, Observe, and to Protect." Their own ten-point program, laid out in June 1968, urged the following: unification of all Chicanos, bilingual education, a Civilian Police Review Board comprised of community members, teaching "the true history of the Mexican American," and hiring police who lived in Mexican-American communities and spoke Spanish.

Another important Latino group appearing at the end of the 1950s, the Young Lords Organization (YLO), largely focused on the concerns and problems confronting Puerto Ricans. Puerto Ricans gangs like the Young Lords, headed by Cha Cha Jimenez, acquired greater political consciousness, becoming involved in substance abuse efforts, food relief, other community enterprises, and direct action or protests related to government and mafia-connected real estate offices, as well as police stations. Jimenez and Fred Hampton, a leader in the Illinois chapter of the Black Panthers, conversed about revolutionary politics. Along with William "Preacherman" Fesperman of the Young Patriots Organization and Carlos Montes of the Brown Berets, they created the Rainbow Coalition.

Influenced by the free breakfast program of the Panthers, the Young Lords undertook a similar effort in East Harlem, the area above the Upper East Side often referred to as Spanish Harlem. They demanded that the city of New York improve garbage collection there. They launched lead poisoning detection tests, and later carried out TB testing in both Spanish Harlem and the Bronx. To draw attention to the plight of the poor, they conducted occupations of both vacant lands and various institutions, including hospitals and churches. In conjunction with the Panthers, the Young Lords initiated the Health Revolutionary Unity Movement at Gouverneur Hospital on the Lower East Side, to organize hospital workers.

The YLO laid out a "13-Point Program and Platform," prefaced by a pronouncement that it was "a Revolutionary Political Party Fighting for the Liberation of All Oppressed People." The Program and Platform called for self-determination for Puerto Ricans, which amounted to independence for the island and liberation within the United States, "self-determination for all Latinos," "liberation of all third world people," and an end to racism. It also lauded community control of Puerto Rican institutions and territory, revolutionary culture, and socialism. The Young Lords supported immediate removal of American soldiers from Puerto Rico, emancipation of all political prisoners, equality for women, an international confederation against anti-communism, and liberation through "armed self-defense and armed struggle."

The relationship of Native Americans to the United States, like that of African Americans and Latinos, had long been torturous. Even prior to the founding of the American nation, white settlers had desired land Native-Americans were associated with, leading to continued clashes and practices that many historians deem genocidal. As some nineteenth-century Americans sought to push Native Americans onto reservations or aside altogether, resistance occurred as well, resulting in the Indian wars whose conclusion was virtually preordained, given the disparity of resources. With the Native American threatening to become the Vanishing American, seemingly well-intentioned but paternalistic reformers like Carl Schurz and Helen Hunt Jackson favored assimilation into the dominant society. What followed was the takeover of Indian land, the tearing apart of communal reservations, and continued ethnocentric and racist stereotypes. The 1924 Indian Citizenship Act provided citizenship and the franchise to all Native Americans, which some did not desire. Led by the Bureau of Indian Affairs (BIA) director, John Collier, FDR's New Deal administration attempted to address the plight of Native Americans, many mired at the bottom of the socioeconomic ladder. The Indian Reorganization Act sought to nurture Native American cultural heritage and tribal self-government. The federal government's policy of termination, initiated in 1953, called for rapidly making Native Americans "subject to the same laws and . . . the same privileges and responsibilities . . . applicable to other citizens of the United States." Over the span of little more than a decade, this furthered termination of 109 Indian tribes but also federal responsibility over 2.5 million acres of trust land.

All along, various Native Americans agitated for their rights. The National Congress of American Indians (NCAI), established in 1944, became the leading pan-Indian political organization and turned into a significant lobbying force. The NCAI fought for the rights of Alaskan natives, opposed voter discrimination, and set up the Indians Claims Commission that emphasized "treaty rights, tribal sovereignty, and identity issues." It relied on legal and political action and drew on the motto, "Indians Don't Demonstrate." During the latter stages of the 1950s, the Six Nations people in New York State employed "passive resistance and militant protests" to stave off construction projects and land seizures, the historian Troy R. Johnson records. Similar battles occurred elsewhere, and hundreds of Native Americans headed for the BIA headquarters, located in the nation's capital, in 1959, to condemn the policy of termination.

The NCAI provided seeds for the Native American activism of the 1960s, the decade in which it called greater attention to the economic and medical concerns of Indians. As the historian Bradely G. Shreve indicates, the National Indian Youth Council (NIYC), which appeared in 1961 in Gallup, New Mexico, and would be noted for gender inclusivity and disavowal of cultural assimilation, provided more impetus for inter-tribal Native American activism. Looking to their elders for guidance, young people in NYIC emphasized the tenets that would be linked to the era's Red Power movement: Indian sovereignty, self-determination, treaty rights, and cultural preservation. Native American college and university students gathered at Indian youth councils, soon determining to contest assimilation. Like black and Latino activists, they resorted to direct action. Beginning in 1964, the NIYC put out *Americans Before Columbus*, an early influential Red Power newspaper. During fish-ins at Washington State that same year, largely initiated by Bruce Wilkie (Makah) and Hank Adams (Assiniboine) and patterned after civil rights sit-ins, the NIYC contested the arrests of tribal members seeking to sustain rights to off-reservation fishing guaranteed by treaties. The NIYC helped to establish the Survival of American Indians Association, designed to carry out more direct-action protests. The struggle in Washington State led to the NYIC first employing the phrase "Red Power," soon associated with the Indian rights movement.

As the fish-ins occurred, a group of Sioux—Allen Cottier, Martin Martinez, Richard D. McKenzie, Walter Means, and Garfield Spotted Elk—engaged in a brief occupation on March 8, 1964, of Alcatraz Island, located off the San Francisco coast. Perceived injustices and lack of government concern, coupled with the ferment of the era, led to materialization of new Native American organizations and political action. United Native Americans (UNA), a pan-Indian group, appeared in the Bay Area in the summer of 1968, determined to promote Native Americans' general welfare. Also during the summer of 1968, the American Indian Movement (AIM) was founded by Dennis Banks, Clyde Bellecourt, Vernon Bellecourt, and George Mitchell, in Minneapolis, to condemn discrimination and police brutality. That December, Mowhawk Indians carried out a blockade at the Cornwall

International Bridge, to protest curbs restraining Mohawk Indians from moving back and forth between Canada and the United States.

In November 1969, just under 100 Native Americans, who proclaimed themselves to be operating on behalf of Indians of All Tribes (IAT), undertook an occupation of Alcatraz Island. This takeover would go on for eighteen months, ending only with an ouster by federal agents. Buildings soon offered messages in keeping with the occupation: "Peace and Freedom. Welcome. Home of the Free Indian Land," "Red Power," and "Custer Had It Coming." The occupiers delivered the "Alcatraz Proclamation," addressed to "the Great White Father and His People 1969." This manifesto expressed a determination to construct centers for Native American Studies, spirituality, and ecology, along with an Indian Training School and an American Indian Museum. Problems soon developed on the island, with additional occupiers arriving, a number suffering from drug addictions, and conditions deteriorating. In the spring, the government shut off electrical power and phone service, and public sympathy waned. The occupation ended when government agents removed the last fifteen individuals still on Alcatraz Island.

Three years later, AIM, led by Russell Means and Dennis Banks, acquired still greater notoriety, particularly with a seventy-one-day siege at the impoverished village of Wounded Knee, South Dakota, located on the Pine Ridge Indian Reservation, which began on February 27, 1973. Over eight decades earlier, the U.S. Cavalry had carried out a massacre of 146 Sioux men, women, and children. AIM members now led 250 Sioux in an effort to draw attention to the plight of Native peoples, but the Wounded Knee takeover and holding of eleven hostages was but one of scores of actions by AIM activists around the country. The seizure hardly ended well, with a U.S. Marshall and an FBI agent shot and two Indians killed.

Garnering far less attention, radical Asian Americans nevertheless were making their distinctive mark as well through the Asian American Movement, which was shaped, to a considerable extent, by the Vietnam War and the civil rights struggle. New student groups, including the Asian American Political Alliance at UC Berkeley, appeared. Its newsletter asserted, "American society is historically racist and one that has systemically employed social discrimination and economic imperialism, both domestically and internationally, exploiting all non-white people in the process of building up their affluent society." A co-founder, Yuji Ichioka, devised the term "Asian American"—"a radical political identity," according to movement participant Gordon Lee—when establishing the pan-Asian group. By the spring of 1968, students at UCLA sought, but to no avail, an ethnic studies department that would possess its own faculty, who would deliver courses dealing with African American, Latino, Asian, and Native American anthropology and history.

Producing their own, self-funded paper, five UCLA students began publishing *Gidra* the following spring, a newspaper discussing the Third World Liberation Front, which desired "eradication of institutional racism"; rescission of the summary firing of the Japanese-American county coroner, Thomas Noguchi; prohibition of "yellow prostitution"; and termination of the racist history Asian Americans had withstood. Between issues, staff members studied capitalism, the Cold War, Marxism, and Maoism. One of the paper's founders, Mike Murase, joined with other Asian Americans to make their presence felt at antiwar gatherings, holding signs recalling a World War II internment camp, Manzanar, and exhorting, "Stop killing our Asian sisters!" They recognized the racist lens through which many American soldiers waged the Vietnam War, with easy references to killing "gooks." Recalling that period, historian Karen Ishizuka relates coming of age in the midst of the Vietnam conflict: "An unholy alliance of racism and imperialism, like nothing before or since, the war united Asians in America who, regardless of our various ethnicities, looked more enemy than American." Asian Americans for Action, developing back East, saw the need for a melding of black power and antiwar opposition, a linkage that the poet Amy Uyematsu recognized in her essay, "The Emergence of Yellow Power," which appeared in *Gidra*.

The sociologist Sharon M. Quinsaat notes that Asian Americans were also participating in community battles, including those involving removal of elderly tenants from the International Hotel located in Manilatown, a once vibrant Filipino community in downtown San Francisco. But beginning in 1968, the I-Hotel, which housed seasonal farm laborers and merchant marines, became a target for the San Francisco Redevelopment Agency. Its head, Justin Herman, was heard to say, "This land is too valuable to permit poor people to park on it." The Asian American Movement insisted on housing rights for indigents elsewhere, including in Los Angeles, Seattle, Philadelphia, and New York City, through organizations like Little Tokyo People's Rights, Yellow Brotherhood, Asian American Hardcore, the East Wind collective, Yellow Seeds, I Wor Kuen ("Righteous Harmonious Fist"), and the Creative Arts Program. Members could be found in Hawaii, attempting to ensure land rights outside urban centers. Asian American activists, drawing on a slogan, "Serve the People," Mao offered as the Cultural Revolution continued in China, demanded that local colleges and universities help stave off evictions. During the fall of 1968, Asian American students at San Francisco State joined in protests and strike activities.

By the winter of 1969, the Red Guard Party, largely made up of young Chinese-Americans, could be found in San Francisco's Chinatown. International events, the Movement's vibrant nature in the Bay Area, and "miserable conditions" in Chinatown set the stage for this new organization. Its members had attempted, as early as 1967, to set up a non-profit, cooperative organization, Leway, Inc., which was intended to funnel moneys for youth-based programs. Standing for "Legitimate Way," Leway was designed to terminate police harassment, but instead itself became a target for the police. Eventually, Leway participants participated in the ongoing struggle at San Francisco State, and engaged in an examination of the Panthers' 10-point program. Having to contend with the newly formed San Francisco Tactical Squad, Leway leaders determined that "an out-front political organization" was required. Their identification with the Chinese Communist Party was profound, but the new Red Guard Party concentrated on "anti-redevelopment struggles," challenging the destruction of the Chinese Playground, picketing as the Kwong Chow Temple was wiped out, and opposing the tearing down of the International Hotel. The party also offered Breakfast for Children and Free Lunch programs, while viewing itself as a participant in "the American revolutionary movement." One of the best known activists, the Japanese immigrant, Shin'ya Ono, a transplant like Harry Chang, who emigrated from Korea and induced several young radicals in the Bay Area to explore both Marxism and racism, served as an editor for *Studies on the Left*, later joining Weatherman before being jailed for participating in the Days of Rage in Chicago.

* * *

One of the largest and most enduring movements of the 1960s revolved around the despoliation human beings were visiting upon the global ecosystem. The environmental movement was yet another with roots in the Progressive period but radicalized during the post-World War II era. From Thoreau's extolling of nature and Walden Pond to George Perkins Marsh's warning in 1864, "The earth is fast becoming an unfit home for its noblest inhabitant," a small but growing number of activists proved determined to protect the American wilderness. Following the Civil War, the explorer John Wesley Powell released *Report on the Lands of the Arid Regions of the West* (1878), George Grinnell's Audubon Society committed to protecting birds and their natural habitats, while John Muir's Sierra Club focused on wilderness preservation and outdoor recreation. Both Theodore Roosevelt and his distant cousin Franklin Delano Roosevelt displayed a determination to set aside vast swaths of forested land and to shield "national monuments." Environmental classics appeared right after World War II, including Fairfield Osborn Jr.'s *Our Plundered Planet* (1948), Aldo Leopold's *A Sand County Almanac and Sketches Here and There* (1949), and Eugene Odum's *Fundamentals of Ecology* (1953).

The Kennedy and Johnson administration proved supportive of environmental protections, with the modern environmental movement in the United States launched by publication of Rachel Carson's *Silent Spring* (1962), which warned of the contaminating effects of pesticides, particularly DDT (dichlorodiphenyltrichloroethane). She wrote, "The most alarming of all man's assaults upon the environment is the contamination of air, earth, rivers, and sea with dangerous and even lethal materials." As the U.S. Senate held hearings on pollution, Abraham Ribicoff told her, "You are the lady who started this," an obvious allusion to how President Lincoln had greeted Harriet Beecher Stowe, author of *Uncle Tom's Cabin*. During her testimony, Carson called for a grass-roots movement to form "citizens' brigades."

During the last half of the 1960s, environmental activism surged in other ways. In 1967, scientists, committed to banning DDT, joined with Art Cooley, Dennis Puleston, and Charlie Wurster to form the Environmental Defense Fund. The next year, the Sierra Club, led by David Brower, battled against the building of government dams in the Grand Canyon. Brower placed full-page ads in the *New York Times*, with one asking, "If They Turn Grand Canyon Into a Cash Register Is Any National Park Safe?" The park ranger and environmental advocate Edward Abbey published *Desert Solitaire*, extolling the southeastern Utah desert and wilderness in general. He viewed the wilderness as an antipode to the "uniformity, artificiality, and technological control" of modern existence.

The entomologist Paul R. Ehrlich's book, *The Population Bomb*, opened with the warning, "The battle to feed all of humanity is over." He predicted that hundreds of millions would soon starve to death, with "an utter breakdown of the capacity of the planet to support humanity." The ecologist Garret Hardin wrote "The Tragedy of the Commons," insisting on the necessity of "relinquishing the freedom to breed, and that very soon." What Ehrlich and Hardin failed to foresee was the Green Revolution, fueled by the biologist Norman Borlaug, who helped to breed varieties of high-yielding crops that staved off anticipated mass famines. In the fall of 1968, Stewart Brand published *The Whole Earth Catalog*, which served as a bible for self-sustaining practitioners. Brand sought to help each reader "share his own education, find his own inspiration, shape his own environment and share his adventure."

Early in 1969, as many as 100,000 gallons of oil began spilling onto the breathtaking coastal line of Santa Barbara, California, following an oil well blowout suffered by Union Oil. The Santa Barbara oil spill helped spur environmental activism on many levels. Get Oil Out! or GOO, a local activist group, demanded an immediate halt of all offshore oil explorations, but the DuBridge Committee, authorized by President Nixon, called for more drilling to relieve pressure in underground reservoirs. As Sun Oil Company began to build a new platform, GOO protestors conducted a "fish-in," but oil exploration continued. A fire in the Cuyahoga River in June also garnered the attention of environmental activists. The sewage and industrial waste-laden river in Northeast Ohio caught fire as train sparks ignited oil-laden debris.

Also in 1969, David Brower, who was much influenced by John Muir's reverence for the wilderness, founded both the League of Conservation Voters and Friends of the Earth. John Nielsen has suggested that "calling David Brower an important activist is like calling Hamlet an important member of the Danish royal court. Brower invented modern American environmental activism." Brower had helped to spur growth of the Sierra Club, battled to protect Dinosaur National Monument, and the Grand Canyon, favored creation of several new national parks and seashores, including Redwood National Park and Point Reyes, and demanded ratification of the 1964 Wilderness Act. Now, Brower sought to create "a global, media-savvy, politically muscular activist group," writes Daniel Coyle, former editor of *Outside* magazine. Friends of the Earth would become "the first truly international environmental group."

In December, having checked out the Santa Barbara spill, Senator Gaylord Nelson discussed the possibility of a national environmental teach-in. He hired twenty-five-year-old Denis Hayes, former president of the Stanford student body and an antiwar activist studying at the Kennedy School of Government, to serve as national coordinator. Hayes put together a staff of eighty-five, including a team of regional coordinators and a media campaign manager—Stephen Cotton, Andrew Garling, Bryce Hamilton, Barbara Reid, and Arturo Sandoval—all drawn from various movements of the era. Senator Nelson wanted "a nationwide demonstration of concern for the environment so large that it would shake the political establishment out of its lethargy and, finally, force this issue permanently onto the national political agenda."

Millions of Americans participated in the first Earth Day celebrations on April 22, 1970, designed to call attention to environmental concerns. A purported ten million public school children joined in "teach-in" programs, while thousands of colleges and community groups held rallies of their own. Nelson considered this the day when "Americans made it clear that they understood and were deeply concerned over the deterioration of our environment and the mindless dissipation of our resources." Mass rallies took place across the country, with 10,000 showing up at the Washington Monument and thousands congregating on Fifth Avenue in Manhattan.

* * *

Receiving sustenance from the temper of the times, a series of additional movements, some that would scarcely have been anticipated even a short while earlier, also appeared. Perhaps unexpectedly, given that Social Security benefits became somewhat more generous and Medicare had been enacted, guaranteeing medical coverage for those sixty-five and older, the elderly comprised their own protest movement as the decade of the 1970s opened. Founder Margaret E. "Maggie" Kuhn, initially involved with the

Young Women's Christian Association in Cleveland before working in New York City for the United Presbyterian Church for twenty-two years, was upset at being forced to retire on turning sixty-five in 1970. She and five other women established the Consultation of Older and Younger Adults for Social Change, whose members were soon referred to as the Gray Panthers. Operating out of Philadelphia, the Gray Panthers battled age discrimination. Even more than that, Kuhn explained, "Gray Panthers are out to make old a beautiful thing, not something to be hidden but something to be declared and affirmed." They stood in solidarity with college students in the Philadelphia area, condemning the war and supporting draft resistance. The Gray Panthers eventually set up a National Media Watch Task Force to oppose stereotyping of older individuals. They also supported affordable housing, national health insurance, reform of nursing homes, and consumer protection.

A young Lebanese-American attorney sparked yet another people's movement that began in the 1960s but attained greater prominence during the following decade and beyond. A graduate of Princeton and Harvard Law School, Ralph Nader sparked the largest consumer movement since the progressive era. Just a year after finishing law school in 1958, he published an article in *The Nation* on car safety, declaring, "It is clear that Detroit today is designing automobiles for style, cost, performance and calculated obsolescence, but not for safety. Doors that fly open on impact, inadequately secured seats, the sharp-edged rearview mirror, pointed knobs on instrument panels and doors, flying glass, the overhead structure—all illustrate the lethal potential of poor design."

Nader acquired national attention with the publication in 1965 of *Unsafe at Any Speed: The Designed-In Dangers of the American Automobile*, a muckraking-like expose. The book opened with the pronouncement, "For over a half a century the automobile has brought death, injury and the most inestimable sorrow and deprivation to millions of people." In early 1966, Nader testified to a Senate subcommittee about automotive safety. Democratic Senator Abraham A. Ribicoff of Connecticut assailed General Motors (GM) on learning that the giant corporation was attempting to dig up dirt on Nader, who had singled out Chevrolet's Corvair as particularly dangerous. Congress began passing legislation mandating more stringent safety standards for automobiles. House Speaker John W. McCormack attributed passage of the National Traffic and Motor Vehicle Safety Act to Nader's "crusading spirit" and belief that "he could do something."

Drawing on the notoriety he had achieved and a substantial settlement from GM, Nader eventually established over two dozen public interest groups, while his staff members were called "Nader's Raiders." He called on law students in 1968 to look into the Federal Trade Commission. His team found the agency "fat with cronyism, torpid through an inbreeding unusual even for Washington, manipulated by the agents of commercial predators,

[and] imperious to governmental and citizen monitoring." The next summer, Nader hired both undergraduate and law students to examine additional government and corporate abuses, including those involving the Interstate Commerce Commission, the Food and Drug Administration, and air pollution. Within a year, over 30,000 students sought 200 summer positions with Nader's groups. In 1969, he set up the Center for Study of Responsive Law and called for a national consumer movement. Later, Nader's Raiders investigated water pollution, First National City Bank (later Citibank), nursing homes, pesticides, and the machinations of California developers and speculators. A series of Nader-sponsored books poured forth. In 1971, hundreds of college students tracked all members of Congress and several important committees, through the Congress Project, which eventually called for passage of a "sunshine law" mandating congressional reforms. Public Citizen also appeared, seeking to "ensure that all citizens are represented in the halls of power." Nader proved instrumental in passage of the Wholesome Meat Act (1967), the Clean Air Act (1970), the Environmental Protection Act (1970), the Occupational Safety and Health Act (1970), the Consumer Product Safety Act (1972), the Safe Drinking Act (1974), and the Freedom of Information Act (1974).

Attempting to speak on behalf of tens of millions of Americans, a disability rights movement unfolded. Long one of the most neglected groups in the nation, disabled individuals had been ridiculed, considered lacking in mental faculties, confined to warehouse-styled institutions, dumped in asylums, compelled to undergo sterilizations, and altogether marginalized. Even exceptional accomplishments by remarkable individuals like the author-activist Helen Keller, who became deaf and blind as an infant, and Franklin D. Roosevelt, who was paralyzed at the age of thirty-nine, failed to dampen stereotypes about the disabled. Veterans disabled owing to service during World War II agitated for government-sponsored rehabilitation, training, and education. Nevertheless, public buildings continued to lack access for the disabled. As the multitude of rights movements flourished in the 1960s, attention was drawn to the plight of the disabled. Sparked by students at UC Berkeley, led by Ed Roberts and a group called "The Rolling Quads," the Independent Living Movement appeared. That movement insisted the disabled "must take the initiative, individually and collectively, in designing and promoting better solutions and must organize themselves for political power. Besides de-professionalization and self-representation . . . de-medicalization of disability, de-institutionalization" were required.

Activists demanded legislation affording rights for the disabled, leading to passage of the 1973 Rehabilitation Act precluding discrimination regarding physical or mental disabilities. The newly created Architectural and Transportation Barriers Compliance Board ordered equal access for the disabled to public services and funding for vocational training. Within two years, Congress agreed to the Education for All Handicapped Children Act, requiring equal access, including mainstreaming, for disabled children to public schools. Later in the decade, activists stepped up the pace of protest, calling on direct action tactics, including lengthy sit-ins at government offices, to demand stronger legislation or government enforcement of existing laws. A group of activists associated with ADAPT (Americans Disabled for Accessible Public Trust, later called Americans Disabled Attendant Programs Today) demanded improved access for the disabled, carrying out demonstrations involving wheelchair users around the country. A precursor, The Gang of Nineteen, had appeared in Denver, exclaiming "We Will Ride" and conducting a blockade.

Two of the most controversial movements of the era, and two of the most short-lived, appeared by the latter stages of the 1960s, those involving prisoner's rights and welfare recipients. For nearly a century, federal courts generally ruled that prisoners lacked constitutional safeguards. But beginning in the early 1960s, the U.S. Supreme Court began countering such a "hands-off" approach. The Black Muslims helped to trigger the movement, filing lawsuits charging that prison officials were denying inmates racial and religious equality. A number of Supreme Court rulings afforded inmates various rights, to the dismay of prison officials and many politicians. *Jones v. Cunningham* (1963) enabled state prisoners to rely on habeas corpus to contest sentencing and prison conditions. *Cooper v. Pate* (1964) indicated that prison officials did not possess carte blanche to handle inmates however they chose to, with an underscoring of the need to safeguard the free exercise of religious rights. The nation's highest court also affirmed, starting with the case of *Johnson v. Avery* (1969), that prisoners could afford each other legal services when those were not provided by prison officials.

The prisoner rights movement was itself shaped by and helped to influence various political and social campaigns during the 1960s and 1970s. The percentage of African Americans behind bars—always disproportionate—increased from the 1950s onward. Malcolm X, Eldridge Cleaver, and George Jackson were among those radicalized by the time they spent as prisoners. Jackson, who co-founded an African American prison gang, joined the Black Panthers, and authored *Soledad Brother* (1970), warned, "This monster—the monster they've engendered in me will return to torment its maker, from the grave, the pit, the profoundest pit. Hurl me into the next existence, the descent into hell won't turn me. . . . I'm going to charge them reparations in blood. I'm going to charge them like a maddened, wounded, rogue male elephant, ears flared, trunk raised, trumpet blaring. . . . War without terms." Incarcerated in Soledad prison, Jackson died during an apparent attempted breakout.

Angered by the recent murder of Jackson, shot while purportedly trying to escape from San Quentin, and influenced by the prison rights movement,

1,000 inmates at the Attica Correctional Facility, located in the north central sector of New York State, took over a pair of cell blocks in September 1971, grabbed thirty guards, and seized the control room. The inmates insisted on better living conditions, an end to racist abuse, and amnesty for the takeover. Negotiations proved fruitless and state troopers and correction officers moved in to regain control of the prison. As the historian Heather Ann Thompson reports, troopers and officers employed force all but indiscriminately, firing at will, engaging in sadistic acts of brutality, and targeting high-profile prisoners like Sam Melville, who, predating Weatherman actions, had directed a series of bombings in New York City, and others who had spoken against ill treatment behind bars. Thirty-nine people, including ten hostages, died as the retaking of prison grounds followed. Such acts continued once the shooting ended, adding to the long-term difficulties encountered by prisoners who bore the trooper-officer onslaught.

Only somewhat less controversial, a national welfare rights movement emerged by the mid-1960s, lasting virtually a full decade. In 1966, former CORE associate national director George Wiley founded the National Welfare Rights Organization (NWRO), most of whose members were poor African American women. Influenced by Frances Fox Piven and Richard Cloward, social work professors at Columbia University, Wiley, himself a former academic and well-known chemist, wanted to further racial justice, with dignity, through the affording of expanded economic opportunities for the indigent. Within three years, NWRO claimed a family membership of 22,000, and conducted a series of public demonstrators, including sit-ins, on behalf of poor Americans of all colors. Over 100,000 individuals participated in NWRO's local campaigns. Although largely situated in the nation's urban "ghettos and barrios," NWRO groups could be found in the rural South, in Appalachia, and in America's midsection. Demanding expanded benefits, adequate day care, clothing, food, furniture, and job-training programs, welfare proponents also called for caseworkers to treat recipients more humanely. A report in the *New York Times* by 1970 indicated that the organization had been involved with "sit-ins in legislative chambers . . . mass demonstrations of several thousand welfare recipients, school boycotts, picket lines, mounted police, tear gas, arrests—and, on occasion, rock-throwing, smashed glass doors, overturned desks, scattered papers and ripped-out phones."

Experienced in union organizing, Johnnie Tillmon, daughter of a migrant sharecropper, demanded that welfare recipients control the organization. Attempting to link up with the women's movement, Tillmon also delivered an essay, "Welfare Is a Women's Issue," which appeared in *Ms.* magazine, founded in 1971 by the feminists Gloria Steinem and Dorothy Pitman Hughes. Tillmon, who replaced Wiley as NWRO's Executive Director at the end of 1972, eloquently stated, "I'm a woman. I'm a black woman. I'm a poor woman. I'm a fat woman. I'm a middle-aged woman. And I'm on welfare. In this country, if you're any one of those things, you count less as a person. If you're all those things, you just don't count, except as a statistic. I am a statistic." The NWRO called for all Americans to be allotted a guaranteed annual income, something that the Nixon administration briefly flirted with, at the behest of domestic adviser Daniel Patrick Moynihan.

Wiley's departure from the organization and financial difficulties led to NWRO's demise, with its doors closed in early 1975. ACORN, a national network of community organizations, fulfilled some of the same purposes, calling for a guaranteed annual income and acquiring many indigent, black, and brown members. Founder Wade Rathke, a former SDS member and a Wiley protege, hoped to build a "cross-class association," that would receive backing from organized labor.

* * *

As the 1960s wound along, the civil rights, New Left, student, and antiwar movements served as inspirations for or were inspired by a host of other examples of progressively-rooted citizen activism, often quite radical in nature. Women, gays, and people of color condemned discriminatory, prejudicial treatment, while seeking, in the face of great opposition and antagonism, to be empowered both individually and collectively. Additional movements arose, fueled by the singular demand to be treated as human beings. Meanwhile, the counterculture, which had flowered during the last half of the 1960s, continued to make its mark, albeit in attenuated form.

Chapter 8

Citizen Activism on Many Fronts

Notwithstanding media representations to the contrary, the 1970s and 1980s resulted in a continued flourishing of American radical movements that were locally based, national in scope, or even international in dimension. Indeed, in the middle of that period the activist Harry Boyte suggested that a "backyard revolution" amounting to a new citizen movement was unfolding in the United States. More recently, the historian Michael S. Foley has indicated that those decades witnessed a profusion of "front porch politics" when millions participated in "citizen advocacy." The new slogan evoking this determination was "think globally, act locally." Activists worked to construct alternative institutions and community-based media. All of this occurred despite the New Left's withering, the counterculture lacking revolutionary potential, and the civil rights movement absent its moral beacon. Nevertheless, many movements that emerged or expanded during the 1960s became more potent or at least attracted more adherents as that decade passed from the scene. A good number emphasized direct action tactics, the kind that the political scientist and pacifist Gene Sharp featured in his landmark study, *The Politics of Nonviolent Action* (1973), which served as a primer for other peace activists.

Both surprisingly and not, given how readily facets of the Movement gravitated to Marxist-Leninist concepts by the end of the 1960s, sectarianism continued to beset the American left. In many ways, this was terribly unfortunate, particularly given the optimistic tenor bordering on utopianism that characterized early SNCC and SDS. The vision of the beloved community and the ideal of participatory democracy faded for many, as Movement activists foresaw resistance and revolution. Such a shift alienated some while attracting others but ensured a still greater fracturing of the Movement. There had always been disagreements whether the beloved community and participatory democracy were possible or simply pie-in-the-sky notions in the presence of diehard segregationists, the vast bulk of the American populace, and liberals of the JFK, LBJ, or even RFK variety. Less than a decade after the founding of SNCC and SDS, many black and white activists, including veterans of those organizations, had grabbed for the Holy Grail that had ground down and poisoned the Old Left. That included belief in a vanguard party, which both the Panthers and the Weather Underground exalted, however differently.

A small but significant number of American radicals considered some variant of Marxism the answer to global ailments. Different vogues came and went, such as viewing Che, Ho, or Mao as inspirations. The death of the first two left the Chinese Communist leader as the leading revolutionary exemplar, with too little concern expressed about the catastrophic costs engendered by purges, the Great Leap Forward, and the ongoing Great Proletarian Cultural Revolution. More tragedies were taking place, including in Southeast Asia, where the Khmer Rouge, the fanatical Cambodian communists led by the Western-educated Pol Pot and supported by Mao's China, undertook a relentless, blood-soaked drive for power. The appeal of Maoism globally, but most surprisingly in Western Europe and the United States, remained, for a time, considerable.

The New Communist Movement appeared in the United States, drawing from former SNCC and SDS members and various radical student organizations that particularly appealed to minority students. Even a small number of CPUSA veterans participated, appreciating the Marxist-Leninist thrust and belief in the eventual dictatorship of the proletariat. The Georgia Communist League, led by organizer Lynn Wells and Bob Zellner, a white activist and early SNCC member; the pro-Maoist Revolutionary Union (RU); and the October League (OL), which included former Revolutionary Youth Movement II (an SDS splinter) leaders Michael Klonsky and Bob Avakian, were all part of the New Communist Movement. The RU and the OL participated in a number of wildcat strikes, as did the League of Revolutionary Black Workers, which melded faith in Marxism-Leninism and black power, operating in Detroit and acquiring strong leaders in the African American attorneys Ken Cockrel and Mike Hamlin, and the still more radical General Gordon Baker and John Watson. The Cleveland-based American Communist Workers Movement drew from the area's draft resistance and radical student activism. Emerging out of Chicago and RYM II, the Sojourner Truth Organization (STO) appreciated the support European radicals offered to militant young workers, carrying out wildcat strikes and engaging in plant takeovers. STO emphasized the notion of "white skin privilege," articulated by Noel Ignatin and non-members Ted Allen and Don Hamerquist, who insisted that drove white supremacy and prevented African American and white workers from joining forces. Hamerquist also highlighted the importance of hegemony as the Italian Marxist Antonio Gramsci had before World War II, while talking about "dual consciousness," the fact that workers possessed both bourgeois and proletarian consciousness.

American Trotskyists were still viewed as heretics by other self-acknowledged communists, but their impact on political developments in the United States was hardly inconsiderable. The Young Socialist Alliance (YSA), the Trotskyist movement's youth branch, was deeply enmeshed in the antiwar campaign. While seeking a large antiwar coalition, the YSA and its parent group, the Socialist Workers Party (SWP), championed an immediate, unconditional pullout of American forces from Southeast Asia. Its members were part of the Movement, including the New Mobe and other leading antiwar organizations. The historian Jim O'Brien credits "the SWP-YSA" with dedicated commitment to the antiwar movement, calling it "the most influential single group in the coalitions that" sponsored the massive antiwar rallies of the period. Many New Left activists viewed "the Trots" with disdain, angered by their staving off of greater militancy, recalls former SDS president, Carl Oglesby.

However, Oglesby also acknowledged that SWP endured, in contrast to SDS. As of 1973, SWP possessed nearly 1,200 members, while its weekly newspaper, the *Militant*, had a circulation of 31,000. In addition to a substantial headquarters in New York City, the SWP had party branches in cities across the United States, many with paid organizers. Each year, the SWP hosted the weeklong Socialist Activist and Educational Conference, with classes and lectures by party leaders. Biannually, a national convention occurred, where a National Committee was elected. To the dismay of some radicals, the SWP devoted considerable attention to the era's people's movements, not only the labor struggle, viewing them as "part of the general struggle against the outmoded capitalist system." That enabled the SWP to appeal to a new cadre of younger activists. Attending to other important issues of the day undoubtedly did as well. The parent organization and YSA provided the nucleus for the U.S. Committee for Justice to Latin American Political Prisoners, providing aid to leftwing prisoners and their families suffering through brutal coups in Chile and Argentina. The Trotskyists similarly offered assistance to support dissidents in Iran and the Soviet bloc, protest apartheid in South Africa, and oppose Zionism.

Opening in Chicago on January 30, 1976, the National Hard Times Conference welcomed 2,200 people from a variety of radical organizations, seeking to refurbish a movement that would link "local and regional struggles" based on the nation's troubled economic circumstances. Among the groups helping to organize the gathering included the Weatherman-spawned Prairie Fire Organizing Committee, the American Indian Movement, the Federation of Marxist-Leninist Organizations, the General Brotherhood of Workers, the Gray Panthers, the Puerto Rican Socialist Party, the United Black Workers, and the Welfare Workers for Justice. Amid acrimony, the attempt to rebuild a broad-based movement fell apart.

Democratic socialists and other progressives vied for backers of their own as the Movement of the later 1950s and the 1960s dissipated. The New American Movement (NAM) appeared in late 1971, evolving out of SDS and second-wave feminism. Displeased about SDS's degeneration into sectarianism and a kind of infantile leftism, New Left veterans desired to foster a "revolutionary democratic socialist-feminist" approach in local battles involving housing, utility rates, and reproductive rights. Key NAM figures included activists Theirrie Cook, formerly of SDS; Michael P. Lerner, a member of the militant Seattle Liberation Front; the radical lawyer Dan Siegel; and Old Left veteran James Weinstein. NAM's founders expressed a commitment to democratic socialism, one involving "economic, racial, and sexual equality." Michael Harrington, author of *The Other America: Poverty in the United States*, a book credited with influencing both JFK's and LBJ's approaches to the subject, founded, in 1973, the Democratic Socialist Organizing Committee (DSOC). He sought to propel the Democratic Party in a leftward direction, toward a "fourth New Deal" aiming for full employment and an expanded welfare state. In 1982, Harrington helped to engineer the merger of NAM and DSOC, resulting in creation of the Democratic Socialists of America (DSA). The DSA insisted on the need for democratic control over economic processes, challenged the Reagan administration's Cold War rhetoric, and backed the civil rights and women's movement, along with labor unions.

* * *

Civil rights, New Left, and feminist activist Heather Booth, with assistance from her husband Paul, the former SDS president, founded in 1973 the Midwest Academy (MA), designed to help train community organizers and encourage progressive groups. The institute sought to encourage "economic, racial, environmental and social justice" by instructing activists how to "alter the relations of power in our society where too much power is concentrated in the hands of too few." Like Saul Alinsky, the famed community organizer, MA turned to grassroots engagement.

Established by black feminists and lesbians, the Boston-based Combahee River Collective coined the term "identity politics," referring to "a politics that grew out of our objective material experiences as black women." Demita Frazier and the twin sisters Barbara and Beverly Smith produced *The Combahee River Collective Statement* (1977), condemning both sexual oppression among African Americans and racism inside the feminist camp. To that end, they blasted capitalism, imperialism, and patriarchy, viewing them as necessarily intertwined, but they also refused to laud lesbian separatism.

In California, former SDS leader Tom Hayden and his wife, the actress-activist Jane Fonda, helped to found the Campaign for Economic Democracy (CED) in 1976, after Hayden's unsuccessful bid for the Democratic Party nomination for a U.S. Senate seat. Also seeking to strengthen a progressive agenda within Democratic Party ranks, the CED quickly built chapters across the state, winning a number of local offices, while Hayden believed, "We're going to take over. . . . The next big generation will be those who came to political life during Vietnam." Insightfully, the CED supported establishment of a public agency, SolarCal, to encourage installation of solar equipment. In the early 1980s, Hayden began a nearly two-decade long tenure in first the California state assembly and then the state senate.

While acquiring notoriety, due its high-profile founders, which other organizations lacked, the CED was hardly the era's only "citizen action" group. Civic organizations appeared across the country such as Massachusetts Fair Share, the Ohio Public Interest Campaign, the Illinois Public Action Council, the Oakland Community Organization, and San Antonio's church-based Communities Organized for Public Service (COPS). Established in 1974 and influenced by Saul Alinsky, COPS sought to improve mostly Latino neighborhoods, demanding the construction of sidewalks, curbs, and drainage systems; the building of libraries, health clinics, and affordable housing; as well as the setting up of public parks. Henry Cisneros, who served as the city's mayor from 1981–1989, indicated, "I can say unequivocally, COPS has fundamentally altered the moral tone and the political and physical face of San Antonio."

On a still more local level, former students, New Left, and civil rights activists took control of municipal governments, including Paul Soglin in Madison, Wisconsin, Gus Newport in Berkeley, and Bernie Sanders in Burlington, Vermont. Having been involved in the thriving Movement at the University of Texas, twenty-six-year-old Jeff Friedman landed on the City Council, thanks to a coalition of students, minorities, and progressives, before becoming known as Austin's "hippie mayor." The now thirty-year-old Friedman exclaimed that the "people of Austin have taken the city." Friedman supported equalizing electrical rates, establishing a public ambulance corps, and ensuring that the people had a voice in the mayor's office. Previously little listened to groups, especially African Americans and Latinos, were no longer largely ignored. Friedman both helped to create and was the beneficiary of Austin's uniquely tolerant makeup.

Congress itself included a small number of leftwing legislators, and more of a progressive cast. A black activist in the Bay Area, Ronald Dellums, an avowed democratic socialist, began a nearly three-decade span in the House of Representatives in 1971, battling against massive military spending and U.S. intervention overseas, while supporting social welfare measures. Well into his career as a national legislator, Dellums helped to establish the Congressional Progressive Caucus (CPC), whose founders also included Maine's Thomas Andrews, Oregon's Peter DeFazio, Illinois' Lane Evans, Vermont's Bernie Sanders, and California's Maxine Waters. Among those soon joining the CPC were California's Bob Filner, George Miller, Nancy Pelosi, Peter Stark, and Lynn Woolsey; Hawaii's Patsy Mink; Massachusetts' Barney Frank and John Olver; New York's Maurice Hinchey, Jerrold Nadler, Major Owens, and Nydia Velazquez; and Washington State's Jim McDermott. Later staunch left-of-center House members included Arizona's Raul M. Grijalva, the District of Columbia's Eleanor Holmes Norton, and California's Barbara Lee.

Genuine progressives sat in the Senate like California's Barbara Boxer; Illinois' Carol Moseley Braun, Barack Obama, and Richard J. Durbin; Maryland's Barbara Mikulski; Massachusetts' Edward M. Kennedy, John Kerry, Elizabeth Warren, and Edward J. Markey; Minnesota's Paul Wellstone and Al Franken; Oregon's Jack Reed; Rhode Island's Sheldon Whitehouse; Vermont's Bernie Sanders; and Wisconsin's Russ Feingold and Tammy Baldwin. In many other Western nations, any number of these legislators would have easily fit inside social democratic or even democratic socialist parties.

*   *   *

Providing information about ideological schisms, national leftwing organizations, or local activities were publications that largely supplanted the underground press tied to the Movement and the counterculture, and carryovers from the early Cold War period like *The Guardian*, *The Monthly Review*, *Dissent*, and *The Village Voice*. *Rolling Stone* magazine's identification with the Movement had often been inconsistent, and its ties to the counterculture shifted course as that version of America's latest bohemia did likewise. *Ramparts* lasted until 1975, but its heyday was long past. Filling the resulting void, to a certain extent, were newer offerings like *In These Times*, founded in 1976 by James Weinstein as an independent socialist newspaper, and *Mother Jones*, established the same year and dedicated to both progressive commentary and investigative journalism.

The American civil rights movement never fully recovered from the loss of Martin Luther King Jr. In late 1971, Jesse Jackson, who had headed the Southern Christian Leadership Conference's economic program, Operation Breadbasket, established People United to Save Humanity (later People United to Serve Humanity, Operation PUSH). Supporting both negotiations and possible boycotts, PUSH attempted to convince large corporations to employ more African Americans, conduct additional business with minorities, provide greater funding to black schools and groups, and augment advertising in African American publications. Members of the Philadelphia-located black liberation group MOVE, founded in 1972 by Korean War veteran John Africa, dwelled communally and subscribed to radical environmentalism. The initial National Black Political Convention met in Gary, Indiana, in 1972, insisting on the need for organization and a "Black Agenda," beyond what liberal Democrats sponsored. Those gathered referred to themselves as "the vanguard in the struggle for a new society," who considered essential "determined national Black power," and identification with liberation movements around the globe. That same year, progressive congresswoman Shirley Chisolm from New York City became the first black Democratic Party presidential candidate. Other progressives, Eleanor Holmes Norton and Marion Wright Edelman, came to head the National Black Feminist Organization and the Children's Defense Fund, respectively.

While the civil rights, Latino, Native American, and Asian American movements soon clearly lacked the verve that once characterized each, women's and gay liberation appeared more vibrant, despite encountering embittered, sometimes deadly opposition. In her introduction to *Sisterhood Is Powerful: An Anthology of Writings from the Women's Liberation Movement* (1970), Robin Morgan explained that the movement was broader still by the end of the 1960s, notwithstanding points of divergence. The movement, she indicated, existed where women discussed "their personal lives," but also "in the cells of women's jails . . . the welfare line . . . the supermarket, the factory, the convent, the farm, the maternity ward, the streetcorner, the old ladies' home, the kitchen, the steno pool, the bed." Bluntly put, the movement was "frightening . . . very exhilarating," involved in "creating history, or rather, *herstory*," and could not be escaped.

Morgan, at the time a member of W.I.T.C.H., also penned the devastating missive, "Goodbye to All That," in response to the sexism that infected the *Rat*, New York City's leading underground newspaper. Members of W.I.T.C.H., Redstockings, and Weatherwomen stormed into the office of *Rat*, demanding production of an issue entirely devoted to women's liberation. "Goodbye to All That" served as the focal point of the issue, which began with a condemnation of *Rat*'s porn photographs, "sexist comic strips," and "'nude-chickie' cover," in addition to its "patronizing rhetoric" regarding the women's movement. The article blasted "the counterfeit male-dominated Left," which included the *Rat* and its "token 'pussy power' or 'clit militancy' articles." Blaming white males for most of "the destruction of human life and environment," Morgan noted that they were also leading "the supposed revolution to change all that." She attacked the peace movement, the radical left, and the counterculture, as sexist, and urged feminists, "Let it all hang out. Let it seem bitchy, catty, dykey, Solanisesque, frustrated, crazy, nutty, frigid, ridiculous, bitter, embarrassing, man-hating, libelous, pure, unfair, envious, intuitive, low-down, stupid, petty, liberating. WE ARE THE WOMEN THAT MEN HAVE WARNED US ABOUT."

Militant feminism received a good deal of attention early in the decade. Radical publications poured forth, such as Jo Freeman's "The BITCH Manifesto," *off our backs*, Kate Millet's Sexual Politics, Shulamith Firestone's *The Dialectic of Sex: The Case for Feminist Revolution*, Germaine Greer's *The Female Eunuch*, Pauli Murray's *The Liberation of Black Women*, Anne Koedt's "The Myth of the Vaginal Orgasm," the Radicalesbians' "The Woman Identified Woman," Gloria Steinem's "What It Would be Like If Women Win," and the Chicago Women's Liberation Union's "Free Abortion Is Every Woman's Right," all in 1970 alone.

The women's movement seemed on the cusp of two sweeping accomplishments: passage of the Equal Rights Amendment (ERA) and liberalization of abortion rights. Endorsed by NOW, the ERA declared that "equality of rights under the law shall not be denied or abridged by the United States or by any State on account of sex." By 1972, the ERA had swept through Congress and was quickly ratified by thirty states, picking up additional backing in five others, before falling short. The Clergy Consultation Service on Abortion, a network of religious leaders, had recently sponsored referral services for women in need of less dangerous abortions, which largely remained illegal. Feminist groups also set up referral groups, while the Abortion Counseling Service of the Chicago Women's Liberation Union formed Jane, an underground feminist-run abortion service. On January 22, 1973, Supreme Court Justice Harry Blackmun, a Nixon appointee, issued the majority ruling in *Roe v. Wade*, affirming that a woman's ability to end a pregnancy during the first trimester was constitutionally protected under a "right of privacy," embedded "in the Fourteenth Amendment's concept of personal liberty." The state was afforded authority to safeguard a woman's health during the second trimester as well as to protect a fetus viable in the final trimester.

The women's movement also insisted that rape laws be revisited, defense attorneys not be allowed to point to a victim's sexual history, police departments establish sex crimes units, and rape crisis centers become available for women. Similarly, activists denounced laws or judicial rulings that seemingly abetted spousal rape, and they helped to set up battered women's shelters around the country. At the shelters, they sought to provide safe spaces, along with information about sexism and violence directed against women. Over 1,600 women gathered for the 1975 Socialist Feminist Conference, held in Yellow Springs, Ohio, recognizing the necessity of supporting an "autonomous women's movement throughout the revolutionary process," while agreeing that socialist feminism was "a strategy for revolution."

Feminists battled against a backlash led by Republican activist Phyllis Schlafly, who stitched together a "STOP ERA" drive and increasingly proved support of anti-abortion efforts. The nation's political and cultural currents were shifting with the Republican Party increasingly veering rightward. Over 14,000 women met at the National Women's Conference in Houston in November 1977, but the mass gathering was something of second-wave feminism's last gasp. Attendees did appear to resolve the conundrum involving sexual preference, which had perplexed the movement. As Steinem later reflected, "Everybody came together," refusing to accept homophobic representations of lesbian or bisexual women."

Sparked by the Stonewall riots, the gay liberation movement became a more visible and vocal presence during ensuing decades. Activists led gay pride parades, initially to commemorate Stonewall and to celebrate the new spirit in the fight for homosexual liberation. The Gay Liberation Front published the newspaper, *Come Out!* As the naming of their publication suggested, GLF members emboldened others "to come out of the closet." The historian John D'Emilio offers, "Coming out provided gay liberation with an army of permanent enlistees." Discussing the impact of small groups of radicals within the new organization, the writer Sherry Wolf quotes from a GLF statement delivered to the *Rat*, the underground paper.

> We are a revolutionary homosexual group . . . formed with the realization that complete sexual liberation . . . cannot come about unless existing social institutions are abolished. We reject society's attempt to impose sexual roles and definitions of our nature. . . . We are going to be who we are. At the same time, we are creating new social forms and relations . . . relations based up brotherhood, cooperation, human love, and uninhibited sexuality. Babylon has forced us to commit ourselves to one thing . . . revolution.

Some GLF members, including Arthur Evans, Jim Owles, and Marty Robinson, broke away, establishing the Gay Activists Alliance (GAA), which determined to work within the existing political system but hardly meekly. Its constitution propounded an agenda "exclusively devoted to the liberation of homosexuals," while declaring "the right to make love with anyone, anyway, anytime," and "the right to treat and express our bodies as we will." Gay members declared, "We declare our Liberation *from* repression and *to* the point where repressive laws are removed from the books and our rights are written into the documents that protect the rights of all people." *Out of the Closets: Voices of Gay Liberation* (1972) included co-editor Karla Jay's affirmation: "If we do share one idea . . . it is that *gay is good*. We affirm our uniqueness. We are proud to be lesbians and homosexuals, and we offer no apologies or explanations of why we are what we are."

Openly gay candidates began running for political office, with Harvey Milk undertaking a bid for a city supervisorial slot in San Francisco in 1973, capturing the Castro district and a number of other progressive areas. The next year, Elaine Noble became a member of the Massachusetts state legislature. In 1976, Milk, shortly after being appointed to the Board of Permit Appeals, made a vigorous, albeit unsuccessful run for a state assembly seat, then helped to devise the San Francisco Gay Democratic Club. Defeating sixteen other candidates, Milk landed on the city's Board of Supervisors on January 8, 1978 and led the push for a civil rights measure outlawing discrimination on the basis of sexual orientation. Milk also fought against Proposition 6, proposed by former gubernatorial candidate John Briggs, which called for the firing of school employees who openly backed gay rights. During Gay Freedom Day, celebrated in San Francisco, Milk urged a crowd to "come out. Come out . . . to your parents . . . to your friends . . . to your neighbors . . . to your fellow workers."

Tragically, on November 27, 1978, Dan White, who had recently resigned from the Board of Supervisors, assassinated both Milk and Mayor George Moscone, a strong supporter of the gay movement. Approximately 40,000 participated in candlelight vigils that evening. A resident of Castro Street stated, "Considering that there had been no planning, this was phenomenal. It assured us that we were not alone. We WERE community and we WERE supported by our fellow citizens." Such a display of support was apparent the following year when around 100,000 individuals joined in the National March on Washington for Lesbian and Gay Rights. The 1980 Democratic Party National Convention included a plank reading, "All groups must be protected from discrimination based on race, color, religion, national origin, language, age, sex or sexual orientation."

The first Earth Day, held a decade earlier on April 22, 1970, demonstrated the potency of the American environmental movement, strongly supported by both female and male activists. Both President Nixon and Congress responded, with the setting up of the Environmental Protection Agency and passage of significant legislation regarding environmental impact reviews, national air quality standards, auto emissions, supersonic transport, clean water, marine mammal protection, ocean dumping, drinking water, wilderness protection, forest management, and endangered species.

Radical environmentalists desired far more. Founded in 1971 in Vancouver by transplanted Americans Irving and Dorothy Stowe, among others, Greenpeace received support from both Quakers and antiwar activists in undertaking a campaign against U.S. nuclear testing in Alaska. The initial Greenpeace action could be likened to that of earlier radical pacifists, involving an attempt to send a boat into the Amchitka testing site. While the U.S. Navy halted the boat, called "the Greenpeace," a rock concert featuring Joni Mitchell, Phil Ochs, and James Taylor raised over $23,000, providing seed money for the new antinuclear organization. By the middle of the decade, Greenpeace was doing battle with whalers, including a Russian fleet, and attempting to save baby harp seals, blocking a sealer's ship, the *Arctic Endeavor*, off Newfoundland's coast. Later, Greenpeace broadened its protests, highlighting both tropical forests and dumping of toxic materials, including nuclear waste, into the ocean.

Concerns about nuclear radioactivity sparked a series of protests, also by the middle of the decade, and intensified over the next several years. In February 1974, Sam Lovejoy resorted to civil disobedience in his fight against nuclear power, knocking down a utilities weather tower located on the Montague Plains, slated site of a double nuclear reactor. His typed statement charged that atomic energy "was dangerous, dirty, expensive, unneeded and," worst of all, threatening to children, thus justifying the tower's destruction. A subsequent trial led to Lovejoy's acquittal, based on technical grounds, with a jury poll later indicating a not guilty would have been rendered. Testifying on his behalf were radical historian Howard Zinn and John Gofman, the Atomic Energy Commission's initial health director, who now claimed that atomic reactors spawned "mass murder."

In 1976, Lovejoy helped found the Clamshell Alliance, which relied on affinity groups and drew from Albert Einstein's call "to take the issue of atomic energy to the village square." Tying together affinity groups, Clamshell devised a "spokescouncil" intended to represent the different groups. Determined to engage in mass nonviolent civil disobedience, the Clamshell Alliance targeted Seabrook, New Hampshire, where nuclear reactors were being built. The Clamshell Alliance's antinuclear activists were committed to stop nuclear power plant construction around the country. Drafting a Declaration of Nuclear Resistance, the Clamshell Alliance, on August 1, 1976, undertook its first protest of several hundred people. A second protest and the eventual occupation of the construction site resulted in mass arrests. The following April, the Clamshell Alliance led 2,000 people at a demonstration, which produced 1,400 arrests. Other antinuclear organizations emerged, including "Oystershell, Sunshell, Abalone, Palmetto, Shad, Crabshell, [and] Trojan." More mass protests and arrests followed at Seabrook, with more than 20,000 people, during the summer of 1978, participating in mostly legal protests.

That was the year the Environmental Life Force (ELF) disbanded, after its founder, John Hanna, was charged with having used explosives and incendiary devices on federal property. Established the previous year, the ELF was intended to be a cell-driven, decentralized group, but it failed to survive Hanna's arrest and conviction. Frustrated by reliance on cancer-causing pesticides and influenced by both Rachel Carson and Robert Van Den Bosch, a UC Berkeley professor of entomology who had written *The Pesticide Conspiracy*, Hanna had elected "to go underground and employ guerrilla tactics in defense of the earth."

The antinuclear movement garnered considerable strength after the partial meltdown on March 29, 1979, of a Three Mile Island Unit 2 reactor near Harrisburg, Pennsylvania. The accident provided impetus to antinuclear activists, and badly damaged the nuclear industry in the United States. It also occurred less than two weeks following release of the high-budget Hollywood film, *The China Syndrome*, starring Michael Douglas, Jane Fonda, and Jack Lemmon, regarding a cover-up of safety violations at a nuclear power plant. A massive antinuclear energy demonstration took place in Washington, D.C., in early May. The Musicians United for Safe Energy collective organized No Nukes, a series of concerts held during September at Madison Square Garden, with antinuclear songs like John and Johanna Hall's "Power" and "Plutonium Is Forever." Mike Nichols later directed *Silkwood* (1983), a film about a young woman working at a plutonium plant, Karen Silkwood, who had died mysteriously several years earlier, possibly the result of being hounded and murdered for her union activism and whistle-blowing related to nuclear power.

The beefing up of safety standards culminated in the eventual halting of a number of partially-constructed plants and the shelving of plans for 100 others. Continued protests kept the issue alive, as through the Abalone Alliance's extensive protests at the site of Pacific Gas & Electric's attempted construction of the Diablo Canyon nuclear power plant along the beach in San Luis Obispo County, California. Clamshell veterans also participated in the Women's Pentagon Action on November 17, 1980, which occurred after the election of Ronald Reagan as president of the United States. Following gigantic Bread and Puppet Theatre female puppets, about 2,000 marched along Arlington Cemetery to the Pentagon, which they encircled, then blocked the entrance to the Mall. They delivered an eloquent "Unity Statement," declaring, "We are gathering at the Pentagon . . . because we fear for our lives. We fear for the life of this planet, our Earth, and the life of our children who are our human future."

Barry Commoner, the antinuclear activist and biologist who had been labeled "the Paul Revere of Ecology" by *Time* magazine and had written the best-selling book, *The Closing Circle*, warning of the need for a recasting of economic priorities to stave off ecological ruin, conducted a quixotic run for the presidency. Commoner was concerned about the perils posed by pesticides, toxins, and pollutants, including radioactive fallout; insisted on the ordinary citizen's right to be apprised of such dangers; and considered sustainability essential. A believer in holistic approaches, respecting nature, and recognizing "there is no such thing as a free lunch," in other words, understanding that the use of fossil fuels damaged the world's carbon cycle, the man later headlined as having "forced environmentalism into the world's consciousness" believed that tackling the environmental crisis required solving "the problems of poverty, racial injustice and war." Running on the newly formed Citizens Party ticket in 1980, Commoner received only 0.25 percent of the votes but hardly damaged his reputation as "a leader among a generation of scientist-activists." His campaign offered "a pro-environment, anti-nuclear, anti-big business platform."

During the 1980 presidential campaign, a new, radical environmental group emerged: Earth First! One of its founders, Dave Foreman, discussed the organization's intentions: "EARTH FIRST will take strong action on related issues such as mining, energy development, off road vehicles, logging, and the MX missile. We will actively campaign for the destruction of dams like Glen Canyon, Hetch Hetchy, Fort Peck, Tellico, and those in Hells Canyon. We do not wish to merely preserve what's left, we want to re-create wilderness." Displeased by mainstream environmentalists, activists drawn to Earth First! favored a militant posture involving well-publicized protests, guerrilla theater, civil disobedience, and ecotage. The latter, drawn from Edward Abbey's 1975 novel, *The Monkey Wrench Gang*, involved destroying road-construction equipment, billboards, traps, and tree-cutting operations through randomly driving deep spikes into trees. As Foreman explained, "A monkey wrench thrown into the gears of the machine may not stop it. But it might delay it. Make it cost more. And it feels good to put it there." Members of Earth First! extolled "biocentrism, or Deep Ecology," and the acting out of the organization's beliefs. Ecoradical Foreman declared, "No Compromise in Defense of Mother Earth."

* * *

With Reagan's ascendancy to the presidency and his determination to shift the country in a more conservative direction, the American left was in for something of a bumpy ride, although citizen activism at times remained fierce. In addition to Reagan's trouncing of the Democratic incumbent Jimmy Carter, Republicans captured the U.S. Senate, thanks to the defeat of liberal stalwarts Birch Bayh, Frank Church, John Culver, John Durkin, Warren Magnuson, George McGovern, and Gaylord Nelson. Moreover, many newly elected Republicans at all levels were staunch conservatives, who owed their electoral success, to a certain extent, to the New Right, a combination of religious fundamentalists, anti-regulatory "free market" advocates, and gay rights and abortion opponents. The latest iteration of the Christian Right, the Moral Majority, led by Jerry Falwell, was a key component, promoting a conservative social agenda through its opposition to abortion, the ERA, gay rights, and pornography, and its backing of a fervent anti-communist foreign policy.

American progressives had to contend with the new administration's determination to whittle away at the welfare state, sharply reduce income tax progressivity, and dramatically increase military spending. Particularly troubling were appointments of rightwing cabinet members committed to weaken the very cabinets and programs they headed; the administration's nuclear arms buildup coupled with a Strategic Defense Initiative involving an anti-

ballistic missile system, known as Star Wars; and Reagan's readiness to
support anti-revolutionary forces under the template of anti-communism.

The initial push back from the American left focused on both domestic
and foreign policy considerations. The Coalition for the Homeless and similar groups cropped up in cities across the United States, soon forming the
National Coalition for the Homeless, as the number of individuals without
residences of their own mushroomed. With the safety net curbed, thousands,
many suffering from mental illness and addiction, were thrown into the
street. The National Union of the Homeless (NUH), made up of activist
organizations, appeared, committed to furthering "economic justice, human
rights, and full liberation" through "a sustained struggle" against "all forms
of exploitation, racism, sexism, and abuse." The NUH aspired to "create not
only the new society, but also the new human being." A combination non-
profit shelter and antiwar organization, the Community for Creative Non-
Violence (CCNV), sought to provide succor for the homeless in Washington,
D.C. Founded by J. Edward Guigan, a young Catholic priest from the Catholic Workers, and "Christian anarchists," CCNV often featured Mitch Snyder,
a former felon who had shared jail time with Daniel and Philip Berrigan.
Desirous of underscoring the plight of the homeless, Snyder, notes the journalist Colman McCarthy, kicked off a number "of fasts, lawsuits and demonstrations."

Many progressives pointed to Central America and a new, lengthening
arms race. Both were caught up in the reigniting of the Cold War, which had
followed, in 1979, the Soviet Union's invasion of Afghanistan. President
Carter had adopted a series of hardline policies in response: increasing the
Pentagon's budget, embargoing the sale of grain to the Soviet Union, re-
questing the Senate to delay ratification of a new arms treaty, and boycotting
the 1980 Moscow Summer Olympics. He also provided assistance to Afghan
rebels, including fundamentalist mujahidin, doing battle with Soviet troops.

A nuclear freeze movement, initiated by a young disarmament researcher,
Randall Caroline Forsberg, appeared by 1980, proving particularly strong in
Western Europe and the United States. Forsberg presented a manifesto, "Call
to Halt the Nuclear Arms Race." Seemingly moderate in its demands, the
movement favored negotiations to bring about a bilateral end of testing,
developing, and deploying nuclear arms. Randy Kehler, a Vietnam War era
draft resister who had spurred Daniel Ellsberg to publish the Pentagon Papers
revealing U.S. machinations in Southeast Asia, led the Nuclear Weapons
Freeze Campaign. Subscribing to the idea of "Think Globally, Act Locally,"
freeze advocates fanned out across the country, forming local groups and
delivering resolutions and referenda before town meetings, city governments,
and state legislatures. They also began holding national conferences and
joined with the Union of Concerned Scientists, Physicians for Social Responsibility, and other groups to highlight the perils posed by nuclear armaments.

The Livermore Action Group engaged in a nonviolent direct action campaign against the Lawrence Livermore National Laboratory, partnering with the University of California. Participants included Ellsberg and the beat poet Lawrence Ferlinghetti. About a million people, drawn to the theme of "Freeze the Arms Race—Fund Human Needs," showed up on June 12, 1982, for a rally in New York City. The freeze campaign obtained signatures of almost two-and-a-half million Americans. By 1983, public opinion polls indicated overwhelming support for the freeze effort, which pollster Pat Caddell deemed "the most significant citizens' movement of the last century." Leading American religious groups backed the movement, along with nearly 400 city councils, over seventy county councils, and a large number of state legislative bodies.

Despite strident rhetoric emanating from the Reagan administration, the president ultimately responded to the nuclear freeze movement, which included massive demonstrations in Western Europe, altering his course of action. That, of course, became apparent during a series of meetings with the new Soviet leader, Mikhail Gorbachev, who developed an intriguing relationship with the American president enabling the two men to discuss curbing the nuclear arms race and for Reagan to proclaim, "A nuclear war cannot be won and should never be fought." That pattern continued under Reagan's successor, George Herbert Walker Bush. As the historian Lawrence Wittner notes, the nuclear freeze drive continued as well, melding with SANE in 1987 to form Peace Action, the nation's largest antiwar and disarmament organization.

But while President Reagan became more receptive to the possibility of disarmament, he remained steadfast in his determination to damage or even topple leftwing governments or groups his administration labeled Marxist. With a particular focus on Central America, where an extended legacy of repression, exploitation, and corruption had led to radical movements and, in certain instances, radical regimes, the Reagan administration insisted on the need to funnel funds to their opponents, no matter how undemocratic or brutal. Thus, even in the face of determined Democratic opposition, it provided assistance to the Contras, a series of rebel groups, many rightwing, who sought to overthrow the newly established revolutionary Nicaraguan government headed by Daniel Ortega and the Sandinistas. Similarly, the Reagan administration backed anti-revolutionary forces in El Salvador in the midst of a civil war, despite the unsavory nature of some of those forces and their leaders, including Robert D'Aubuisson, a fanatical anti-communist and apparent head of death squads.

Progressive groups in the United States and Western Europe particularly condemned American operations in Central America. The Committee in Solidarity with the People of El Salvador (CISPES) had appeared in 1980, committed to contesting U.S. backing for the Salvadoran junta and to supporting the revolutionary Farabundo Marti National Liberation Front and leftwing popular organizations. Progressives similarly condemned the Contras and defended the Sandinistas, with a number of Americans going to either Nicaragua or El Salvador to provide assistance to people's movements. The political satirist P. J. O'Rourke coined the term "Sandalistas" to describe the foreigners sporting sandals and casual attire in Nicaragua, but many were well-intentioned young people like twenty-seven-year-old engineer Benjamin Linder, an American volunteer murdered there, as the Contra War continued. Several thousand Sandalistas, among them many Americans, remained in Nicaragua through the end of the decade. As Stephen Solnit, a young computer specialist from the Bay Area, indicated, "Everybody came down to support the revolutionary process." The eventual political toppling of the Sandinistas in 1990 would prove unsettling to the youthful expatriates. The Pledge of Resistance, for its part, condemned U.S. policy regarding both El Salvador and Nicaragua. One member, Brian Wilson, a Vietnam veteran, participated in a blockade of a munition train at the Concord Naval Weapons Station that failed to stop, causing the loss of both of his lower legs.

The Reagan administration's seeming attempt to turn the clock back, pertaining to domestic programs, proved equally unsettling to left-of-center Americans. This involved a whole array of issues, such as attempting to gut environmental and safety regulations, deliberately weakening labor unions, challenging the welfare state, dabbling in racism, attacking abortion rights, pandering to the Religious Right, and refusing to address the AIDS epidemic.

* * *

The Rainbow Coalition of the 1980s, which featured Jesse Jackson's presidential bids in 1984 and 1988, offered a more racially diverse version of the earlier progressive campaigns run by Eugene McCarthy, Robert F. Kennedy, and George McGovern. Only McGovern had obtained the Democratic Party presidential nomination, McCarthy and Jackson coming up short and RFK falling victim to the politics of assassination. But all their campaigns were significant, with Jackson's effort particularly noteworthy as he was the first African American to make a serious bid for the nomination of a major American political party. A controversial figure because of statements like a reference to New York City as "Hymietown," support from the anti-Semitic leader of the Nation of Islam, Louis Farrakan, and sharp criticisms of Israel, Jackson was nevertheless a significant political player. The historian David Chappell offers that Jackson "had the advantage of having a larger following than any of his critics—and was arguably more practical as well as more courageous, in that he dared to rally discontented masses of not just black voters but, increasingly, Hispanic, poor white, and other have-not constituencies against the popular rightward trend" of the era. Jackson's 1984 campaign followed the previous year's March on Washington that displayed, according to the *New York Times*, a coming together of "groups—labor, blacks, Hispanic Americans, women, antinuclear activists and environmentalists, among others," often recently battling one another.

Jackson's presidential bids occurred during a period when urban America appeared out-of-step with national politics, at least regarding the holding of office by black mayors as the Reagan Revolution continued. Philadelphia's Wilson Goode, Detroit's Coleman Young, Atlanta's Maynard Jackson and Andrew Young, Los Angeles' Tom Bradley, and Chicago's Harold Washington attempted to enact progressive policies. Putting together what he referred to as his "Rainbow Cabinet," Washington sought to empower the previously disfranchised: women, blacks, Latinos, indigent ethnic whites, and the disabled.

At the end of the decade, critical race theoretician and law professor Kimberle Williams Crenshaw presented the theory of intersectionality to examine how African American women were doubly cursed. Drawing on Catherine MacKinnon's contention regarding the sexual harassment of women and MacKinnon's recognition that multiple strands of inequality afflicted various individuals, Crenshaw believed women suffered racism at the hands of their white sisters, and sexism through paternalistic anti-racist groups. This emerged, indicates *The Guardian*'s Eleanor Robertson, even in legislation designed to attack discrimination and services afforded to victims of domestic violence.

* * *

In the face of continued homophobia and seeming indifference from the Reagan White House, gay activists maintained their struggle on behalf of lesbian and gay rights, as tennis champion Billie Jean King came out of the closet and the *San Francisco Chronicle*'s Randy Shilts acquired notoriety as "the first openly gay reporter with a gay beat in the American mainstream press." However, in addition to ferocious campaigns associated with the Christian Right, homosexuals had to contend with the modern equivalent of the plague, as the HIV/AIDS epidemic began besetting the gay community. Reflecting on the issue of the "gay cancer," a group of gay men and their friends met in the Greenwich Village apartment of the writer Larry Kramer and formed the Gay Men's Health Crisis, which set up the initial AIDS hotline. But gay activists, including Kramer, finally had enough, forming, in March 1987, the AIDS Coalition to Unleash Power (ACT-UP) at Manhattan's Lesbian and Gay Community Services Center. ACT-UP employed direct action tactics, held die-ins, initiated lawsuits against discriminating companies, and countered misleading information about the disease. Early protests were directed against Wall Street and the White House. In October

1987, at least 200,000 demonstrators participated in the Second National March on Washington for Lesbian and Gay Rights, demanding additional federal support for research and treatment of AIDS and for a cessation of discriminatory practices. Founder Cleve Jones and other participants displayed the Names Project AIDS Memorial Quilt, revealing nearly 2,000 separate panels, representing only a small portion of the American fatalities resulting from the disease.

Shilts published the first full account of the tragedy, *And the Band Played On: Politics, People, and the AIDS Epidemic* (1987). A *New York Times* review noted that the pandemic was in its seventh year and would likely get "much worse." H. Jack Geiger, a socially conscious physician, repeated Shilts's charge "that AIDS did not just happen to America—it was allowed to happen" and amounted to a "national failure" that caused "needless death." Both Geiger and Shilts underscored the recalcitrance on the part of the Reagan administration and public health agencies, but also cast blame on gay community leaders who "played politics with the disease, putting political dogma ahead of the preservation of human life." Those leaders did so by denying the existence of the disease and calling efforts to change behavior "sexual fascism." The mass media proved indifferent until Hollywood actor Rock Hudson perished from the disease in 1985. Even *And the Band Played On* lacked perspective at times, underplaying AIDS' devastating impact on minorities and the poor during "the great second wave."

* * *

Just as AIDS coursed through the gay community to devastating effect, violence continued to impact the American left in a variety of ways during the latter stages of the 1970s and throughout the next decade. In February 1977, an arsonist attacked St. Paul's Planned Parenthood Clinic, which offered information about abortion. The following January, the Northwest Women's Center in Columbus, Ohio, suffered considerable fire damage triggered by arson, while the firebombing of a recently vandalized abortion clinic in Cleveland occurred the next month. An arsonist caused chemical burns to the face of a clinic worker, Aurelia Elliott. Philadelphia police undertook a raid on the black liberation group, MOVE, on August 9, 1978, resulting in the death of a police officer, several injuries, and lengthy prison sentences for nine members of the radical group. Charismatic cult leader Jim Jones, who had moved his Peoples Temple from San Francisco to Jonestown, Guyana, promising a socialist utopia, ordered his followers to engage in "revolutionary suicide." After the killing of progressive California Congressman Leo Ryan and four others, who went to Guyana to ascertain if communards were being held against their will, Jones, on November 18, 1978, directed the killing of over 900 people, one-third of them children. Members of the KKK and the American Nazi Party shot and murdered five Communist Workers Party members and textile plant union organizers on November 3, 1979, in Greensboro, North Carolina. That followed a series of rallies against the KKK, including one that day titled "Death to the Klan."

On March 14, 1980, Dennis Sweeney, a cofounder of the Resistance but a man suffering from paranoid schizophrenia, murdered his mentor, Allard K. Lowenstein, who had helped chart Freedom Summer and the "Dump Johnson" movement designed to prevent LBJ's renomination, before becoming a one-term congressman. On December 8, 1980, a crazed fan fatally shot John Lennon, who, as the Beatles imploded, followed up "Revolution" with "Give Peace a Chance," "Working Class Hero," "Power to the People," "Imagine," "Happy Xmas (War Is Over)," "Attica State," and "John Sinclair."

Having pulled off a number of robberies, bombings, and prison breaks, some lethal, former members of the Black Liberation Army and the Weather Underground undertook a holdup of a Brinks armored car in Nanuet, New York, that left two policemen and a guard dead. Calling themselves the Revolutionary Armed Task Force or the Family, ex-Weather Underground participants Kathy Boudin, Judith Clark, David Gilbert, and Susan Rosenberg, as well as Marilyn Buck, called "the chief gunrunner and the only white member of the BLA," conducted the heist on October 20, 1981, which netted $1,589,000. The ringleader, BLA activist Mutulu Shakur, evaded arrest for several years. Captors tied to the Army of God, an extremist anti-abortion group, kidnapped Dr. Hector Zevallos of the Hope Clinic in Granite City, Illinois, and his wife Rosalie Jean, on August 13, 1982, holding them for eight days. On November 7, 1983, a bomb went off on the second floor of the U.S. Senate Chambers. Federal agents eventually singled out the Resistance Conspiracy, which included Marilyn Buck, Linda Evans, and Laura Whitehorn, as having bombed the Capitol, Ft. McNair, and the Washington Navy Yard. Edward Markley, a Catholic priest, attacked an abortion clinic in Birmingham, Alabama, on June 15, 1984, and assaulted three workers.

The politics of assassination came into play yet again three days later, when a white supremacist group murdered Alan Berg, the progressive radio talk show host. In Pensacola, Florida, opponents of abortion bombed a pair of physicians' offices and a clinic on December 25, 1984. Over 500 police officers conducted another raid on MOVE headquarters in Philadelphia on May 13, 1985, discharging more than 10,000 bullets within an hour-and-a-half, following gunfire from the house. When high-pressure hoses and tear gas proved ineffective, the police commissioner ordered that the house be bombed. As it burned, firefighters were instructed to let the blaze continue. Sixty-one houses were razed, and eleven MOVE members, including founder John Africa and five children, were killed. No charges were brought against city officials.

* * *

Events overseas also continued to influence the American left. The collapse of the communist regimes in Eastern Europe and the breaking apart of the Soviet Union dramatically affected the Western left in general, ironically both strengthening free market proponents and curbing democratic socialism's appeal. It also caused Francis Fukuyama to muse about the end of history. Like the American political economist, various progressively-inclined politicians in the West seemingly subscribed to the idea that Western liberal democracy represented humankind's apotheosis. Social democrats had mixed success with Third Way politics that enabled Tony Blair to win the first of three consecutive terms as British Prime Minister, Gerhard Schroder to become chancellor of Germany, Romano Prodi to serve as prime minister of Italy, Francois Mitterand to continue as President of France, and Felipe Gonzales to reign as prime minister of Spain. In Scandinavia, Sweden's Ingvar Carlsson and Goran Persson and Norway's Gro Harlem Brundtland stood as prime ministers. Their rule coincided with the last half of George Herbert Walker Bush's presidency or that of Bill Clinton, the first a moderate Republican, the other a moderate Democrat associated with the Democratic Leadership Council, which sought to curb the party's supposed leftward turn from the late 1960s. However, all of these figures headed in a generally middle-of-the-road direction, undoubtedly constrained by the growing costs of the welfare state and the continued move in the direction of privatization that began gathering momentum two decades earlier. Clinton concentrated on balancing the federal budget rather than increasing entitlements and actually campaigned on a promise to "end welfare as we know it." He proceeded to support termination of Aid to Families with Dependent Children, a key component of the 1935 Social Security Act.

What was true under Jimmy Carter, another moderate Democratic president, took place over much of Clinton's presidency: a failure of the American left to coalesce or at least grow as it had when Wilson, FDR, JFK, and LBJ were in the Oval Office. That was also less the case while Harry Truman served as president, but then his tenure coincided with the emergence of the Cold War and the ferocity of the postwar red scare. Nevertheless, the left was not altogether absent or silent, including in the cultural realms as will be discussed somewhat more in the next chapter.

Another significant, sometimes troubling, somewhat understandable development materialized in the 1990s regarding American foreign policy, although it too wasn't entirely novel. Liberals and radicals had divided, as they had during World War I, over the Vietnam War, even regarding the horrors committed by Cambodia's Khmer Rouge, about possible U.S. interventionism. Once again, American progressives splintered in their response to first the possibility and then the reality of an attack on Iraq's Saddam Hussein during the Gulf War that began in January 1991. The journalist, John R. MacArthur, indicates that liberals had been pushing since the start of the previous decade for additional "aggressive 'humanitarian' interventions that" could surmount international law, national sovereignty, and UN peacekeeping endeavors. The French jurist Mario Bettati and his countrymen, Bernard Kouchner, a '68er who cofounded Doctors Without Borders, and Bernard Henri-Levy, a leader of the New Philosophers school, favored humanitarian intervention. A number of progressives, both overseas and in the United States, accepted President George Herbert Walker Bush's rationale that Saddam, who had invaded oil-rich Kuwait, "was the new Hitler." More supported intervention in strife-torn Somalia, Haiti, Kosovo, and Serbia. The 1994 genocide in Rwanda, where the West failed to act, seemed to provide yet another justification for liberal interventionism. Support for humanitarian intervention in various instances emanated from distinguished figures on the American left side of the ideological spectrum such as Paul Berman, British expatriate Christopher Hitchens, the English historian turned New York City resident Tony Judt, Anthony Lake, and Samantha Powers.

* * *

In the meantime, the environmental, women's, and gay liberation movements retained some of their verve, while continuing to face backlashes. The UN delivered a report in 1990 warning that global warming was indeed taking place. That same year, 140 nations participated in a celebration of Earth Day's twentieth anniversary, and Gallup revealed that 76 percent of Americans polled considered themselves environmentalists. Earth First! undertook Redwood Summer, seeking "Freedom Riders for the Forest" who would employ guerrilla theater and tactics to prevent the felling of old redwood trees by timber companies. One of the Earth First! leaders, forty-year-old Judi Bari, endured a car bombing attack on May 24, 1990, that maimed and disabled her as she drove through Oakland. Amazingly, the FBI and the Oakland police went after Bari, her fellow passenger Darryl Cherney, and other members of Earth First! Seeking damages from the Bureau and the Oakland police department, Bari and Cherney charged that they had suffered false arrest and a violation of their Fourth Amendment right regarding unlawful searches. "This case is not just about me or Darryl or Earth First," she claimed. "This case is about the rights of all political activists to engage in dissent without having to fear the government's secret police." On October 19, 1998, ELF burned a ski resort in Vail, Colorado, resulting in $12 million in property damage.

Relying on a "leaderless resistance" structure, emerging out of Earth First! and following the Animal Liberation Front's lead, the Earth Liberation Front (ELF) appeared in 1992, initially in the United Kingdom, then on the

European continent and in the United States. Eventually called the nation's greatest domestic terrorist threat, the ELF carried out arson attacks against logging companies and development projects it viewed as corrosive to the environment. Founded by John Hanna, the ELF relied on self-contained autonomous small unit cells.

Later in the decade, twenty-three-year-old Julia Butterfly Hill climbed a nearly 200-foot tall California Coast Redwood tree, remaining there for two years to stave off its destruction. A tree felled by the Pacific Lumber Company crushed twenty-four-year-old David "Gypsy" Chain, an Earth First! activist who was protesting logging near the Grizzly Creek Redwoods State Park. The radical environmental group also torched about forty Hummers and sport utility vehicles at a dealership in West Covina, California, in 1993, justifying the action as designed "to remove the profit motive from the killing of the natural environment." ELF activists Craig Rosebraugh and Leslie James Pickering established the Liberation Collective in Portland, Oregon. Condemning capitalism, Rosebraugh stated that "animal rights issues, environmental issues, social justice, are all related." The ELF declared its determination to "inflict economic damage on those profiting from the destruction and exploitation of the natural environment," and a readiness "to reveal and educate the public on the atrocities committed against the earth and all species that populate it."

American feminists experienced mixed results, with 1992 labeled the Year of the Woman due to the record number of women elected to the U.S. Senate. This came in the wake of the previous year's confirmation hearings involving Supreme Court nominee Clarence Thomas, selected by President George Herbert Walker Bush to replace Thurgood Marshall. While the attorney Anita Hill testified that Thomas had made sexually inappropriate statements when she worked for him, the Senate Judiciary Committee chose to believe his recounting of their shared history in a classic case of "he said, she said." In another setback for women's rights—former Black Panther supporter Thomas had shifted far rightward and was hardly supportive of the women's movement—the Supreme Court approved of various state restrictions regarding abortion rights.

As if in reaction to the televised Hill-Thomas confrontation and the Supreme Court rulings, 500,000–750,000 pro-choice women participated in The March for Women's Lives, held in Washington, D.C., on April 5, 1992. NOW president Patricia Ireland explained, "The reality is that we're tired of begging men in power for our rights. If the courts won't protect them, then Congress has got to enact laws to protect a woman's rights. And if Congress doesn't, then we're going to elect pro-choice women to Congress." In mid-August 1994, Women of African Descent for Reproductive Justice issued page-long ads declaring the issue to be "life and death . . . for many Black women," thereby deserving "as much recognition as any other freedom." The group's statement, addressed to congressional representatives and signed by such individuals as former Congresswoman Shirley Chisholm; Maxine Waters, a future member of the House; and political strategist Donna Brazile, insisted that heath care reform required funding "the full range of reproductive services," including abortion and contraception. Also responding to the treatment endured by Hill, the writer Rebecca Walker, daughter of a Jewish civil rights attorney and famed author Alice Walker, conveyed her readiness "to fight back," indicating that once again she had "been radicalized, politicized, shaken awake." She insisted, "The fight is far from over. Let this dismissal of a woman's experience move you to anger. Turn that outrage into political power. Do not vote for them unless they work for us. Do not have sex with them, do not break bread with them, do not nurture them if they don't prioritize our freedom to control our bodies and our lives." The younger Walker declared, "I am not a postfeminism feminist. I am the third wave."

Gay liberation also experienced ups and downs during the 1990s, with the adoption of the "Don't Ask, Don't Tell" policy by the U.S. Armed Forces, far less progressive than Bill Clinton's pre-election promise to discard prohibitions regarding gays in the military. Homophobia remained rampant in the halls of Congress, with North Carolina Senator Jesse Helms damning gays as "degenerates" or "weak, morally sick wretches." Mississippi Senator Trent Lott, the Republican Majority Leader, likened homosexuality to alcoholism "or sex addiction . . . or kleptomania." In 1996, Congress passed the Defense of Marriage Act, which defined marriage as involving the union of a man and a woman. President Clinton signed it into law. Two years later, thugs brutalized Matthew Shepard, a gay, twenty-one-year-old student at the University of Wyoming, torturing him and cracking his skull; he died six days following the beating.

The decade was also marked by the use of the acronym LGBTQ, standing for lesbian, gay, bisexual, transgender, and queer, as well as new militancy associated with ACT UP but also organizational offshoots. Those included Queer Nation, which emerged in 1990, and the Lesbian Avengers, first appearing two years later. New Yorker Michelangelo Signorile, who had helped to found *OutWeek*, a gay magazine to which he contributed a weekly column, "Gossip Watch," also helped to found Queer Nation. The journalist Randy Shilts indicated that the organization "makes everybody else look reasonable," employing tactics varying from "nights out" to civil disobedience. Viewing with disdain traditional gay groups and enraged by mounting anti-gay violence and negative media representations, Queer Nation adopted a determinedly defiant stance challenging homophobic companies and governmental bodies. Queer Nation clearly elected to operate through "an in your face" approach, overseeing protests, engaging in disruptions, and outing closeted individuals. Other gays soon adopted Queer Nation's favored expression: "We're here. We're queer. Get used to it." During its early demonstrations, Queer Nation also wielded a banner reading "Dykes and Fags Bash Back." The group Lesbian Avengers, for its part, sprang up in New York City too, determined to engage in direct action and overcome lesbian invisibility. It was displeased as well about misogyny within the gay community. One of its founders, Ana Simo, had spoken of the need for "a group totally focused on high-impact street activism, not on talking." The call for the first meeting was addressed to "LESBIANS! DYKES! GAY WOMEN!" and insisted, "We're wasting our lives being careful. Imagine what your life could be. Aren't you ready to make it happen?" On April 24, 1993, 20,000 women participated in the initial Dyke March, held in Washington, D.C., while 10,000 showed up in San Francisco.

Another ostracized group, the disabled, continued to fight back against prejudices and discriminatory treatment, carrying out acts of civil disobedience, featuring rallies and demonstrations, and sponsoring Disability Pride Marches, the first two occurring in Boston at the onset of the 1990s. These took place as new federal legislation, the Americans with Disabilities Act (1990), required the affording of "reasonable accommodations" for the disabled regarding public transit, but also prohibited discriminating against "a qualified individual with a disability." The ADA passed after more than 1,000 disabled protestors crawled up the Capitol building steps demanding action. Four Senators, two from each major party and all with disabled relatives—Edward M. Kennedy, Tom Harkin, Bob Dole, and Lowell Weicker—helped to bring about Senate passage of the bill.

* * *

Left intellectuals continued to make their mark by the 1990s, many of them through the various institutions they had once challenged, even berated: American colleges and universities. Pacifica Radio established *Democracy Now!* in 1996, the journalists Amy Goodman, Juan Gonzales, and Nermeen Shakih serving as hosts. The program tracked corporate and governmental misdeeds, as well as a range of progressive movements. The nonprofit independent newscenter *Common Dreams* appeared in 1997, striving for participatory engagement while championing a free press. In his probing examination of American radicals, John Diggins explores the arrival of what he labels the Academic Left. With the coming apart and dissipating of the Movement, many Sixties radicals resumed their academic training or returned to it, like New Left activists or Black or Brown Power proponents Bill Ayers, Kathleen Cleaver, Angela Davis, Bernadine Dohrn, Todd Gitlin, Jose Angel Gutierrez, Tom Hayden, Ericka Huggins, Michael Kazin, Maurice Isserman, Howard Machtinger, and Mark Rudd. This demonstrated the determination of many activists to undertake "the long march through the institutions," earlier called for by the German New Left militant Rudi Dutschke. That notion was in keeping with Gramsci's examination of cultural hegemony and occurred in many professions and institutions beyond the Ivory Tower.

Some also considered, as social commentator Roger Kimball explores in *Tenured Radicals: How Politics Has Corrupted Our Higher Education*, the growing emphasis on race, class, and power, or identity politics, discussed by grassroots organizer L. A. Kauffman, both in 1990. Such emphases did increasingly show up in various classes, departments, even entire colleges or universities, which served as a corrective to the ethnocentric, patriarchal approaches and practices that long characterized the American academy, as they did life in the United States generally. Critics expressed concern too about the growth of Studies programs, particularly those involving women, African Americans, Latinos, Native Americans, and gays. Many faculty involved with such programs combined teaching and scholarship with activism. Earlier than Kimball and Kauffman, the historian Russell Jacobs worried about the passage of New Left radicals into the professoriate, but he expressed larger concerns regarding their narrowing of perspectives and involvement in the construction of "institutional fiefdoms" rather than operating as public intellectuals.

Intellectual discourse underwent marked changes, as new or altered concepts involving class, gender, power, memory, and thought itself impacted various disciplines. The great English historian E. P. Thompson helped to trigger a new working-class history, and more scholars determinedly wrote history from below, with attention to previously little considered groups, such as women, the poor, and the altogether marginalized. The concept of hegemony, associated with Gramsci, proved increasingly appealing within the social sciences and to former New Leftists entering the professoriate. The French philosopher Michael Foucault, associated with postmodernism, the American anthropologist Clifford Geertz, and the American historian Hayden White pushed at the boundaries of academic explorations, with examinations of power relations, symbols, and objectivity. The cultural turn, involving the essence of meaning and language, led some to worry about the loss of ethical standards altogether, including regarding some of the most horrific events in recorded history. Much of this proved highly controversial, inside and outside the Academy, but helped to call into question embedded patriarchal and hierarchical sensibilities. Also noteworthy was the American Social History Project's multi-volume series, *Who Built America?* Sparked by the labor historian Herbert G. Gutman and representative of the new social history and history from below, *Who Built America?* emphasized the role of the "ordinary American" in the workplace, whether at home, on the farm, in factories, and in both small and large businesses.

A very small number of left-oriented professors became American media sensations, producing best-selling books, hitting the lecture tour, or delivering commentary through radio or television programs. Having demanded his fellow intellectuals oppose the Vietnam War, Noam Chomsky continued criticizing U.S. foreign and domestic policies, but also insisted on the need to protect human rights across the globe. Consequently, he condemned both the Indonesian military takeover of East Timor and the Cambodian Khmer Rouge. Civil and antiwar activist, Boston University historian Howard Zinn wrote *A People's History of the United States* (1980), a revisionist exploration that initiated a cottage industry of a kind.

* * *

As the New Left and the Movement dissipated and a series of other campaigns continued, so too did what various analysts called a backyard revolution or front porch politics in which citizen advocacy thrived. Ideological battles remained in place, with Marxism surprisingly retaining its appeal for some, democratic socialism or social democracy vying for various hearts and minds, and liberation campaigns for women, gays, environmentalists, and anti-nuclear activists possessing vibrancy of their own. Acts of civil disobedience and massive street protests remained visible, but radicals and stalwart progressives also engaged in electoral politics.

Leftwing citizen activism, progressive policies, and progressive politicians hardly went uncontested. Numerous left-of-center groups or organizations were vilified by ideological opponents, continuously subjected to charges of being anti-family, terrorists, un-American, communists, and more. Rhetoric alone didn't always suffice as Harvey Milk, George Moscone, Alan Berg, and Judi Bari discovered. But electoral campaigns could prove unsettling too, as demonstrated by the battles against the ERA, abortion rights, and gay rights.

Chapter 9

Resurgent Radicalism: The Global Left

"It was the uprising that began the 21st century," and "unleashed a new global spirit of democratic resistance and revolution," contends the Institute for Policy Studies' Ben Manski. The decade's social movements were well-represented in Seattle, with workers and environmentalists, organizers from urban centers and farmers, and people from both "the Global North and the Global South" appearing linked. Many considered this latest effort part of the global justice movement, which involved striving, as the renowned systems theorist Buckminster Fuller had put it, "to make the world work for 100% of humanity in the shortest possible time, through spontaneous cooperation, without ecological offense or the disadvantage of anyone." Drawing on radical but nonviolent environmental battles out West, young rebels, subscribing to the slogan "This is What Democracy Looks Like!" accomplished what they set out to do: prevent the World Trade Organization (WTO) from convening, at least temporarily. They called on what were then novel tactics like "the 'people's mic,' 'action spokescouncils,' and independent media." The activists also turned to "the Old Left, trade unions, new movements and anarchist groups" for inspiration, the sociologist Immanuel Wallerstein states. They belonged to what can best be analyzed as the Global Left, one whose reach transcended boundaries of all sorts—national, class, racial, sexual—while being linked through new technological devices that allowed messages to spread all but instantaneously.

The protests proved to be "an important watershed for Internet-mediated activism," the political economist Matthew Eagleton-Pierce suggests. Many paid the price for their engagement, with 147 arrested and an untold number of individuals on the receiving end of police assaults. Nevertheless, those activists sparked an array of mass protests condemning capitalism, before meetings of government and corporate leaders at sites ranging from Austin,

Boston, and Washington, D.C., to Davos, London, Sao Paolo, Seoul, and Melbourne. Global Trade Watch's Mike Dolan, who helped organize anti-WTO protests, indicated a year after the Seattle uprising, "The coalition is intact and empowered, and actions are springing up all over the place." Political scientist David Olson affirmed, "This is a global phenomenon." A public report from the Canadian Security Intelligence Service acknowledged that something was afoot: "Seattle and Washington reflect how large the antagonistic audience has become, and the lengths to which the participants will go in their desire to shut down or impede the spread of globalization." The Seattle protests also resulted in formation of the World Social Forum, linking individuals and groups connected to the global justice movement.

For several days, beginning on November 28, 1999, marches and demonstrations condemning the WTO occurred in Seattle, Washington. Considered the start of the antiglobalization movement, the Seattle WTO protests involved sustainability, the environment, consumer protection, and workers' rights. They comprised, L. A. Kauffman contends, "the most ambitious direct-action undertaking in thirty years." As many as 100,000 people participated, most peacefully. However, a black bloc group of anarchists, attired in black apparel, masks, sunglasses, and padded motorcycle helmets, engaged in acts of vandalism, including involving police vehicles. They singled out stores like Nike, Nordstrom, and Starbucks, trashing windows and setting trash cans afire. Police resorted to batons, rubber bullets, tear gas, and pepper spray, while some demonstrators hurled water bottles and sticks. An AFL-CIO sponsored labor rally at the Seattle Center culminated in a march of more than 35,000 to the downtown sector.

Resistance had been anticipated at the WTO gathering, with *The Nation* offering a full issue concerning what it anticipated as the forthcoming "Battle in Seattle." The magazine appreciated that "corporate-managed globalization" had resulted in American protests "of European-style militancy." Nevertheless, the size and dimension of the actual protests must have been disconcerting to advocates of globalization, as "riots, rallies and marches against it" arose in twenty countries, at a minimum. Nor could they have been happy with the formation of the Direct Action Network, which sought to link nonviolent affinity groups subscribing to direct democracy, a termination of neoliberalism, and global solidarity.

Little pleasing too were protests occurring in Washington, D.C., in April 2000, directed against the International Monetary Fund and the World Bank. Among those marching were "two hundred masked-up teenage ninja revolutionaries" carrying black and red flags and a large banner referring to the group as the "Revolutionary Anti-Capitalist Bloc." Although far fewer than the Seattle protestors, the Washington contingent engaged in "a running, wall tagging, barricade building, cop baiting rampage," Jack Jones declares. Confronting the "teenage shock troops" hollering "Capitalism sucks" were 3,000 cops with tear gas and billy clubs.

* * *

During the run-up to the 2000 presidential election, more than 20,000 demonstrators came to Washington, D.C., in October to participate in the World March of Women, which demanded termination of both poverty and violence against women. Long planned and following the International Women's Day in early March, the October protests occurred worldwide. The National Organization of Women, which continued to push for ratification of the ERA, helped organize the Washington gathering. At the same time, NOW activists campaigned diligently to defeat Republican nominee George W. Bush.

Ultimately, NOW's efforts proved unavailing as the U.S. Supreme Court, following a bitterly contested race pitting Bush against Democratic Party candidate Al Gore, proclaimed the Republican the victor. The race came down to Florida, where the poorly designed ballot undoubtedly led to the misdirecting of thousands of votes by Jewish residents to rightwing candidate Pat Buchanan, viewed as no friend of Israel if not thoroughly anti-Semitic. Also hurting Gore was the third-party candidacy of Ralph Nader, who obtained 97,488 votes in Florida, a state Gore supposedly lost by a few hundred votes. Nader also amassed more than 22,000 votes in New Hampshire, where Bush prevailed by just over 7,000 votes; New Hampshire's four electoral votes too could have made Gore president. Running on the Green Party ticket and receiving support from a number of celebrities, while championing universal healthcare, strong labor unions, and environmental protections, Nader collected almost three million votes nationwide. Voter disfranchisement additionally prevented millions of potential voters, many people of color, from being able to participate in the 2000 election.

The new Bush administration foundered early and was the subject of protests involving feminists led by NOW, which put together a "Zap Action for Women's Lives," with 30,000 demonstrating in Washington, D.C. about the new president's stance on reproductive rights. Environmentalists were no happier, as the White House encouraged additional oil exploration and the building of both coal and nuclear power plants, while favoring reduced research funding involving renewable energy and conservation.

But the horrific attacks on September 11 caused Americans to rally around the administration, even though it had proven lax in responding to threats about impending terrorist attacks on the United States. The Bush administration adopted policies injurious to civil liberties, weakening the Freedom of Information Act, increasing surveillance of ordinary Americans, conducting warrantless wiretapping, setting up a No-Fly List, arresting and temporarily detaining purported "material witnesses" to crimes, preventing various scholars from coming to the United States, and expanding the National Security State.

In addition to passing measures such as the Patriot Act, supposedly designed to provide "appropriate tools required to intercept and obstruct terrorism," Congress authorized the president to employ force against those behind or involved in the September 11 attacks or who sheltered them. Only California Representative Barbara Lee, a member of the Congressional Black Caucus, opposed the authorization, fearing "an open-ended war" that lacked "a focused target" or "an exit strategy." Encouraged by the neoconservatives, a group of intellectuals who insisted Saddam Hussein was involved with the 9/11 attacks on New York City and Washington, D.C., notwithstanding all evidence to the contrary, the Bush administration supported military operations in both Afghanistan and Iraq. Afghanistan had housed Osama bin Laden's terrorist organization Al Qaeda, while Saddam, a secular dictator and a Sunni, brutally dealt with his country's Shiite majority. But the neoconservatives pointed to a supposed nexus between Osama and Saddam, and, along with Vice-President Richard "Dick" Cheney, helped convince Bush to attack Iraq.

Immediate opposition to U.S. military operations engendered harsh criticisms. Writing on September 12, 2001, Noam Chomsky indicated, "The September 11 attacks were major atrocities," while contending that far more deaths had resulted from Bill Clinton's destruction of Sudanese pharmaceutical supplies. He warned of impending "harsh security controls," as well as possible diminution of civil liberties and personal freedoms and was concerned that "the crime is a gift to the hard jingoist right." On Bill Maher's talk show *Politically Incorrect*, the host declared days after the attack, "We have been the cowards, lobbying cruise missiles from 2,000 miles away. That's cowardly. Staying in the airplane when it hits the building? Say what you want about it, it's not cowardly." The popularity of Maher's program plummeted and it was cancelled months later. Writing in *The New Yorker*, Susan Sontag offered, "If the word 'cowardly' is to be used, it might be more aptly applied to those who kill from beyond the range of retaliation, high in the sky, than to those willing to die themselves in order to kill others." Letters to the editor proved "overwhelmingly negative," at least at first.

The American left, including expats Christopher Hitchens and Tony Judt, split over how to respond to 9/11. International law expert Richard Falk, one of the foremost legal critics of U.S. operations in Vietnam, questioned Chomsky's analysis. Chomsky, Falk worried, was "so preoccupied with the evils of US imperialism that . . . it's not possible for him to acknowledge . . . some US military intervention may actually have a beneficial effect." The war in Afghanistan, Falk concluded, was "just and necessary," although he considered employment of devices such as cluster bombs "in clear violation of the laws of war." New Left veteran Paul Berman wrote, "America's crime, its real crime, is to be America itself," by exuding "the dynamism of an ever-changing liberal culture." Chastizing what he viewed as "the radical failure of the left's response to the events of the previous fall, Michael Waltzer, co-editor of *Dissent* magazine, wondered, "Can there be a decent left in a super-power?" The war, *The Nation*'s Katha Pollitt admitted, "is a real crisis for the left, in that finally there is an enemy who has attacked us, as opposed to any enemy that's in our heads, and one that's completely unsympathetic to the goals of the left." Hitchens, who had a complicated history with the left but considered himself part of it, condemned the director Oliver Stone's talk of "the revolt of September 11." Hitchens also slammed Chomsky's response to 9/11, charging that the famed linguist had discarded "every standard that makes moral and intellectual discrimination possible." Judt backed the war in Afghanistan but expressed grave reservations regarding the Bush administration's impending invasion of Iraq.

The sociologist Victoria Carty notes that activists drew on "cyber-activism and cyber-organizing" to form transnational protest connections. Web-oriented "Peaceful Tomorrows, Win Without War, and MoveOn" served as significant antiwar online organizations committed to creating "a broad, global movement toward peace and justice." Peaceful Tomorrows, made up of 9/11 victims' family members, fretted about military retaliation. Win Without War, which brought together almost fifty progressive groups, expressed a commitment to tackling both terrorism and arms proliferations, while opposing "unilateral military preemption." MoveOn fired off an online petition urging Congress not to retaliate "by bombing Kabul and" killing "people oppressed by the Taliban." Doing so would make the American people "like the terrorists we oppose."

Less than three weeks after the attacks on the World Trade Center and the Pentagon on September 11, thousands gathered in Washington, D.C., for an "Anti-War, Anti-Racist" rally sponsored by Act Now to Stop War and End Racism (ANSWER), chanting "We will not be silent!" or "We want justice, we want peace, US out of the Middle East." In early October, thousands participated in rallies in New York City and San Francisco, warning about a military response to 9/11 and the administration's announced War on Terror. During the spring of 2002, a coalition of groups, including pacifist organizations, participated in the April 20th Stop the War Mobilization. Not all were pleased by ANSWER's involvement, particularly its urging of "Free Palestine, No War on Iraq." The progressive Jewish magazine *Tikkun* later discussed "Authoritarianism and Anti-Semitism in the Anti-War Movement," pointing to ANSWER's vilification of both Jews and Israel.

A growing number of progressive political bloggers, including Markos Moulitsas of *Daily Kos*, delivered critical analyses of U.S. engagement in the Near East; their online outposts were also part of what the political strategist Jerome Armstrong referred to as netroots. Activists held antiwar, anti-capi-

talist rallies on October 31, in both the United States and the United Kingdom. On November 17, 2002, activists formed Code Pink: Women for Peace,
a self-described "grassroots peace and social justice movement" seeking "to
end US-funded wars and occupations, to challenge militarism globally, and
to redirect our resources into health care, education, green jobs and other life-
affirming activities."

With the Bush administration readying for war, mass rallies took place
across the world. Millions turned out on February 15, 2003, expressing opposition to an anticipated attack on Saddam Hussein's Iraq in responding to the
call "the world says no to war!" Demonstrators participating in "the first
global demonstration," as former British Labour cabinet member Tony Benn
referred to it, cried out, "Not in our name!" Two million people congregated
in London, 800,000 gathered in Paris, 500,000 massed in Berlin, 300,000
appeared in Rome, 250,000 came together in Sydney, and 200,000 demonstrated in Barcelona. Approximately 200,000 marched in San Francisco and
another 400,000 in New York City, where animated, even hopeful anarchists,
pacifists, students, veterans, musicians, and regular urban dwellers, including
"Soccer Moms Against the War," participated. Heading to the rally in New
York, South Africa's Archbishop Desmond Tutu exclaimed, "Peace! Peace!
Peace!" and urged that the United States "listen to the rest of the world."
Many signs in rallies across the country read "Can you justify blood for oil!"
MoveOn and Win Without War sparked the sending of thousands of phone
calls and faxes to U.S. Senators with the admonition, "DON'T ATTACK
IRAQ!"

Antiwar protests took place both at home and abroad in the immediate
aftermath of the United States' invasion of Iraq in March 2003. Many of the
demonstrations overseas were massive in scale, while 50,000 gathered in
Boston only days after the bombing began. Violent and nonviolent protest
occurred in Oakland. MoveOn initiated a large-scale transnational email
campaign to gather signatures for a proclamation stating, "As we grieve for
the victims of this war, we pledge to redouble our efforts to put an end to the
Bush Administration's doctrine of preemptive attack and the reckless use of
military power." Other online groups like "Bring Them Home Now, Military
Families Speak Out, Mothers Against War, and VoteVets" sought to challenge "the sanitized 'official' version of the war," anticipating testimony by
returning veterans of the conflict. Critical analyses could be heard through
Radiopower.org, which in 2002 began delivering progressive talk radio programs, while the Sirius Left satellite channel started broadcasting. The next
year, *Air America Radio* initiated operations, delivering progressive talk
radio programming.

With the fall of Saddam Hussein's regime, opposition to the war hardly
abated. In late October, thousands turned out for demonstrations in the United States and elsewhere. Michael Moore's scathing documentary *Fahrenheit*

9/11, about the War on Terror, was released in the United States on June 25, 2004. Having condemned the U.S. invasion of Iraq, former Vermont governor Howard Dean undertook a bid for the Democratic Party presidential nomination, relying on fundraising through the Internet. His campaign caught fire initially, then faltered, and he departed the race. According to some estimates, nearly a million people protested in New York City on August 29, as the Republican National Convention prepared to renominate George W. Bush. Running against Bush was former VVAW leader John Kerry, the junior senator from Massachusetts, who played up his Vietnam War experience, which was turned against him by Republican operatives who nastily called into question his heroics. Also damaging to Kerry was his party's identification with gay rights, accelerated since San Francisco Mayor Gavin Newson, in February 2004, directed city and county officials to issue marriage licenses to gay couples, kicking off another stage in the cultural wars dividing the nation. The city experienced a "Winter of Love," with thousands of same-sex marriages conducted.

Weeks before the election, Arlington National Cemetery was the scene of "A Trail of Mourning and Truth from Iraq to the White House," involving veterans and Gold Star families, which included Cindy Sheehan, whose son Casey died in Iraq. Neil Young blasted the Bush administration, producing such songs as "Living with War" and "Let's Impeach the President." Green Day crafted *American Idiot* and the Dixie Chicks, "Not Ready to Make Nice," both embittered indictments of President Bush. Nevertheless, the "swiftboating" of John Kerry, an ironic reference to his service as a much-decorated naval veteran, and the turnout by Christian conservatives, adverse to the idea of gay marriage, abetted Bush's reelection.

While some displayed an initial reluctance to criticize U.S. military engagement, the Iraq War's steadily ruinous nature ensured that opposition continued. As Iraq imploded, charges of war criminality materialized, including regarding the prison at Abu Ghraib outside of Baghdad where prisoners were subjected to harsh interrogations and abuse that some insisted involved torture. Investigative accounts, including by Seymour Hersh in *The New Yorker*, tracked instances of American soldiers brutalizing Iraqis. Large demonstrations against the war continued, a number held on anniversaries of the invasion. The antiwar movement, political scientist Michael Heaney indicates, "was pretty well sustained from 2003 through about 2006," with massive protests, "coordinated activity and lobbying," "numerous active coalitions," and considerable grassroots mobilization. Denunciations of the Bush administration could be heard at the annual gatherings of Netroots Nation, kicked off by Daily Kos and intended for progressive political activists, who met a series of potential Democratic Party presidential candidates. Jon Stewart, host of *The Daily Show*, and *Real Time with Bill Maher*, programs noted for their sardonic humor, regularly offered biting criticisms of the Iraq War.

Condemnations of the Bush administration also centered on its handling of the economy, regressive tax policy, gutting of environmental regulations, packing of federal courts with rightwing jurists, and readiness to resort to perverse political attacks questioning its opponents' patriotism. The unfortunate response in 2005 to Hurricane Katrina, which devastated New Orleans, further empowered the administration's critics, who already accused it of war crimes and civil liberties' violations. Events since 9/11 only drove Tony Judt to a still more critical perspective, at the same time he lauded genuine social democracy and a humane welfare state, the strength of both of which were increasingly called into question.

* * *

The campaign and election of Barack Obama, the first African American to receive the nomination of a major political party, blunted the antiwar movement. Some of that was due to Obama's early opposition to the war, as expressed during a speech on October 2, 2002, in which the then Illinois state senator began by indicating he was not opposed to all wars, including the Civil War that helped to eradicate slavery and World War II, when his grandfather "fought in the name of a larger freedom . . . over evil." Obama also stated that he supported the Bush administration's determination following 9/11 "to hunt down and root out those who would slaughter innocents in the name of intolerance." What he opposed was "a dumb war . . . a rash war . . . the cynical attempt by" neocons "and other armchair, weekend "warriors" who sought "to shove their own ideological agenda down our throats, irrespective of the costs in lives lost and in hardships borne." Damning Saddam Hussein as "brutal . . . ruthless," a butcherer of his own people, Obama nevertheless insisted that the Iraqi dictator posed "no imminent and direct threat to the United States or to his neighbors." Instead of going after Saddam, Obama declared, President Bush should "finish the fight with bin Laden and al-Qaida." Bush should also make "our so-called allies in the Middle East," referring to Saudia Arabia and Egypt, "stop oppressing their own people, and suppressing dissent."

His early and continued opposition to war in Iraq helped Senator Obama capture the Democratic Party presidential nomination, besting New York Senator Hillary Clinton, the former First Lady who had supported the U.S. invasion. Obama's campaign received a boost from the large number of young people who assisted his campaign, as they acquired both "unprecedented access to new digital tools" and "training in organizing," indicates the journalist Sarah Jaffe. Obama's own earlier experience as a community organizer in Chicago was wielded against him during the presidential campaign, and efforts were made to tie him to former Weather Underground leaders Bill Ayers and Bernadine Dohrn, neighbors of Obama in Chicago's historic Hyde

Park area. Obama maintained American troops in Iraq and intensified the fighting in Afghanistan but antiwar rallies diminished in size and intensity. Yet according to sociologists Michael T. Heaney and Fabio Rojas, the number of participants at antiwar gatherings actually began to decline as early as 2007.

Civil rights veteran Marshall Ganz notes that Obama failed to employ the activists who helped land him in the White House, in contrast to how labor unions furthered the New Deal under Franklin D. Roosevelt and the civil rights movement provided support for passage of the Voting Rights Act that Lyndon B. Johnson came to favor. Markos Moulitsas suggests, "What happened when Obama won? We all went home."

That proved disconcerting to progressives as the president's opponents were relentless and sometimes downright perverse. Various foes continued to attack him as they had during the campaign, as some kind of socialist and an un-American, whose very citizenship was called into question, especially by New York real estate tycoon Donald Trump. Senate Minority Leader Mitch McConnell of Kentucky expressed his determination to ensure that Obama was a one-term president, and rightwing foes, backed by large pools of "dark money," whose origin remained undisclosed, conducted unprincipled campaigns at all levels. Republicans won back local, state, and federal offices, taking over many small cities, statehouses, and Congress, at different points. The 2010 elections enabled Republicans to grab control of state legislatures and governorships, which provided the means to gerrymander elections over the next decade. Once in office, new hard right governors like Maine's Paul LePage, New Jersey's Chris Christie, Ohio's John Kasich, Michigan's Rick Snyder, Wisconsin's Scott Walker, Florida's Rick Scott, and Texas' Rick Perry waged war on public service employees, teachers' unions, public education, social welfare measures, voting rights, the environment, workers, and consumer protection. Even attempts to fight back, such as efforts to recall Walker, generally proved unavailing.

While *Fox News* attracted a right-leaning audience, pleased with the reactionary turn in state after state and delighted by Fox's blistering criticisms of Obama, progressive viewers tuned into MSNBC for *Countdown with Keith Olbermann*. The host offered something rare on network television: insightful, articulate, angry commentary from the left-side of the American political spectrum. Later Olbermann suggested, "I think I helped open a door for criticism against Bush and particularly the politicizing of terror in 2005, 2006, 2007." *Air America* Radio continued its run until early 2010, challenging the right's stranglehold on talk radio. Former *Saturday Night Live* comedian Al Franken finished his program on *Air America*, running for a senatorial seat from his home state of Minnesota. Politically charged documentarian Michael Moore put out *Sicko* (2007), a slap at the American health care system; *Slacker Uprising* (2008), a recounting of his tour of American colleges, intended to get-out-the-vote; and *Capitalism: A Love Story* (2009), covering the impact of the nation's economic system's boom-and-bust nature. Canadian-born author Naomi Klein, a favorite on American colleges and universities, produced *The Shock Doctrine: The Rise of Disaster Capitalism* (2007), which was published shortly before the economy began crumbling. The United We Dream Network appeared in 2008, eventually becoming the nation's "largest immigrant youth-led organization," demanding that immigrant youth and families be treated fairly. The left, however, experienced setbacks as well, including unrelenting assaults on abortion rights, birth control, and a progressive organization like ACORN, which had done much good but was incessantly assaulted by rightwingers displeased by its commitment to social and economic justice, an increased minimum wage, and affordable housing. False allegations of corruption and a cutting off of federal funds eventually proved too much, causing ACORN to cease operations.

Amid the economic collapse that began as the 2008 presidential election neared a close, first the Tea Party on the right side of the ideological spectrum and then Occupy Wall Street arose, the latter challenging wealth inequality, corporate dominance, and corruption. The near economic depression was the worst the nation had experienced since the 1930s, and the recovery was slow, because of the severity of the downturn, deep-seated structural problems, and the propensity of Republicans to stymie President Obama's efforts to stimulate growth and create jobs. Then there was Obama's reluctance and that of many of his leading advisers to push for more forceful change. Even as the economy began to improve, more affluent Americans, particularly the wealthiest of all, benefitted disproportionately as they had during the past four decades. Anger about stagnant or plummeting wages, job losses, home foreclosures, deindustrialization, and globalization fueled both the Tea Party and Occupy. Beginning in Manhattan's Financial District, Occupy soon appeared in over 100 communities across the United States, and more than 1500 cities globally. Its backers argued that the wealthiest one percent unfairly reaped the greatest economic bounty, in both good and bad times, and wielded too much political power.

While the billionaire Koch brothers—David and Charles—along with legitimate concerns about the state of the economy, fueled the Tea Party's rise, Occupy's roots were both simpler and more complex. Political activists, including Kalle Lasn, co-founder and editor-in-chief of the leftwing anti-consumerism publication, *Adbusters*, produced the initial calls for a demonstration in front of Wall Street. Lasn and his compatriots were displeased that Tea Party members were "passionately strutting their [sic] stuff," as the American political left was "sort of hiding somewhere." They reasoned that an uprising could occur in the United States "because a) the political left needs it and b) because people are losing their jobs . . . their houses, and young people cannot find a job." They were displeased that "the financial fraudsters on Wall Street" who spawned the economic debacle "haven't even been brought to justice yet." Consequently, "We felt this was the right moment to instigate something." Published shortly after the 1999 WTO protests in Seattle, Naomi Klein's book, *No Logo: Taking Aim at the Brand Bullies* served as a movement template for alter-globalization or alternative globalization.

Lasn placed a poster in the July 2011 edition of his magazine, urging 20,000 people to pour into lower Manhattan to "incessantly repeat one simple demand in a plurality of voices," and he turned to a listserv of 90,000 "culture-jammers" around the world. As Lasn, a Canadian resident born in Tallinn, indicated, for two decades "our network" had "been interested in cultural revolution and just the whole idea of radical transformations." The Arab Spring of late 2010 and 2011, characterized by pro-democracy demonstrations and uprisings in North Africa and Middle East, provided another backdrop. It led Lasn and others to believe "that a few smart people using Facebook and Twitter can put out calls and suddenly get huge numbers of people to get out into the streets and start giving vent to their anger." Anonymous, a body of international activist hackers who believed in "the free flow of information," also assisted the Arab Spring, joining with dissidents to share videos, prevent governments from carrying out phishing campaigns, and restore access to censored sites. Another inspiration was the Paris-oriented Situationist movement in Europe that developed between 1957 and 1972, which offered through Guy Debord's *The Society of the Spectacle* the notion that "a very powerful meme—a very powerful idea—," along with a ripe moment, could "ignite a revolution." The Situationists had influenced the near revolution in France during the spring of 1968, but Lasn saw the present budding movement as potentially "the second global revolution that we've been dreaming about for the last half a century."

Those gathering in Zucotti Park, beginning on September 17, 2011, engaged in free-flowing debate, as the apparently "leaderless, demandless movement" emerged. With amplification largely prohibited, Occupiers employed the "People's Mic," repeating pronouncements sentence by sentence to enable those beyond the speaker to hear. Participants were devoted to decision-making by consensus, and committed to "horizontalism," associated with the idea of the New York City General Assembly (NYCGA) and an absence of hierarchy. National Public Radio noted that the demonstrations had a variety of labels, in addition to Occupy, such as "American Autumn" or "The 99 Percent." Focusing on "the 1%," although that threw together comfortable, even affluent individuals with the super-rich, Occupy spread across the United States. And influenced by Occupy, activists and organizers determined to foster genuine democracy, relying on nonviolent civil resistance, formed 99Rise. It sought to drive big money out of American politics.

Other progressive groups continued to appear during President Obama's first term. Employing direct action tactics, the Dream is Coming pressured both the administration and immigrant rights supporters. The United We Dream Network helped to goad Obama into establishing the Deferred Action for Childhood Arrival (DACA) program. DACA provided certain legal protections for undocumented immigrants who arrived in the United States before turning sixteen, enabling each to acquire work authorization and a social security number. Also relying on civil disobedience, GetEQUAL insisted on "full legal and social equality" for the LGBTQ community. The Progressive Change Campaign Committee set up the P Street Project, intending it to be, as co-founder Adam Green indicated, a "permanent Hill lobbying shop that constructs 'inside-outside' strategy with members of Congress around progressive legislation."

Following yet another slaying of an unarmed black teenager, Trayvon Martin, this time at the hands of a neighborhood watch captain in Florida, demonstrators held the "Million Hoodie March" in New York's Union Square on March 21, 2012. About 1,000 marchers, many wearing hooded sweatshirts like the one Martin had on when shot, called out, "We want arrests!" and "We are all Trayvon." Speaking to a crowd at Union Square, his father, Tracy Martin, said, "We're not going to stop until we get justice. My son did not deserve to die." Barely an hour after the rally nearly a million signatures had been collected for an online petition demanding a criminal investigation of George Zimmerman, the man who killed Martin.

During the spring of 2013, Reverend William J. Barber II of Goldsboro, North Carolina, initiated the Moral Mondays movement, which involved civil disobedience at the statehouse. The protests pertained to measures passed by the legislature to curb social welfare measures and restrict voting rights. President of North Carolina's NAACP chapter, Barber worried about tax reductions for the wealthy, diminished spending on public education, and the repeal of the Racial Justice Act, passed four years earlier, which enabled death row inmates to challenge racially discriminatory sentences. Called "the moral voice of the South," Barber contested what he deemed the "immoral" determination to curb the Affordable Health Care Act (the ACA, also known as Obamacare), stating, "I never want to have health insurance and see other members of the human family denied."

Appearing in mid-2013 and led by Patrisse Cullors, Alicia Garza, and Opal Tometi, three black organizers, #BlackLivesMatter (B.L.M.) drew from civil rights activist Diane Nash's observation, "Freedom, by definition, is people realizing that they are their own leaders." It emerged in the wake of the latest in a succession of black men and women wrongly killed by police or vigilantes, with no justice forthcoming. State violence, the organization charged, led to black poverty, genocide, and mass incarceration, as well as to unending assaults on black women, families, homosexuals, and transgender individuals. #BlackLivesMatter became "a platform and organizing tool," used by other groups also concerned about racism. B.L.M. was particularly troubled by "state-sanctioned violence," and how it resulted in the taking of the lives of too many young African Americans, including Trayvon Martin, Tanisha Anderson, Sandra Bland, Mike Brown, Mya Hall, Tamir Rice, and Walter Scott. The killing of eighteen-year-old Brown by Darren Wilson, a white police officer, in Ferguson, located in the metropolitan area of St. Louis, Missouri, resulted in an outpouring of rage, demonstrations, and civil unrest. Determined to stand by the African American communities in Ferguson and St. Louis, B.L.M. founders saw the necessity of "organizing and building Black power across the country." Associated with B.L.M., #StayWoke emphasized the need to appreciate how racism, sexism, and classism impacted so many individuals. #StayWoke tracked systematic racial abuses involving the police and the prison system, but also urged readers to understand how privilege or its absence affected American society.

Responding to repeated incidents of police brutality meted out to scores of young African Americans, San Francisco 49er quarterback Colin Kaepernick delivered a profound statement of his own. During preseason contests, Kaerpernick refused to stand during the playing of the national anthem, declaring, "I am not going to stand up to show pride in a flag for a country that oppresses black people and people of color." The 2016 regular season saw numerous other National Football League (NFL) players follow Kaerpernick's lead, just as he was acting as the National Basketball Association star Mahmoud Abdul-Rauf had years earlier.

* * *

The 2016 presidential campaign included Senator Bernie Sanders, a self-described democratic socialist, competing in the Democratic Party primaries against former Secretary of State and First Lady Hillary Clinton. Attracting rabid adherents, Sanders condemned wealth inequality, the American middle class's increasingly precarious state, corporate preeminence, sweeping domestic government surveillance, and trade deals that hurt workers and the environment alike. Mostly relying on small donations, Sanders also demanded pro-union legislation, paid leave, acknowledgment of climate change, public funding of elections, universal health care, and greater investments in education, from preschool through college. Sanders pushed hard for a $15 an hour federal minimum wage standard, which activists increasingly demanded. Like Clinton, Sanders supported LGBT rights, which had received a boost from the 2015 Supreme Court ruling of *Obergefell v. Hodges* solidifying the right to same-sex marriage. He also called for decriminalization of marijuana, termination of the death penalty, reform of the American criminal justice system, gun control, racial justice, and immigration reform.

Sanders additionally favored a progressive foreign policy, one that backed a two-state solution on Israeli-Palestinian land and warned against the United States being "involved in perpetual warfare in the Middle East." Receiving over thirteen million votes, Sanders won twenty-three of fifty-seven primaries or caucuses, a remarkable feat for a political figure long viewed as on the far-left side of the political spectrum.

During the 2016 presidential campaign, Donald J. Trump clearly pandered to the Alt Right (Alternative Right), individuals and groups situated on the extreme right favorably disposed to racism, anti-Semitism, and white supremacy. These included right-wing militias, white nationalists, self-professed patriot groups, segregationists, members of the Ku Klux Klan, and Nazis. They employed platforms ranging from the neo-Nazi website, *The Daily Stormer*, to alt-right blogging. They engaged in vicious trolling during the campaign that led to the sending of pictures of gas chambers to journalists considered unfriendly to Trump; those pictures contained images of the journalists and sometimes of their children. Trump's campaign received a boost from the release by WikiLeaks, Julian Assange's intelligence network once admired by many progressives, of documents, including private emails, related to the Democratic Party and Hillary Clinton.

America's cultural wars continued. Macklemore's "Sam Love" served as an ode to marriage equality, including for LGBTQ individuals, and the hip-hop group A Tribe Called Quest's "We the People" referred to the nativism, racism, and homophobia that surged once again during the 2016 presidential campaign. Briana Marela called on "There Is a War" by Leonard Cohen to warn of severe economic disparities, while the celebrated folksinger Joan Baez put out "Nasty Man," about "a future dictator" who possessed "dangerous pathological disorders." In "Formation" and "Alright," African American artists like Beyonce and Kendrick Lamar expressed outrage over blacks unjustifiably killed by the police. MSNBC, despite a tilt away from the progressive orientation associated with Keith Olbermann, who had been fired in 2011, still offered trenchant analyses of Trump on programs hosted by Chris Matthews, Chris Hayes, Rachel Maddow, Lawrence O'Donnell, and Joy Reid, among others. Thom Hartmann, Jim Hightower, Mike Malloy, Stephanie Miller, Bill Press, Randi Rhodes, Ed Schultz, *Democracy Now!*, and *Pacifica Radio* continued offering alternative perspectives on national and international news. *Rag Radio*, a weekly syndicated radio program based out of Austin, Texas, maintained the Movement spirit associated with the legendary underground newspaper, *The Rag*. Host and *Rag* founder Thorne Dreyer deftly interviewed hundreds of guests, among them former SDS leaders Tom Hayden, Todd Gitlin, Bill Ayers, and Bernardine Dohrn; progressive stalwarts Jim Hightower, Gar Alperovitz, and Bernie Sanders; and underground figures Paul Krassner, Ed Sanders, Gilbert Shelton, and John Sinclair.

Zines, defined by author Stephen Duncombe as "noncommercial, nonprofessional, small-circulation magazines" put out by "their creators," flourished as they had for decades. Eventually, "radical, marginalized people" employed zines "to express themselves," indicates multimedia journalist Danny Lewis. Earlier zines served as communication devices for African Americans in the 1920s, oppressed lesbians in the 1950s, Asian-American radicals in the 1960s, punks in the 1970s, the underground feminist movement associated with Riot Grrl in the latter part of the 1980s and the early 1990, and amid the anti-WTO protests that took place in Seattle at the end of the decade. More recent zines such as *Freeing Ourselves: A Guide to Health and Self Love*, the Secret Society of Femmes' *BROS FALL BACK*, and *Black Women Matter* tackled gender identity, patriarchy, and the killing of black women by police officers.

Progressive, even radical ideas also received an airing through edgy comedians, as had long been the case. In keeping with the earlier "sicknik" humor of Mort Sahl, Lenny Bruce, and Dick Gregory, entertainers like Bill Maher, Stephanie Miller, Samantha Bee, and Trevor Noah, who replaced Jon Stewart as host of *The Daily Show*, ridiculed racists, homophobes, and sexists. Maher's *Real Time* on HBO, *Full Frontal* with Samantha Bee, and *The Stephanie Miller Show*, a national syndicated radio program, delivered searing attacks on Trump, whom they considered unhinged and possessing fascistic propensities.

99Rise gave way to Democracy Spring, which by early 2016 included a coalition of more than 120 progressive groups, and "regional organizing hubs" scattered throughout the United States. By April, over 1,300 individuals conducted a sit-in on the U.S. Capitol steps, amounting to the most massive civil disobedience of the new century. That summer, additional sit-ins occurred, along with an extended National Training session involving volunteer leaders.

Progressives experienced internecine squabbles, something the Trump campaign attempted to exacerbate. Writing in *The Atlantic*, Peter Beinart pointed to the issue of political correctness, mentioning that the University of California had recently declared the term "melting pot" a "microaggression." Trump congratulated himself for his refusal to "be politically correct" after intemperately responding to the mass killing by a Muslim shooter of forty people at an Orlando gay nightclub. That also followed Trump's reference to women he disliked as "'fat pigs, 'dog,' 'slobs,' and 'disgusting animals.'"

Discussion of PC had emerged a quarter of a century earlier with concerns expressed about American universities becoming so afflicted. After fading for a time, concerns about PC dogmatism resurfaced late during the Obama administration with discussions of "safe spaces," trigger warnings, which were being embedded in college syllabi, and worries about controversial speakers. Those led some to fear that the range of discussion was being circumscribed, with rightwingers denounced and occasionally unable to deliver lectures due to disruptions at colleges or universities. Comedians like Bill Maher and Chris Rock, neither at all sympathetic to the right, also found it increasingly uncomfortable to appear at certain campuses, particularly elite ones where the new cultural wars seemed to be raging.

* * *

Trump's unanticipated victory in November 2016, following a campaign marked by his repeated use of derogatory statements about Mexicans, a federal judge, his Republican opponents, Gold Star parents, the handicapped, women, and Democratic nominee Clinton, produced an outpouring of grief and a readiness to counter the president-elect. A new movement began in late December with the online publication of *Indivisible: A Practical Guide for Resisting the Trump Agenda*, a twenty-three page guide crafted by former congressional staff members. In contrast to the Tea Party, which became inextricably intertwined with the Republican Party, Indivisible sought to remain apart from the Democratic Party. Ex-Obama staff members Jon Favreau, Jon Lovett, and Tommy Vietor formed *Crooked Media*, which delivered a twice-weekly podcast, *Pod Save America*, soon referred to as "the left's answer to conservative talk radio." Along with Dan Pfeiffer, who had been a top adviser to Obama, they had also presented the *Keepin' it 1600* podcast.

Concerns only intensified following Trump's poorly attended and ill-received inaugural address on January 20, 2017, during which he painted a foreboding, even sinister depiction of the country he was about to lead. Referring to a national landscape beset by poverty, "rusted-out factories," badly educated students, "crimes and gangs and drugs," Trump insisted, "This American carnage stops right here and stops right now." Employing the language of World War II-era isolationists, he declared, "From this moment on, it's going to be America First."

The very next day, the Women's March on Washington, which dwarfed the size of the inaugural address, attracted an enormous crowd of more than half-a-million demonstrators, with hundreds of additional rallies held across the United States. Over 400,000 appeared in New York City, 175,000 in Boston, 250,000 in Chicago. Many participants, a large number defiantly wearing pink "pussyhats," considered themselves part of "the Resistance," as concerted opposition to Trump was called. At one point, "Mothers of the Movement," all of whom had suffered the loss of a child because of police violence, went onstage at the Capitol Mall. The actress-activist Ashley Judd recalled Trump's unabashed admission to sexually harassing women, declaring that private parts "ain't for grabbing. They are for birthing new generations of filthy, vulgar, nasty, proud, Christian, Muslim, Buddhist, Sikh, you name it, for new generations of nasty women."

The historian Timothy D. Snyder delivered his own warning in a small but poignant book, *On Tyranny: Twenty Lessons from the 20th Century*, released the month following Trump's inauguration. Pulling no punches, Snyder, a Holocaust scholar, cautioned that Trump did indeed have designs on becoming an American strongman. Tellingly, Snyder warned, "Americans today are no wiser than the Europeans who saw democracy yield to fascism, Nazism, or communism in the twentieth century." "Hitler's language" like that of Trump's, Snyder indicated, "rejected legitimate opposition." Snyder also worried about the constant use of certain words or phrases that enabled "a narrowing of vocabulary and thought that only empowers the strongman."

Only months into the Trump administration, Reverend William Barber initiated a new Poor People's Campaign. "Fifty years ago," Barber, another eloquent black minister, explained, "Dr. Martin Luther King Jr. called for a radical 'revolution of values,' inviting a nation to stand against the evils of militarism, racism, and economic injustice." Attempting to recapture the spirit of King's Poor People's Campaign that occurred during the last several months of the great civil right leader's life, Barber declared, "We are calling for national moral revival." Barber's socially committed brand of Christianity was in keeping with that of Jim Wallis, the founder of Sojourners, a national faith-based organization that emphasized the need for "sociopolitical engagement." Like Barber, Wallis readily resorted to civil disobedience to contest injustice and war.

The Reverend Barber, Wallis, and other progressives continued to push back against the determination of congressional Republicans and the Trump White House to destroy the Affordable Care Act. ADAPT members staged protests, as they had during previous administrations, conducting a "die-in" outside the Senate office of Republican Majority Leader Mitch McConnell in mid-2017. One woman cried out, "No cuts to Medicaid!" as police lifted her from a wheelchair. Organizer Nancy Salandra bemoaned the fact that "we are still fighting for our freedom from incarceration," referring to the institutionalization of many of the disabled.

Indivisible soon amounted to thousands of chapters across the country, whose members went after representatives and senators favoring repeal of the ACA, which would deny millions of Americans health coverage. Even Senate minority leader Charles Schumer of New York began urging "resistance," while the new Democratic National Committee Chair Tom Perez called for movement "into the ballot box." *Rolling Stone*'s Tim Dickinson wrote that "the passionate activism of hundreds of thousands of progressives" had accomplished "the impossible in Washington, D.C.," preventing

Republicans, in control of all branches of the federal government, from re-
pealing Obamacare.

A training institute that followed the lead of the aging strategist Frances
Fox Piven, Momemtum sought to serve as "movement incubator," schooling
progressive organizers in how to construct "massive, decentralized social
movements." Momentum pointed to the necessity of addressing the nation's
"unprecedented inequality" regarding both wealth and power. Swing Left
particularly targeted congressional seats where the 2016 results had been
close, to try and ensure that the Democrats regained control of the House.
EMILY's List maintained its efforts to elect liberal female candidates, An-
nie's List did the same in Texas, while Emerge America trained progressive
women running for office. Calling on small donors, ActBlue and Blue America strove to do that for liberal candidates in general. Run for Something
targeted rookie progressive candidates. Rock the Vote continued urging
young people to become politically engaged. Latino Victory sought to augment progressive Latino representation from the local level to the presidency.
Our Revolution helped to keep the spirit of Bernie Sanders's presidential
candidacy alive. For Our Future focused on grassroots involvement. Netroots
Foundation strove to unite "online citizens across America, inject progressive voices into the national conversation, and advance the values of justice,
equality and community in our nation's politics." The Harry Potter Alliance
highlighted a series of important issues such as climate change, economic
justice, and immigration reform. Progressive discussion board platforms included *Liberal Forum*, *Reddit: Progressive*, and *Thom Hartmann Message
Boards*. Liberal and progressive blogging remained plentiful, like that of
Matt Bai, Paul Krugman, Robert Kuttner, BillMoyers.com, John Nichols,
Greg Palast, Robert Reich, David Remnick, *AMERICAblog*, *Down with Tyranny!*, *Forward Progressives*, *The Hightower Lowdown*, *The Progressive
Latino*, and *Women's Liberation Front*.

The advent of the Trump presidency led to "explosive growth" for Antifa,
according to the journalist Peter Beinart. The new administration's obvious
dangerous qualities caused some situated within the mainstream left to view
militant antifascists more sympathetically. As the historian Mark Bray notes,
Antifa extolled "radical pan-leftist politics" by "communists, socialists and
anarchists" committed to blunting white supremacists. Harking back to fascism's rise during the 1920s and 1930s, Antifa identified with militant leftists
of that era and also with young leftists who fought against neo-Nazis during
the 1980s. Organizer Scott Crow revealed, "The idea in Antifa is that we go
where they (right-wingers) go," and strive "to shut down" hate speech.

Organizations like Anti-Racist Action (ARA), Torch, the Hoosier Anti-
Racist Movement (HARM), and Antifa, somewhat later, had conveyed a
readiness to battle, sometimes literally, violent rightwing groups. First
emerging in Minneapolis and St. Paul in 1987, ARA determined to fight Nazi

skinheads, referred to as "boneheads," in the area. Declaring "Never let the Nazis have the street," ARA chapters developed in the Midwest and out West. HARM brought together far left activists, providing assistance at homeless shelters, offering security for gay marchers, and engaging in other community action.

* * *

As the second decade of the twenty-first century continued, American radicalism appeared reenergized, belying earlier trends when left-of-center forces tended to achieve the greatest momentum when progressives sat in the Oval Office. This resulted from having either a seemingly irrational individual or one brutally calculating enough to appeal to many of the worst elements in the nation. Having been removed from his national television program, Keith Olbermann eventually turned to podcasts, delivering penetrating political and social commentary about Donald Trump on *The Resistance*, a web series sponsored by *GQ* (*Gentlemen's Quarterly*).

During the early stages of his presidency, Trump continued to curry favor with unsavory, far right groups exuding racism, anti-Semitism, and misogyny. Groups like Antifa and Redneck Revolt, a newly created "anti-racist, anti-fascist communist defense formation," responded in mid-August 2017 as white supremacists marched through Charlottesville, Virginia. Antifascist groups battled with rallygoers, who had gathered earlier, shouting in Nazi-like fashion, "Our blood, our soil!" Thirty-two-year-old Heather Heyer died and nineteen others suffered injuries when rallygoer James Alex Fields Jr. drove his Dodge Challenger into a crowd of pedestrians. Following the incidents, the president initially refused to condemn the white supremacists, seen as part of the Alt-Right, extreme right-wingers enamored with and emboldened by first candidate and now President Trump. Rather, Trump attacked what he called "the alt-left" and declared, "I think there is blame on both sides," but he soon said, "You also had some very fine people on both sides." As criticism of both neo-Nazis and Antifa poured forth, Todd Gitlin noted that the vast majority of "politically motivated killings" over the past decade had been carried out "by right-wing extremists."

In the wake of highly publicized accounts of sexual harassment and assault, which Trump and other prominent figures had repeatedly been accused of, the Me Too movement appeared in the fall of 2017, with several celebrities, including the actress and singer Alyssa Milano, helping to spread the word through Twitter accounts. Milano first employed the hastag #MeToo, after public accounts of Hollywood film producer Harvey Weinstein's sexual abuse of scores of women began to appear. Milano was unaware that black activist Tarana Burke had employed that hastag eleven years earlier, and it had been used online by "a grassroots movement against sexual abuse of women of color," according to the author Linda Hirshman. But the timing was now particularly propitious, given both the charges delivered against Trump and his misogynistic treatment of women, including his leading political opponent, throughout the previous year's presidential campaign that nevertheless landed him in the White House. Countless women could identify with tales of sexual impropriety, as too many had experienced sexual assault or harassment themselves.

Time magazine named "The Silence Breakers" 2017 Person of the Year, with a cover of five women, all dressed in black, including the actress Ashley Judd, who had also been abused. As *Time* indicated, "this reckoning . . . has actually been simmering for years, decades, centuries." Sick of inappropriate bosses and co-workers, tired of worrying about retaliation, disgusted with "the code of going along to get along," these women had begun "a revolution of refusal, gathering strength by the day . . . their collective anger has spurred immediate and shocking results: nearly every day, CEOs have been fired, moguls toppled, icons disgraced. In some cases, criminal charges have been brought." The movement produced unanticipated results at times, as when Minnesota Senator Al Franken, one of the upper chamber's most trenchant critics of Donald Trump, was compelled to resign following a series of accusations involving sexual misconduct.

The National Abortion Rights Action League, Planned Parenthood Federation of America, and Pro-Choice America also insisted that progressive candidates had to fight against attempts to restrict reproductive rights. NARAL issued a statement of principles, backed by several other groups, declaring that progressives must counter attacks on contraception and abortion access, including by the growing number of state legislatures dominated by supposed "pro-life" politicians.

In early 2018, Bob Bland, who had co-chaired the previous January's Women's March, declared, "Last year we marched and we resisted and we organized, and now we're going to bring that collective power to the polls. Moving into 2018, we need to look beyond just 'resistance.'" The Women's March promised additional public demonstrations but also kicked off #PowerToThePolls, seeking to register one million voters.

High school students too increasingly adopted an activist stance following the latest in a long stream of mass shootings carried out in American educational institutions. After the slaughter of seventeen people by a lone gunman at Marjory Stoneman Douglas High School in Parkland, Florida, students conducted a National Walkout Day, engaged in "die-ins," and, on March 24, held a gigantic March for Our Lives in Washington, D.C. Everytown for Gun Safety, founded earlier, maintained its operations, determined to help "end gun violence and build safer communities," but Congress, dominated by unbending Republicans, barely responded, while the National Rifle Association and its rightwing allies rallied gun rights activists.

On April 3, 2018, Timothy Snyder's latest book *The Road to Unfreedom: Russia, Europe, America* appeared, emphasizing the linkage between Vladimir Putin's disinformation efforts and Donald Trump's boldfaced lies. But Snyder also underscored how Russia engaged in "a cyberwar to destroy" the European Union and the United States. That included manipulative efforts on behalf of the Brexit referendum in the British Isles, far right and far left candidates in France and Germany, and Trump's presidential run, as well as his "sado-populism" that would lead to sharp reductions in educational support and health care for many who voted for him.

* * *

Increasingly, progressive figures, including those who referred to themselves as socialists, decided to run for political office. Membership in the Democratic Socialists of America mushroomed following Trump's victory; a Gallup poll indicated that young people increasingly viewed capitalism less favorably and socialism more positively. The Working Families Party (W.F.P.), founded twenty years earlier and a supporter of progressive candidates, offered its backing, drawn from a coalition of advocacy groups, community organizations, and unions, to the actress Cynthia Nixon in her bid to overtake New York Governor Andrew Cuomo for the Democratic Party nomination. Following the victory by twenty-eight-year-old community organizer Alexandria Ocasio-Cortez (AOC), a democratic socialist who ran against the incumbent, Joseph Crowley, in the Democratic Party primary in New York's 14th congressional district, *New York Times* columnist Michelle Goldberg prophesied, "Millennial Socialists Are Coming," referring to other radical young women competing for seats in the Pennsylvania state legislature.

On June 30, 2018, hundreds of thousands protested across the nation against the Trump administration's "zero tolerance" immigration stance, which led to the separation of over 2,000 children from their families. At a rally in Los Angeles, John Legend sang the soulful "Preach," quickly referred to as "an anthem for our times." Before delivering his new song, Legend insisted on the need for "opening your eyes to injustice" and taking a stand. The president, cabinet officials, and aides displayed an appalling lack of concern regarding the human costs of the administration's hardened position, which clearly appeared designed to appeal to Trump's base.

The 2018 congressional elections resulted in a forty-seat pickup by the Democrats, which would have been greater still but for marked gerrymandering. Among the newly elected members of Congress were AOC and Michigan's Rashida Tlaib, both women of color supported by Democratic Socialists of America. At the state level, other DSA candidates won office, including Mike Sylvester in Maine, Gabriel Acevero and Vaughn Stewart in Maryland, Julia Salazar in New York, and Elizabeth Fiedler, Sarah Innamorato, and Summer Lee in Pennsylvania. A whole array of other DSA-backed candidates prevailed as well, along with DSA-endorsed ballot initiatives. Black Voters Matter helped to engender a sensibility that "the South is rising," with black, brown, and Asian voters combining with progressive whites to nearly elect African American gubernatorial candidates, Stacey Abrams and Andrew Gillum just coming short in Georgia and Florida, respectively.

* * *

Shortly following the congressional elections, *Tablet Magazine*, an online Jewish magazine, presented a series of articles by Paul Berman on American radicals, which grappled with a series of cogent issues, including worries about anti-Semitism splintering the left in the United States as it appeared to be doing in Europe. Berman pointed to recent anti-Zionist stances by the American Studies Association, the National Women's Association, and DSA, where young activists were taking control. According to Berman, at the previous year's DSA convention, some delegates cried out, "From the river to the sea/Palestine will be free!" Berman feared the presence of "an obsessive anti-Zionism in pockets of the left." In timely fashion, journalism professor Susie Linfield published a book in early 2019, *The Lions' Den: Zionism and the Left from Hannah Arendt to Noam Chomsky.*

In his third essay, Berman recalled Richard Rorty's 1999 slim but classic work, *Achieving Our Country: Leftist Thought in Twentieth-Century America.* As others would do, Berman pointed to Rorty's prescient warning that economic transformations would adversely impact non-elite workers, who would determine "the system has failed and start looking around for a strongman to vote for." That individual would promise that once in power, "the smug bureaucrats, tricky lawyers, overpaid bond salesmen, and postmodernist professors will no longer be calling the shots." Rory feared that should that strongman take office, the gains garnered in the past four decades by minorities and gays would be eviscerated. Moreover, "jocular contempt for women will come back into fashion. The words 'nigger' and 'kike' will once again be heard in the workplace. All the sadism which the academic Left has tried to make unacceptable to its students will come flooding back. All the resentment which badly educated Americans feel about having their manners dictated to them by college graduates will find an outlet."

* * *

The March 4–17, 2019, issue of *New York* magazine featured a lengthy article by Simon Van Zuylen-Wood, "Pinkos Have More Fun," an analysis of what the author called "the New New Left." Van Zuylen-Wood pointed to

Chapo Trap House, a leftwing podcast; *Lux*, a forthcoming Marxist-feminist magazine; *Red Yenta*, a socialist dating site; the publication *Jacobin*; and the recently shuttered online media enterprise and blog network *Gawker*, all geared for the growing number of young people attracted to left-of-center venues. "Young socialism lives" on *Twitter*, Van Zuylen-Wood suggested. He discussed DSA's explosive growth, having experienced a leap to 50,000 members from less than one-eighth that number just two years earlier. This latest iteration of the American left, Van Zuylen-Wood declared, desired Medicare For All, a Green New Deal, extensive criminal justice reform, and a shifting of national priorities to allow for free public child care, free education all the way through college, and affordable housing. While some readily adopted the label of Dirtbag Left, others favored the symbol of a single rose emoji on Twitter, exhibiting support for democratic socialism. Young activists remained torn about which path to undertake to usher in socialism, with many remaining distrustful of electoral politics and sharply critical when figures like AOC strayed from the seeming path of enlightenment as she purportedly did in posting favorable words about Senator John McCain following his death. Nevertheless, more DSA members readied to undertake political runs of their own and Bernie Sanders again initiated a presidential run.

Meanwhile, other progressive movements, including those with international appeal, continued to emerge, a process fueled by social media and the Internet. Many involved Millennials (born 1977–1994), the largest cohort of American young people after the Baby Boomers, and members of Generation Z (born 1995–2012), the nation's most diverse and rapidly growing youth group. Comprised of activist youth, Sunrise Movement emerged during the spring of 2017, determined to draw attention to the climate crisis. It began when fueled by a small grant from the Sierra Club and was spurred by members of the Fossil Fuel Divestment Student Network. Co-founders Sara Blazevic and Varshini Prakash spearheaded divestment sit-ins at Swarthmore College and the University of Massachusetts, respectively. Newly elected Congressman Ro Khanna of California declared about the Sunrise activists, "I love 'em. They are young, passionate activists. For them, climate change isn't theoretical."

International in scope as well, School Strike 4 Climate appeared in 2018, when the Swedish ninth grader Greta Thunberg, following the lead of March for Our Lives activists, refused to attend school leading up to her country's general election. Perched outside the Swedish general assembly, she held a sign reading "Skolstrejk for klimater," urging a student strike regarding climate change. Quickly gathering momentum, Youth Strike 4 Change became a global phenomenon, leading to the March 2019 Global Climate Strike for the Future, joining students worldwide, again including in the United States.

The Extinction Rebellion, which sprang up in the United Kingdom and later elsewhere, including the United States just before the 2018 midterms, resorted to nonviolent direct action in places like Oxford Circus and Piccadilly Circus in central London, demanding a commitment to greatly diminished carbon emissions. Speaking to a gathered throng at Marble Arch, Thunberg insisted, "We are now facing an existential crisis, the climate crisis and ecological crisis, which have never been treated as crises before, they have been ignored for decades."

In April 2019, Sunrise Movement threw its support toward Audrey Denney, a young congressional candidate in Northern California hoping to wrest a seat away from the far rightwing Republican incumbent, Doug LaMalfa, who charged that "bad science" guided those who spoke of climate change. California's first congressional district, represented by LaMalfa, had suffered a devastating series of wildfires with much of the town of Paradise virtually destroyed by an inferno. Extinction's Facebook page was headlined, "INTERNATIONAL REBELLION." By January 26, 2019, the U.S. version was holding "a nationwide day of nonviolent civil disobedience and protests."

Perhaps more surprisingly, the American labor movement, long dormant and having diminished markedly over the past five decades, itself displayed signs of renewed energy and growth as the 2020 presidential election approached. The investigative journalist Bob Hennelly discussed new multiracial union militancy, what he called "a rising labor tsunami" involving "teachers, nurses, college adjuncts, reporters, factory workers, Uber/Lyft drivers, cafeteria workers in Silicon Valley, even prison inmates." All experienced financial uncertainties, exacerbated by the growing maldistribution of wealth and income. Responding, laborers engaged in a series of significant work stoppages, with the largest number of strikers—many of them teachers across the country—in over three decades.

During late April 2019, former Planned Parenthood chair Cecile Richards, Black Lives Matter co-founder Alicia Garza, and National Domestic Workers Alliance executive director Ai-jen Poo established the multiracial, intergenerational Supermajority. They envisioned the mass training and mobilizing of two million female organizers and local activists, over the course of the next twelve months. Women, Richards explained, felt "newly empowered and frankly motivated to take action," while Garza stated, "Women are mad as hell and we've been in resistance mode for two years. Now it's time to equip people." Supermajority's founders foresaw "a women's 'new deal,'" and "time for women to run things." On college and university campuses such as Swarthmore, students associated with #AskForBetter insisted on greater support for sexual assault victims.

Also at the end of April, Congress held its first hearing on Medicare for All, with activist Ady Barkan, afflicted by amyotrophic lateral sclerosis—

popularly known as Lou Gehrig's disease—grabbing the lion's share of attention. Forced to rely on a text-to-voice computer program, Barkan related his family's struggle with private insurers and the American health care system. Revealing that his family was compelled to spend over $100,000 annually to cover out-of-pocket expenses for home care, Barkan argued that Medicare for All would afford all Americans quality health care and prevent a stripping of "so much dignity" and "our common humanity."

By the summer of 2019, the Movement for Black Lives, drawing from over fifty organizations, demanded "reparations for past and continuing harms" inflicted on African Americans. "White America must recognize that justice for black people cannot be achieved without radical change to the structure of our society," the actor-activist Danny Glover affirmed, before asserting that reparations comprised "a moral, democratic, and economic imperative."

By early July, tens of thousands throughout the country demanded the closure of ICE-run detention centers holding migrants. More than 1,000 protestors, many of them Jews involved with #JewsAgainstIce and #NeverAgainAction, tied up traffic in Boston during rush hour, with one participant warning, "When Jews say never again, we fucking mean it." Over 1,000 protestors, many tied to Never Again Action or Movimiento Cosecha, a band of nonviolent immigrant rights organizers, closed entrances to ICE headquarters situated in the nation's capital. Credo Action, which mobilized progressive activists, demanded House Democrats move to impeach Donald Trump following his latest rants against the four young progressive congresswomen referred to as The Squad—Ocasio-Cortez, Ilhan Omar, Ayanna Pressley, and Rashida Tlaib. Ramping up rhetoric before the next year's presidential election, Trump absurdly slandered the four women—all U.S. citizens, three born in the country, one naturalized—accusing them of hating the United States and urging them to "go back and help fix the totally broken and crime infested places from which they came." *Haaretz*'s Chemi Shalev likened Trump's declaration to Nazi practices regarding Jews, prior to the Holocaust.

At the same time, Amanda Taub and Max Fisher, writing in the *New York Times*, suggested that "2019 might be the year of the protest," with mass protests, often fueled by mass media, occurring around the world, demanding greater accountability from office holders. However, social scientist Zeynep Tufekci of the University of North Carolina indicated that social media-driven protests appeared particularly prone to collapse or cooptation. Nevertheless, on Friday, September 20, millions of demonstrators—many of them youth activists—appeared in the streets in more than 150 countries, just prior to the United Nations Climate Action Summit, with a full week of protests slated along with a second global strike the next Friday. This wave was tied to the Greta Thunberg-spawned Fridays for Future movement, which urged schoolchildren to strike each Friday while insisting governments take action regarding climate and environmental concerns.

* * *

The early twenty-first century American left appeared determined to withstand falsehoods, smears, and race-baiting associated with rightwing groups around the globe, while reflecting the strengths of the indigenous radical tradition. Clearly cognizant of earlier missteps, its independent-minded practitioners were determinedly devoted to democratic ideals and practices, even to the point of questioning the worth of leaders in various instances. They also continued to be viewed as outsiders, and to identify with those seen in the same light, whether that involved young activists, LGBTQ individuals, women, people of color, and those residing along the economic margins of an affluent society. And yet the unprecedented readiness of the Trump administration to engage in lawless, unconstitutional behavior imperiled both the fate of the American republic and those most ready to challenge the dangerous drift toward authoritarianism. A leftwing renaissance, if not quite comprising a fourth great American left, seemed possible, but so did a marked rightward shift that could imperil one of the world's longstanding democracies as the 2020 presidential election approached.

Bibliography

GENERAL SOURCES

Sweeping histories include Sidney Lens's *Radicalism in America* (New York: Thomas V. Crowell Company, 1969), James Weinstein's *Ambiguous Legacy: The Left in American Politics* (New York: New Viewpoints, 1975), Milton Cantor's *The Divided Left: American Radicalism, 1900–1975* (New York: Hill and Wang, 1978), John Patrick Diggins's *The Rise and Fall of the American Left* (New York: W. W. Norton & Company, 1992), Michael Kazin's *American Dreams: How the Left Changed a Nation* (New York: Alfred A. Knopf, 2011), and Howard Brick and Christopher Phelps's *Radicals in America: The U.S. Left since the Second World War* (Cambridge: Cambridge University Press, 2015). Three collections contain illuminating biographical sketches: *American Radicals: Some Problems and Personalities* (New York: Monthly Review Press, 1957); *The American Radical* (New York: Routledge, 1994); and Peter Dreier's *The 100 Greatest Americans of the 20th Century: A Social Justice Hall of Fame* (New York: Nation Books, 2012).

CHAPTER 1: SOCIALISTS, WOBBLIES, AND VILLAGE REBELS

Kevin Kenny's definitive *Making Sense of the Molly Maguires* (New York: Oxford University Press, 1998) delves into the anarchist Irish immigrants, who sought to ensure dignity for fellow coal miners but were executed for capital crimes and because of ethnic hostilities. *The Great Strikes of 1877* (Urbana: University of Illinois Press, 2008) contains a series of well-crafted essays. Leon Fink's *Workingmen's Democracy: The Knight of Labor and American Politics* (Urbana: University of Illinois Press, 1985) relates an attempt to construct a national labor union, which envisioned an economic

217

order rooted in cooperation and possessed a largely open admission policy. Distinguished labor historian James Green's *Death in the Haymarket: A Story of Chicago, the First Labor Movement and the Bombing that Divided Gilded Age America* (New York: Pantheon Books, 2006) deals with the explosion on May 1, 1886, which crippled that anarchist movement. Paul Avrich's *The Haymarket Tragedy* (Princeton, NJ: Princeton University Press, 1984) also delivers a penetrating example of working-class history. George G. Suggs Jr.'s *Colorado's War on Militant Unionism: James H. Peabody and the Western Federation of Miners* (Detroit: Wayne State University Press, 1967) spotlights the heated nature of labor struggles out West. Nick Salvatore's *Eugene V. Debs: Citizen and Socialist* (Urbana: University of Illinois Press, 1982) includes the tale of the American Railway Union's effort to foster industrial unionism.

The incredibly rich historiography on late nineteenth century American farmers' movements includes Lawrence Goodwyn's *Democratic Promise: The Populist Moment in America* (New York: Oxford University Press, 1976), Worth Robert Miller's *Oklahoma Populism: A History of the People's Party in the Oklahoma Territory* (Norman: University of Oklahoma Press, 1987), Robert C. McMath Jr.'s *American Populism: A Social History, 1877–1898* (New York: Hill and Wang, 1992), and Charles Postel's *The Populist Vision* (New York: Oxford University Press, 2007).

Carlos A. Schwantes's *Coxey's Army: An American Odyssey* (Lincoln, NE: University of Nebraska Press, 1985) and Benjamin F. Alexander's *Coxey's Army: Popular Protest in the Gilded Age* (Baltimore: Johns Hopkins University Press, 2015) explore the starry-eyed ragtag group of unemployed individuals who sought to march to Washington, D.C., a year into the terrible depression of the 1890s. James Green's terrific "history from the bottom up" *Grass-Roots Socialism: Radical Movements in the Southwest, 1895–1943* (Baton Rouge: Louisiana State University Press, 1978) accomplishes what its author sets out to do: "write an important missing chapter in the history of the American Socialist party."

During the post-Civil War era, intellectuals, highbrow and not, contributed immeasurably to American radical movements. John L. Thomas's *Alternative America: Henry George, Edward Bellamy, Henry Demarest Lloyd and the Adversary Tradition* (Cambridge: Belknap Press, 1983) provides a revealing account of the radical reformers who penned *Progress and Poverty*, *Looking Backward*, and *Wealth against Commonwealth*, which set the stage for the Single-Tax movement, the Bellamy Club, or different versions of American socialism. The Social Gospel movement is thoughtfully examined in Ronald C. White and C. Howard Hopkins's *Social Gospel: Religion and*

Reform in Changing America (Philadelphia, Temple University Press, 1976) and Robert H. Craig, *Religion and Radical Politics: An Alternative Christian Tradition in the United States* (Philadelphia: Temple University Press, 1992).

L. Glen Seretan's *Daniel DeLeon: The Odyssey of an American Marxist* (Cambridge: Harvard University Press, 1979) and David Herreshoff's *The Origins of American Marxism: From the Transcendalists to De Leon* (Detroit: Wayne State University Press, 1967) emphasize the impact of "scientific socialism" on radicals in the United States. But American socialism's story comes alive through various seminal works: David Shannon's *The Socialist Party of America: A History* (New York: MacMillan, 1955), James Weinstein's *The Decline of Socialism in America, 1912–1925* (New York: Vintage Books, 1967), Mari Jo Buhle's *Women and American Socialist, 1870–1920* (Urbana: University of Illinois Press, 1981), and most recently, Jack Ross's *The Socialist Party of American: A Complete History* (Lincoln: Potomac Books, 2015). *Failure of a Dream? Essays in the History of American Socialism* (Berkeley: University of California Press, 1984) poses the key question anew, "Why no socialism in America?" The sometime friend, sometime competitor of American socialists, the anarchist Emma Goldman is explored in a number of fine studies, still topped by Richard Drinnon's lyrical *Rebel in Paradise: A Biography of Emma Goldman* (Chicago: University of Chicago Press, 1961).

Melvyn Dubofsky's *We Shall Be All: A History of the Industrial Workers of the World* (Chicago: Quadrangle Books, 1969) remains the standard. J. Anthony Lukas's brilliant *Big Trouble: A Murder in a Small Western Town Sets Off a Struggle for the Soul of America* (New York: Touchstone, 1997) explores the murder of ex-Idaho governor Frank Steunenberg and the resulting trial of Haywood, defended by Darrow and condemned by President Theodore Roosevelt.

The historical literature on the young Lyrical Leftists of the early twentieth century is rich. Fine general studies include Arthur Frank Wertheim's *The New York Little Renaissance: Iconoclasm, Modernism, and Nationalism in American Culture, 1908–1917* (New York: New York University Press, 1976), Robert F. Humphrey's *Children of Fantasy: The First Rebels of Greenwich Village* (New York: John Wiley & Sons, 1978), Edward Abraham's *The Lyrical Left: Randolph Bourne, Alfred Stieglitz, and the Origins of Cultural Radicalism in America* (Charlottesville: University of Virginia Press, 1986), Steven Watson's *Strange Bedfellows: The First American Avante-Garde* (New York: Abbeville Press, 1991), Christine Stansell's *American Moderns: Bohemian New York and the Creation of a New Century* (New York: Metropolitan Books, 2000), and the invaluable compendiums

1915, The Cultural Moment: The New Politics, the New Woman, the New Psychology, the New Art & the New Theatre in America (New Brunswick: Rutgers University Press, 1991), and *Echoes of Revolt: The Masses, 1911–1917* (Chicago: Ivan R. Dee, 1989).

Another collection, *Greenwich Village: Culture and Counterculture* (New Brunswick: Rutgers University Press, 1993), presents the geographical setting for the Lyrical Left. Leslie Fishbein's *Rebels in Bohemia, The Radicals of The Masses, 1911–1917* (Chapel Hill: University of North Carolina Press, 1982), Rebecca Zurier's *Art for the Masses: A Radical Magazine and Its Graphics, 1911–1917* (Philadelphia: Temple University Press, 1988), and *Echoes of Revolt: The Masses, 1911–1917* display something of the fabled publication's lively nature. Biographies of individuals at the center of the era's cultural rebellion are particularly strong and plentiful, including Casey N. Blake's *Beloved Community: The Cultural Criticism of Randolph Bourne, Van Wyck Brooks, Waldo Frank and Lewis Mumford* (Chapel Hill: University of North Carolina Press, 1990), William L. O'Neill's *The Last Romantic: A Life of Max Eastman* (New York: Oxford University Press, 1978), Linda J. Lumsden's *Inez: The Life and Times of Inez Milholland* (Bloomington: Indiana University Press, 2004), and Robert A. Rosenstone's extraordinary *Romantic Revolutionary: A Biography of John Reed* (New York: Random House, 1975).

CHAPTER 2: REPRESSION AND THE POSTWAR AMERICAN LEFT

My biography *Roger Nash Baldwin and the American Civil Liberties Union* (New York: Columbia University Press, 2001) discusses his determination to provide legal protections for conscientious objectors and other war opponents, through the American Union Against Militarism's Civil Liberties Bureau. Baldwin took charge of the AUAM, an organization Roland Marchand's *The American Peace Movement and Social Reform, 1889–1918* (Princeton, NJ: Princeton University Press, 1973) and Charles Chatfield's *For Peace and Justice: Pacifism in America, 1914–1941* (Knoxville: University of Tennessee, 1971) explore. The Working Class Union's condemnation of conscription is deciphered in *Opponents of War, 1917–1918* (Madison: University of Wisconsin Press, 1957) by H. C. Petersen and Gilbert C. Fite.

Dubofsky's *We Shall Be All* tracks the conspiracy trials besetting the IWW. The resort to repressive tactics of a governmental and an extra-legal nature emerges in William Preston's *Aliens and Dissenters: Federal Suppression of Radicals, 1903–1933* (Cambridge: Harvard University Press, 1963), Stephen J. Whitfield's *Scott Nearing: Apostle of American Radicalism* (New York:

Columbia University Press, 1974), Paul Murphy's *World War I and the Origin of Civil Liberties in the United States* (New York: W. W. Norton & Co., 1979), Samuel Walker's monumental *In Defense of American Liberties: A History of the ACLU* (New York: Oxford University Press, 1990), David M. Rabban's illuminating *Free Speech in Its Forgotten Years, 1870–1920* (Cambridge, England: Cambridge University Press, 1997), and my Baldwin study.

Shannon's *The Socialist Party of America* examines the SPA's wartime electoral successes and setbacks. Christopher Lasch's *The American Liberals and the Russian Revolution* (New York: Columbia University Press, 1962) and David Caute's *The Fellow-Travellers: Intellectuals Friends of Communism* (New Haven: Yale University Press, 1988) astutely trace the response by Western liberals and radicals to triumphant Bolshevism. But so do these historiographically significant chronicles: Shannon's *The Socialist Party of America*, Irving Howe and Lewis Coser's *The American Communist Party* (New York: Praeger, 1962), and Theodore Draper's *The Roots of American Communism* (New York: Viking, 1957) and *American Communism & Soviet Russia* (New York: Viking, 1957). The postwar red and black scare dramatically impacted the American left. Robert K. Murray's *Red Scare: A Study in National Hysteria, 1919–1920* (New York: McGraw-Hill Inc., 1955) remains seminal.

Walker's *In Defense of American Liberties* and my *Roger Nash Baldwin and the American Civil Liberties Union* chart the emergence of that organization. The SPA's new direction under a Protestant minister turned radical is considered in W. A. Swanberg's *Norman Thomas: The Last Idealist* (New York: Scribner, 1976). Another former minister-leading social activist, A. J. Muste, was instrumental in forming the Conference for Labor Action. Jo Ann Robinson's *Abraham Went Out: A Biography of A.J. Muste* (Philadelphia: Temple University Press, 1982) follows his complex involvement with an array of social movements.

CHAPTER 3: HEYDAY OF THE OLD LEFT

The story of the Old Left is complicated, filled with great hopes and crushing disappointments, soaring idealism, and crass cynicism. The general histories—Diggins's *The Rise and Fall of the American Left*, Cantor's *The Divided Left*, and Kazin's *American Dreamers*—cover this facet of American radicalism well. The great English historian Eric Hobsbawn captures the utopian, even millennial nature of the Old Left, or at least that of many of its adherents, in *Revolutionaries* (New York: Pantheon Books, 1973). The shifts and turns of the CPUSA, soon the dominant American radical organization, crop up in James E. Goodman's *Stories of Scottsboro* (New York: Pantheon, 1994), Harvey Klehr's *The Heyday of American Communism: The Depression Decade* (New York: Basic Books, 1984), and Fraser Ottanelli's *The Communist Party of the United States: From the Depression to World War II* (New Brunswick: Rutgers University Press, 1989).

The Bonus Army, another disheveled group of veterans who marched on Washington, D.C., is scrutinized in Jerome Tuccille's *The War Against the Vets: The World War I Bonus Army during the Great Depression* (Lincoln: Potomac Books, 2018). The response by American intellectuals, many of whom underwent a sharp shift leftward during the Great Depression, is appraised in several enlightening works. Among the most incandescent, stylistically, are Daniel Aaron's *Writers on the Left: Episodes in American Literary Communism* (New York: Harcourt Brace & World, 1961), Malcolm Cowley's *Exile's Return: A Literary Odyssey of the 1920s* (New York: Viking, 1962), his *The Dream of the Golden Mountains: Remembering the 1930s* (New York: Viking Adult, 1980), and yet another of his books, *The Long Voyage: Selected Letters of Malcolm Cowley, 1915–1987* (Cambridge: Harvard University Press, 2014). Richard Pells's *Radical Visions and American Dreams: Culture and Social Thought in the Depression Years* (New York: Harper and Row, 1973) and Judy Kutulas's *The Long War: The Intellectual People's Front and Anti-Stalinism, 1930–1940* (Durham, NC: Duke University Press, 1995) recount the ideological tribulations of many American intellectuals during the period.

Alan Brinkley's *Voices of Protest: Huey Long, Father Coughlin, & the Great Depression* (New York: Alfred A. Knopf, 1982) and Edwin Amenta's *When Movements Matter: The Townsend Plan & the Rise of Social Security* (Princeton, NJ: Princeton University Press, 2006) feature the mid-1930s' figures who helped push Roosevelt leftward, resulting in a second New Deal. Greg Mitchell's *The Campaign of the Century: Upton Sinclair's Race for Governor of California and the Birth of Media Politics* (New York: Random House, 1992) spotlights the famed writer's bid for political office. Mid-1930s' labor battles, both influenced by and influencing radical activists, appear in Bruce Nelson's *Workers on the Waterfront: Seamen, Longshoremen, and Unionism in the 1930s* (Urbana: University of Illinois Press, 1990).

The antiwar movement of the 1930s, greatly impacted by fratricidal struggles, surfaces in several fine studies, including Charles Chatfield's *For Peace and Justice* and Lawrence S. Wittner's *Rebels Against War: The American Peace Movement, 1933–1983* (Philadelphia: Temple University Press, 1984). Robert Cohen's *When the Old Left Was Young: Student Radicals and Ameri-*

ca's First Mass Student Movement, 1929–1941 (New York: Oxford University Press, 1993) provides encyclopedic coverage.

The Popular Front dominated radical politics and culture from the mid-1930s until the signing of the Nazi-Soviet Pact. The following provide a taste of the American version: Pells's *Radical Visions and American Dreams,* Theodore Draper's "The Popular Front Revisited," *New York Review of Books* (May 30, 1985), letters by Paul Buhle and others responding to Draper, *New York Review of Books* (August 15, 1985), Michael Denning's *The Cultural Front: The Laboring of American Culture in the Twentieth Century* (New York: Verso Press, 1997), and Buhle and David Wagner's *Radical Hollywood: The Untold Story Behind America's Favorite Movies* (New York: New Press, 2002).

Robert A. Rosenstone's *Crusade of the Left: The Lincoln Battalion in the Spanish Civil War* (New York: Pegasus, 1969), Peter N. Carroll's *The Odyssey of the Abraham Lincoln Brigade: Americans in the Spanish Civil War* (Palo Alto: Stanford University Press, 1994), and Adam Hochschild's *Spain in Our Hearts; American in the Spanish Civil War, 1936–1939* (New York: Houghton Mifflin Harcourt, 2016) present sharply-honed accounts of American volunteers in the conflict that was an early staging ground for World War II.

The sectarianism that has long afflicted the American left intensified following announcement of the Nazi-Soviet pact in late August 1939, as related in Les K. Adler and Thomas G. Paterson's vital essay, "Red Fascism: The Merger of Nazi Germany and Soviet Russia in the American Image of Totalitarianism, 1930s–1950s" (*American Historical Review* 75, April 1970). Ideological divisions, however, had been present throughout the decade as a number of important studies, including Frank A. Warren's *Liberals and Communism: The Red Decade Revisited* (Bloomington: Indiana University Press, 1966) and Alan Wald's *The New York Intellectuals: The Rise and Decline of the Anti-Stalinist Left from the 1930s to the 1980s* (Chapel Hill: University of North Carolina Press, 1987), demonstrate. *The God That Failed* (New York: Columbia University Press, 2001) contains explanations by the writers Louis Fischer, Andre Gide, Arthur Koestler, Ignazio Silone, Stephen Spender, and Richard Wright for their attraction to and eventual revulsion regarding communism. My *Izzy: A Biography of I.F. Stone* (New Brunswick, NJ: Rutgers University Press, 1992) scrutinizes the twists and turns of the American left during the 1930s, including those pitting Stalinists and fellow travelers against anti-Stalinists. David Caute's *The Fellow-Travellers* and Paul Hollander's *Political Pilgrims: Travels of Western Intellectuals to the Soviet Union, China, and Cuba* (New York: Oxford University Press, 1981) telling unveil the allure of communism for too many intellectuals in the West.

Wartime American radicalism involved further gyrations, as Maurice Isserman explains in *Which Side Were You On? The American Communist Party during the Second World War* (Middletown, CT: Wesleyan, 1982). Donna T. Haverty-Stacke's *Trotskyists on Trial: Free Speech and Political Persecution Since the Age of FDR* (New York: New York University Press, 2016) explores the politically-motivated prosecution of twenty-nine members of the Socialist Workers Party in 1941, which the CPUSA applauded. Markowitz's *The Rise and Fall of the People's Century* (New York: Free Press, 1973) spotlights Wallace's call for a People's Century. The radical pacifists who refused to adhere to Selective Service directives are studied in Lawrence Wittner's *Rebels Against War*. Gregory D. Summer's *Dwight Macdonald and the Politics Circle: The Challenge of Cosmopolitan Democracy* (Ithaca: Cornell University Press, 1996) looks at his subject's experiment in independent radical journalism. My *Smokejumpers of the Civilian Public Service in World War II: Conscientious Objectors as Firefighters for the National Forest Service* (Jefferson, NC: McFarland & Company, Inc., 2006) considers a group of dedicated individuals who served their country in their own fashion.

CHAPTER 4: AMERICAN RADICALISM
AND THE EARLY COLD WAR

Its altered stance as World War II neared an end is noted in David A. Shannon's *The Decline of American Communism: A History of the Communist Party of the United States* (Chatham Bookseller, 1959). Insightful studies of the rich and ever-growing literature on the early postwar red scare include Athan G. Theoharis's *Seeds of Repression: Harry S. Truman and the Origins of McCarthyism* (Chicago: Quadrangle Books, 1971), Stephen J. Whitfield's *The Culture of the Cold War* (Baltimore: Johns Hopkins Press, 1991), and Landon R. Y. Storrs's *The Second Red Scare and the Unmaking of the New Deal Left* (Princeton, NJ: Princeton University Press, 2012). A new anticommunist organization, Americans for Democratic Action, emerged left-of-center, as Steven M. Gillon explains in *Politics and Vision: The ADA and American Liberalism, 1947–1985* (New York: Oxford University Press, 1987).

Revelations since the Soviet Union's collapse have verified earlier charges that various American communists and fellow travelers were, indeed, involved with espionage. Important works include Harvey Klehr, John Earl Haynes, and Fridrikh Igorevich Firsov's *The Secret World Of American*

Communism (New Haven: Yale University Press, 1995); Allen Weinstein and Alexander Vassiliev's *The Haunted Wood: Soviet Espionage in America—The Stalin Era* (New York: Random House, 1998); and Thomas Powers's "The Plot Thickens" (*New York Review of Books*, May 11, 2000).

Conflicting tales by Whittaker Chambers and Alger Hiss continue to fascinate historians, while troubling those on both the political right and left. Among the most intriguing accounts are Chambers's *Witness* (New York: Random, 1952), Hiss's *In the Court of Public Opinion* (New York: Alfred A. Knopf, 1957), Allen Weinstein's *Perjury: The Hiss-Chambers Case* (Stanford: Hoover Institution Press, 1978), and Sam Tanenhaus's *Whittaker Chambers: A Biography* (New York: Random House, 1997).

Hiss and Chambers warred in a number of venues, including the House Un-American Activities Committee. Eric Bentley has compiled the priceless *Thirty Years of Treason: Excerpts from Hearings Before the House Committee on Un-American Activities, 1938–1968* (New York: The Viking Press, 1971). Walter Goodman's *The Committee: The Extraordinary Career of the House Committee on Un-American Activities* (New York: Farrar, Straus & Giroux, 1968) is rich in its own right, while Robert Justin Goldstein's *Political Repression in Modern America: From 1870 to 1976* (Boston: G. K. Hall & Co., 1978) and David Caute's *The Great Fear: The Anti-Communist Purge under Truman and Eisenhower* (New York: Simon & Schuster, 1978) offer sweeping examinations of their subjects, with considerable attention to HUAC.

The Old Left's weakened state was displayed during the 1948 presidential campaign, when former Vice-President Henry Wallace undertook a third-party bid. Curtis Daniel MacDougall's path-breaking three-volume *Gideon's Army* (New York: Marzani & Munsell, 1965), Markowitz's *The Rise and Fall of the People's Century*, and John C. Culver's *American Dreamer: The Life and Times of Henry A. Wallace* (New York: W. W. Norton & Company, 2000) underscore the new Progressive Party's impotent nature.

The more virulent phase of the red scare known as McCarthyism began in early 1950 and has been dissected in such fine works as David M. Oshinsky's *A Conspiracy So Immense: The World of Joe McCarthy* (New York: The Free Press, 1983) and Ellen Schrecker's *Many Are the Crimes: McCarthyism in America* (Princeton, NJ: Princeton University Press, 1998). Ronald Radosh and Joyce Milton's *The Rosenberg File: A Search for the Truth* (New York: Henry Holt & Co., 1983) and Walter Schneir's *Final Verdict: What Really Happened in the Rosenberg Case* (Brooklyn: Melville House, 2010) spin the story of Julius and Ethel Rosenberg. My book *The Social Gospel of*

E. Nicholas Comfort: Founder of the Oklahoma School of Religion (Norman: University of Oklahoma Press, 1997), strives to explain how red-baiting helped to destroy a once vibrant community in the American heartland.

Izzy, Maurice Isserman's *If I Had a Hammer: The Death of the Old Left and the Birth of the New Left* (New York: Basic, 1987), and Leilah Danielson's *American Gandhi: A.J. Muste and the History of Radicalism in the Twentieth Century* (Philadelphia: University of Pennsylvania Press, 2014) trace the passing of one great American left and the attempts to birth another one. Lawrence Wittner's *Rebels Against War: The American Peace Movement, 1933–1983* and Charles Chatfield's *The American Peace Movement: Ideals and Activism* (Boston: Twayne Publishers, 1992) highlight the role played by dedicated pacifists in movements ranging from civil rights to the anti-nuclear campaign. Matthew Laser's *Pacifica Radio: The Rise of an Alternative Network* (Philadelphia: Temple University Press, 1999) discusses the revolutionary impact of Pacifica Radio. Milton Katz's *Ban the Bomb: A History of SANE, the Committee for a Sane Nuclear Policy, 1957–1985* (New York: Praeger, 1986) offers a full chronicle of the anti-nuclear organization.

Mark Tushnet's *The NAACP's Legal Strategy against Segregated Education, 1925–1950* (Chapel Hill: University of North Carolina Press, 1987) provides insights into the courtroom struggle waged by the nation's foremost civil rights organization, often notwithstanding great obstacles and threats. Aldon D. Morris's *The Origins of the Civil Rights Movement: Black Communities Organizing for Change* (New York: Free Pres, 1984) and Robert Weisbrot's *Freedom Bound: A History of America's Civil Rights Movement* (New York: W. W. Norton & Company, 1989) offer fine chronicles of the early civil rights campaign. Stephen J. Whitfield's *A Death in the Delta: The Story of Emmett Till* (New York: Free Press, 1988) grippingly recaptures the horrific murder of the fourteen-year-old African American boy.

Danielle L. McGuire's stunning *At the Dark End of the Street: Black Women, Rape, and Resistance—a New History of the Civil Rights Movement from Rosa Parks to the Rise of Black Power* (New York: Knopf, 2010) graphically captures the decades-long battle by women against the sexual violence that cemented the Southern system of racism and discrimination. *The Montgomery Bus Boycott and the Women Who Started It: The Memoir of Jo Ann Gibson Robinson* (Knoxville: University of Tennessee Press, 1987) traces nonviolent resistance's application in the heart of Old Dixie. The biographical treatments of King and the organization he created, the Southern Christian Leadership Conference, are plentiful, many even memorable, including David J. Garrow's *Bearing the Cross: Martin Luther King Jr. and the Southern Christian Leadership Conference* (New York: William Morrow & Co.,

1986) and Taylor Branch's *Parting the Waters; America in the King Years, 1954–63* (New York: Simon & Schuster, 1988). *The Autobiography of Malcolm X: As Told to Alex Haley* (New York: Ballantine Publishing Group, 1965), brilliant if not wholly accurate, depicts the evolution of the human rights activist. Timothy B. Tyson's *Radio Free Dixie: Robert F. Williams and the Roots of Black Power* (Chapel Hill: University of North Carolina Press, 1999) points to an approach more akin to Malcolm X's.

CHAPTER 5: REVOLT OF THE YOUNG (AND OTHERS)

The New Left is tackled in a variety of books, with the most expansive coverage found in Irwin Unger's *The Movement: A History of the American New Left, 1959–1972* (New York: Dodd, Mead, 1974), Maurice Isserman's *If I Had a Hammer*, Wini Breines's *Community Organization in the New Left, 1962–1968: The Great Refusal* (New Brunswick: Rutgers University Press, 1989), and William L. O'Neill's *The New Left: A History* (Hoboken: Wiley-Blackwell, 2001). The best microcosmic studies, focusing on Berkeley, Madison, Seattle, Austin, and Philadelphia, respectively, are W. J. Rorabaugh's *Berkeley at War: The 1960s* (New York: Oxford University Press, 1989), *History and the New Left: Madison, Wisconsin, 1950–1970* (Philadelphia: Temple University Press, 1990), Walt Crowley's *Rites of Passage: A Memoir of the Sixties in Seattle* (Seattle: University of Washington Press, 1995), Doug Rossinow's *The Politics of Authenticity: Liberalism, Christianity, and the New Left in America* (New York: Columbia University Press, 1998), and Paul Lyons's *The People of This Generation: The Rise and Fall of the New Left in Philadelphia* (Philadelphia: University of Pennsylvania Press, 2003).

Morris's *The Origins of the Civil Rights Movement* invaluably recalls early sit-ins. The story of the Greensboro sit-in and the movement it spawned, including the founding of the Student Nonviolent Coordinating Committee, has been presented in many worthwhile accounts. These include William H. Chafe's *Civilities and Civil Rights: Greensboro, North Carolina, and the Black Struggle for Equality* (New York: Oxford University Press, 1980), Clayborne Carson's *Struggle: SNCC and the Black Awakening of the 1960s* (Cambridge: Harvard University Press, 1981), and Wesley C. Hogan's *Many Minds, One Heart: SNCC's Dream for a New America* (Chapel Hill: University of North Carolina Press, 2007). Many leading civil rights activists also participated in freedom rides, which built on the 1947 Journey of Reconciliation. Particularly strong works include August Meier and Elliott Rudwick's *CORE: A Study in the Civil Rights Movement, 1942–1968* (New York: Oxford University Press, 1973) and Raymond Arsenault's *Freedom Riders: 1962 and the Struggle for Racial Justice* (New York: Oxford University

Press, 2006). Laura Visser-Maessen's *Robert Parris Moses: A Life in Civil Rights and Leadership at the Grassroots* (Chapel Hill: University of North Carolina Press, 2016) depicts its subject's voting rights crusade in Mississippi, while Doug McAdams's *Freedom Summer* (New York: Oxford University Press, 1988) evokes Mississippi Freedom Summer, which Moses helped to orchestrate. An abundance of sometimes luminous writings explore Dr. King's continued quest to transform the Deep South and the American nation, among them Taylor Branch's *Pillar of Fire: America in the King Years, 1963–65* (New York: Simon & Schuster, 1998) and *At Canaan's Edge: America in the King Years, 1965–68* (New York: Simon & Schuster, 2006). David J. Garrow's *Protest at Selma: Martin Luther King, Jr., and the Voting Rights Act of 1965* (New Haven: Yale University Press, 1978) considers the march that helped bring about an end to *de jure* segregation in the United States. Joshua Bloom's *Black Against Empire: The History and Politics of the Black Panther Party* (Berkeley: University of California Press, 2016) imparts a definitive narrative of the militant organization.

In *A Prophetic Minority* (New York: Dutton Adult, 1966), the journalist and former member, Jack Newfield, crafts a soulful, early history of SDS. Kirkpatrick Sale's exhaustive *SDS* (New York: Random House, 1973) remains definitive, but Todd Gitlin's *The Whole World Is Watching: Mass Media in the Making and Unmaking of the New Left* (Berkeley: University of California Press, 1980), Wini Breines's *Community and Organization in the New Left, 1962–1968: The Great Refusal* (South Hadley, MA: J. F. Bergin, 1982), and James Miller's *Democracy Is in the Streets: From Port Huron to the Siege of Chicago* (New York: Simon & Schuster, 1987) contribute to explorations of both SDS and the New Left. The literature on the antiwar movement is also deep and lengthening, featuring exemplary studies like Nancy Zaroulis and Gerald Sullivan's detailed *Who Spoke Up? American Protest against the War in Vietnam, 1963–1975* (Garden City: Doubleday, 1984), Charles DeBenedetti's comprehensive *An American Ordeal: The Antiwar Movement of the Vietnam Era* (Syracuse: Syracuse University Press, 1990), and Tom Wells's massive *The War Within: America's Battle over Vietnam* (Berkeley: University of California Press, 1994). Antiwar activists Michael Ferber and Staughton Lynd's *The Resistance* (Boston: Beacon, 1971) remains vital, although Michael S. Foley's *Confronting the War Machine: Draft Resistance during the Vietnam War* (Chapel Hill: University of North Carolina Press, 2003) is another seminal undertaking.

CHAPTER 6: THE YEAR OF REVOLUTION AND BEYOND

Professional historians and laypersons alike remain drawn to 1968, as attested by the sheer volume of works. Global perspective include George Katsiasficas's *The Imagination of the New Left: A Global Analysis of 1968* (Boston: South End Press, 1987), David Caute's *The Year of the Barricades: A Journey through 1968* (New York: Harper and Row, 1988), Robert V. Daniels, *Year of the Heroic Guerillas: World Revolution and Counterrevolution in 1968* (New York: Basic Books, 1989), Mark Kurlansky's *1968: The Year That Rocked the World* (New York: Ballantine Books, 2003), Jeremi Suri's *The Global Revolutions of 1968* (New York: W. W. Norton & Company, 2007), Elaine Carey's *Protests in the Streets: 1968 Across the Globe* (Indianapolis: Hackett Publishing Company, Inc., 2016), Richard Vinen's *1968: Radical Protest and Its Enemies* (New York: Harper, 2018), and my (co-author Blaine T. Browne) *1968: The Rise and Fall of the New American Revolution* (Lanham: Rowman and Littlefield, 2018). Paul Berman's *A Tale of Two Utopias: The Political Journeys of the Generation of 1968* (New York: W. W. Norton, 1996) explores the story of '68ers after the ebbing of "utopian exhilaration."

Various topics have been carefully dissected, with the following a sampling of some of the most insightful treatments. David Farber's *Chicago '68* (Chicago: University of Chicago Press, 1994) clearly relates the Yippies' plan to disrupt that year's Democratic National Convention. Jessica Mitford's *The Trial of Dr. Spock* (New York: Alfred A. Knopf, 1969) follows the case of the Boston Five, backers of the Resistance, the group of young men refusing to accept Selective Service System directives. Francine due Plessix Gray's opinion piece in the September 25, 1969, issue of *The New York Review of Books* coined the phrase "The Ultra-Resistance" to categorize the Berrigan brothers and others determined to more forcefully condemn the draft. Michael S. Foley's *Confronting the War: Draft Resistance during the Vietnam War* (Chapel Hill: University of North Carolina Press, 2003) meticulously portrays the story of opposition to conscription amid the Vietnam conflict. Michael K. Honey's *To the Promised Land: Martin Luther King and the Fight for Economic Justice* (New York: W. W. Norton & Company, 2018) and Sylvie Laurent's *King and the Other America: The Poor People's Campaign and the Quest for Economic Equality* (Berkeley: University of California Press, 2018) movingly recall King's final campaign. Miriam Pawel's *The Crusades of Cesar Chavez: A Biography* (New York: Bloomsbury Press, 2014) recounts those of the United Farm Workers' chieftain. Jack Newfield's *Robert Kennedy: A Memoir* (New York: E. P. Dutton, 1969) still provides the sharpest, albeit loving analysis of the murdered presidential candidate. Richard Hoffer's *Something in the Air: American Passion and Defiance in the*

1968 Mexico City Olympics (New York: Free Press, 2009) recalls Tommie Smith and John Carlos's black power protest.

SDS's sharp turn leftward and the heightened militancy of white and black radicals became starkly apparent in 1968 and continued for some time afterward. Kirkpatrick Sale's *SDS* discusses the revolutionary shift, as do Bryan Burrough's *Days of Rage: America's Radical Underground, the FBI, and the Forgotten Age of Revolutionary Violence* (New York: Penguin Press, 2015), Arthur M. Eckstein's *Bad Moon Rising: How the Weather Underground Beat the FBI and Lost the Revolution* (New Haven: Yale University Press, 2016), Clara Bingham's *Witness to the Revolution: Radicals, Resisters, Vets, Hippies, and the Year America Lost Its Mind and Found Its Soul* (New York: Random House, 2016), and Heather Ann Thompson's *Blood in the Water: The Attica Prison Uprising of 1971* (New York: Pantheon, 2016). Richard Stacewicz's *Winter Soldiers: An Oral History of the Vietnam Veterans Against the War* (New York: Twayne Publishers, 1997), Andrew E. Hunt's *The Turning: A History of Vietnam Veterans Against the War* (New York: New York University Press, 1999), and Gerald Nicosia's *Home to War: A History of the Vietnam Veterans Movement* (New York: Crown, 2001) offer chronicles of VVAW members, many increasingly militant. Jeffrey Toobin's *American Heiress: The Wild Sage of the Kidnapping, Crimes and Trial of Patty Hearst* (New York: Doubleday, 2016) carries the story deeper into the 1970s, when revolutionary dreams became even more twisted and perverse.

CHAPTER 7: ONE, TWO, MANY MOVEMENTS

Howard Brick and Christopher Phelps's *Radicals in America: The US Left since the Second World War* (New York: Cambridge University Press, 2015) spans its particular subject matter most fully. The following works best analyze the American version of bohemia that thrived from World War II into the early 1970s: Theodore Roszak's classic *The Making of a Counter Culture: Reflections on the Technocratic Society and Its Youthful Opposition* (New York: Doubleday, 1969), Timothy Miller's *The Hippies and American Values* (Knoxville: University of Tennessee Press, 2011), W. J. Rorabaugh's *American Hippies* (New York: Cambridge University Press, 2015), and my *Sex, Drugs, and Rock 'n' Roll: The Rise of America's 1960s Counterculture* (Lanham: Rowman and Littlefield, 2015). Abe Peck's *Undercovering the Sixties: The Life and Times of the Underground Press* (New York: Pantheon Books, 1985), *Voices from the Underground* (East Lansing: Michigan State University Press, 2011–2012), John McMillian's *Smoking Typewriters: The Sixties Underground Press and the Rise of Alternative Media in America* (New York: Oxford University Press, 2011), and *Celebrating the Rag: Aus-*

tin's Iconic Underground Newspaper (Austin: New Journalism Project, 2016) offer enthralling windows into the era's underground press. *The Hidden 1970s: Histories of Radicalism* (New Brunswick: Rutgers University Press, 2010) contains articles on movements that carried on into the new decade.

Jonathan Eig's sprightly *The Birth of the Pill: How Four Crusaders Reinvented Sex and Launched a Revolution* (New York: W. W. Norton & Company, 2014) contends that the scientific discovery sparked a social metamorphosis. The literature covering feminism's second wave is profuse, and among the most significant volumes are Sara Evans's *Personal Politics: The Roots of Women's Liberation in the Civil Rights Movement and the New Left* (New York: Alfred A. Knopf, 1979), Alice Echols's *Daring to Be* (New York: Viking Adult, 2000), Ruth Rosen's *The World Split Open: How the Modern Women's Movement Changed America* (New York: St. Martin's Press, 2004), and Breanne Fahs's *Firebrand Feminism: The Radical Lives of Ti-Grace Atkinson, Kathie Sarachild, Roxanne Dunbar-Ortiz, and Dana Densmore* (Seattle: University of Washington Press, 2018).

Still valuable, Donn Teal's *The Gay Militants* (New York: Stein & Day, 1971) captures the zeitgeist when the homosexual revolution exploded onto the American scene. Marc Stein's *Rethinking the Gay and Lesbian Movement* (New York: Routledge, 2012) carefully follows the movement's early roots and development. So does Lillian Falderman's sweeping study, *The Gay Revolution: The Story of the Struggle* (New York: Simon & Schuster, 2015). David Carter's terrific *Stonewall: The Riots That Sparked the Gay Revolution Bad: Radical Feminism in America, 1967–1975* (Minneapolis: University of Minnesota Press, 1989) and Martin Duberman's fascinating *Stonewall* (New York: Dutton, 1993) relate the epochal event that ignited a social movement. John D'Emilio's *Sexual Politics, Sexual Communities* (Chicago: University of Chicago Press, 1983) remains the standard work.

Studies covering radical Latino, Native American, and Asian American movements, like those of women and gays, are vibrant. F. Arthur Rosales's *Chicano! The History of the Mexican American Civil Rights Movement* (Houston; Arte Publico Press, 1996) and Maylei Blackwell's *!Chicana Power! Contested Histories of Feminism in the Chicano Movement* (Austin: University of Texas Press, 2011) deliver fine overviews of that movement. More specialized treatments, also quite good, include Miriam Pawel's *The Union of Their Dreams: Power, Hopes, and Struggle in Cesar Chavez's Farm Worker Movement* (New York: Bloomsbury Press, 2009), Juan Gomez-Quinones and Irene Vasquez's *Making Aztlan: Ideology and Culture of the Chicana and Chicano Movement, 1966–1977* (Albuquerque: University of New

Mexico Press, 2014), and Darrel Wanzer-Serrano's The *New York Young Lords and the Struggle for Liberation* (Philadelphia: Temple University Press, 2015).

Paul Chaat Smith and Robert Allen Warrior's *Like a Hurricane: The Indian Movement from Alcatraz to Wounded Knee* (New York: New Press, 1996) vigorously explores the Native American movement that began flourishing at the end of the 1960s. Troy R. Johnson's *The Occupation of Alcatraz Island: Indian Self-Determination and the Rise of Indian Activism* (Urbana: University of Illinois Press, 1996) investigates the 1969 takeover on Alcatraz Island that fueled Native American militancy. Daryl Joji Maeda's *Rethinking the Asian American Movement* (New York: Routledge, 2011) and Karen L. Ishizuka's *Serve the People: Making Asian America in the Long Sixties* (London: Verson, 2018) document a still too little explored brand of activism that emerged during the 1960s.

Other progressive movements emerged at that point, some flourishing later. Roger Sanjek's *Gray Panthers* (Philadelphia: University of Pennsylvania Press, 2009) focuses on elder activism, including that spearheaded by Maggie Kuhn. Justin Martin's *Nader: Crusader, Spoiler, Icon* (New York: Basic Books, 2002) highlights the solitary figure associated with a consumer revolution. Fred Pelka's *What We Have Done: An Oral History of the Disability Rights Movement* (Boston: University of Massachusetts Press, 2012) offers a distinct contribution, presenting histories of the too frequently ignored disability rights movement. Literature covering environmentalism is abundant and flourishing, including Kirkpatrick Sale's *The Green Revolution: The American Environmental Movement, 1962–1992* (New York: Hill and Wang, 1993) and Thomas R. Wellock's *Preserving the Nation: The Conservation and Environmental Movements, 1870–2000* (Wheeling, IL: Harlan Davidson, Inc., 2007). The prison rights movement that also appeared during the 1960s is the subject of Dan Berger's *Captive Nation: Black Prison Organizing in the Civil Rights Era* (Chapel Hill: University of North Carolina Press, 2014) and Lisa M. Corrigan's *Prison Power: How Prison Influenced the Movement for Black Liberation* (Tuscaloosa: University Press of Mississippi, 2016). Frances Fox Piven and Richard A. Cloward's *Poor People's Movements: Why They Succeed, How They Fail* (New York: Vintage Books, 1979) and Premilla Nadasen's *Rethinking the Welfare Rights Movement* (New York: Routledge, 2012) probe the welfare rights movement.

CHAPTER 8: CITIZEN ACTIVISM ON MANY FRONTS

The Hidden 1970s, Harry Boyte's *The Backyard Revolution: Understanding the New Citizen Movement* (Philadelphia: Temple University Press, 1980), Barbara Epstein's *Political Protest and Cultural Revolution: Nonviolent Direct Action in the 1970s and 1980s* (Berkeley: University of California Press, 1991), David R. Swartz's *Moral Minority: The Evangelical Left in an Age of Conservatism* (Philadelphia: University of Pennsylvania Press, 2012), and Michael S. Foley's *Front Porch Politics: The Forgotten Heyday of American Activism in the 1970s and 1980s* (New York: Hill and Wang, 2013) convincingly refute the notion that the American left waned dramatically following the 1960s. Howard Brick and Christopher Phelps's *Radicals in America* carefully follows the various sectarian organizations that emerged out of the ashes of the New Left.

Along with New Left veterans Heather Booth and Steve Max, Boyte presents *Citizen Action and the New American Populism* (Philadelphia: Temple University Press, 1986). *How We Get Free: Black Feminism and the Combahee River Collective* (Chicago: Haymarket Books, 2017) contains essays by and interviews with lesbian feminist activists who established one of the most significant women's liberation groups in the mid-1970s. John Anderson and Hilary Hevenor's *Burning down the House: MOVE and the Tragedy of Philadelphia* (New York: W. W. Norton & Co., 1990) grippingly recaptures the battle between the revolutionary group and Philly police. Joyce Antler's vital *Jewish Radical Feminism: Voices from the Women's Liberation Movement* (New York: NYU Press, 2018) relates the impact of Jewish women on second-wave feminism. Lillian Faderman's *The Gay Revolution: The Story of the Struggle* (New York: Simon & Schuster, 2015) produces a large history of the battle for gay and lesbian rights, while Randy Shilts's *And the Band Played On: Politics, People, and the AIDS Epidemic* (New York: St. Martin's Press, 1987) remains, in many ways, definitive. Jim Downs' *Stand by Me: The Forgotten History of Gay Liberation* (New York: Basic Books, 2016) recalls gay activities and genuine tragedies, including the too infrequently remembered arson murder of thirty-two men. Robert W. Fieseler's *Tinderbox: The Untold Story of the Up Stairs Lounge Fire and the Rise of Gay Liberation* (New York: Liveright, 2018) grippingly recounts that terrible event, which occurred in mid-1973 at a New Orleans bar.

Keith Makoto Woodhouse's *The Ecocentrists: A History of Radical Environmentalism* (New York: Columbia University Press, 2018) highlights those activists determined to arrest ecological crises through genuinely radical tactics and the application of radical ideas. Harvey Wasserman's *Energy War: Reports from the Front* (Brooklyn: Lawrence Hill, 1979) discusses the antinuclear movement, while Natasha Zaretsky's *Radiation Nation: Three Mile Island and the Political Transformation of the 1970s* (New York: Columbia University Press, 2018) explores the impact of the 1979 nuclear accident in Central Pennsylvania. Dan Liberman's *A Third Party Can Succeed in America* (Bethesda, MD: Altinst Books, 2012) covers Barry Commoner's 1980 presidential bid. David S. Meyer's *A Winter of Discontent: The Nuclear Freeze and American Politics* (New York: Praeger, 1990) examines the anti-nuclear movement that rose and then faded during the early Reagan years. Gary Rivlin's *Fire on the Prairie: Chicago's Harold Washington and the Politics of Race* (New York: Henry Holt & Co., 1992) dissects the mayor's crafting of a multiracial coalition that served as "a grand experiment with national ramifications."

CHAPTER 9: RESURGENT RADICALISM

Howard Brick and Christopher Phelps's *Radicals in America*, Sarah Jaffe's *Necessary Trouble: Americans in Revolt* (New York: Nation Books, 2017), and L. A. Kauffman's *Direct Action: Protest and the Reinvention of American Radicalism* (London: Verso, 2017) offer the most astute extended analyses of American radicalism of the past two decades. *From ACT UP to the WTO: Urban Protest and Community Building in the Era of Globalization* (London: Verson, 2002) diligently pursues the run-up to the Seattle protests of November 1999. *The Battle of the Story of the Battle of Seattle* (Oakland: AK Press, 2009) presents recollections by global justice activists. Lesley J. Wood's *Direct Action, Deliberation, and Diffusion: Collective Action after the WTO Protests in Seattle* (Cambridge: Cambridge University Press, 2012) continues the story initiated by the Global Justice Movement attack on the World Trade Organization.

Michael T. Heaney and Fabio Rojas's *Party in the Street: The Antiwar Movement and the Democratic Party after 9/11* (Cambridge: Cambridge University Press, 2015) focuses on the opposition to the Near Eastern wars that occurred in the wake of the attacks on New York City and Washington, D.C. Paul Berman's typically elegant *Terror and Liberalism* (New York: W. W. Norton & Co., 2003) displays the anguish of a man of the left who believed that liberal ideals were under assault, requiring the War on Terror that the Bush administration and the British government under Tony Blair championed. A different kind of assault involved the unceasing vilifying of ACORN, which had assisted countless numbers of indigent individuals and families across the nation as John Atlas's *Seeds of Change: The Story of ACORN* (Nashville: Vanderbilt University Press, 2010) relates.

Todd Gitlin's *Occupy Nation: The Roots, the Spirit, and the Promise of Occupy Wall Street* (New York: HarperCollins, 2012) lauds the Occupy movement's "incandescent compound of indignation, joy, outrage, hope, ingenuity, and resolve," while Mark Bray's *Translating Anarchy: The Anarchism of Occupy Wall Street* (Washington, DC: Zero Press, 2013) provides an insider's look.

Keeanga-Yamahtta Taylor's *From #BlackLivesMatter to Black Liberation* (Chicago: Haymarket Books, 2016), Wesley Lowery's *They Can't Kill Us All: Ferguson, Baltimore, and a New Era in America's Racial Justice Movement* (New York: Little, Brown and Company, 2016), and Christopher J. Lebron's *The Making of Black Lives Matter: A Brief History of an Idea* (New York: Oxford University Press, 2017) examine the movement that arose following yet another spate of deaths of young African Americans at the hands of the police.

The publication of cultural critic Susie Linfield's *The Lions' Den: Zionism and the Left from Hannah Arendt to Noam Chomsky* (New Haven: Yale University Press, 2019) was all too timely as Donald Trump, however opportunistically and hypocritically, attempted to wield the cudgel of anti-Semitism to splinter American progressives. Linda Hirshman's *Reckoning: The Epic Battle Against Sexual Abuse and Harassment* (Boston: Houghton Mifflin, 2019) tracks the roots and unfolding of the movement against sexual depredations that culminated in #MeToo and the challenge to male privilege.

Index

Abbey, Edward, 177
abortion, 146–147, 172; bombings related to, 182; extremists against, 183
Abu Ghraib, 197
Achieving Our Country (Rorty), 212
ACLU. *See* American Civil Liberties Union
ACORN. *See* Association for Community Organizations for Reform
Act Now to Stop War and End Racism (ANSWER), 195
Addams, Jane, 29
affirmative action, 5
Affordable Health Care Act, 202, 207
Afghanistan, 178, 194
A.F.L. *See* American Federation of Labor
African Americans, 45, 59, 61, 94, 162, 181, 205; B.L.M. and, 202–203; CORE for, 68; Jim Crow against, 36–37, 68, 77, 84; lynching related to, 60–61; as mayors, 181; NWRO and, 163; police and, 235; race riots and, 42. *See also* Black Panther Party
agents provocateurs, 8
AIDS Coalition to Unleash Power, 181
AIM. *See* American Indian Movement
"Alcatraz Proclamation," 155
Ali, Muhammad, 108, 112
American Civil Liberties Union (ACLU), 25, 45, 64

American Federation of Labor (A.F.L.), 8, 14, 41, 58–59
American Forum for Socialist Education, 82
American Friends Service Committee, 90
American Indian Movement (AIM), 154–155
American Peace Mobilization, 65
American Railway Union, 8–9, 10, 11
Americans Disabled for Accessible Public Trust, 161
Americans for Democratic Action, 73, 224
American Soviet espionage, 224
American Student Union, 57, 65
Americans with Disabilities Act (1990), 188
American Union against Militarism (AUAM), 28, 29, 35, 36
anarchism, 25, 43, 44
ANSWER. *See* Act Now to Stop War and End Racism
anti-draft movements, 114, 115–116, 122; Boston Five in, 120–122, 123; March on the Pentagon in, 116–117
anti-globalization campaign, 6
antinuclear pacifists, 90–91, 174
Anti-Racist Action, 208–209
anti-Semitism, 215, 235
antiwar movements, 41, 56–57, 130–131, 137; Iraq related to, 195–196; IWW, 33–35; SPA and, 31, 32, 38. *See also*

About the Author

Robert C. Cottrell has written more than 20 books, including biographies of ACLU icon Roger Nash Baldwin and Negro League founder Rube Foster, as well as a dual biography of Hank Greenberg and Jackie Robinson. He is the author most recently of *Sex, Drugs, and Rock 'n' Roll: The Rise of America's 1960s Counterculture* and *1968: The Rise and Fall of the New American Revolution*. He is presently completing a book titled *Martyrs of the Early American Left: Inez Milholland, Randolph Bourne, and John Reed*.